HOW MUCH LONGER WILL A WOMAN HAVE A RIGHT TO HER OWN BODY?

There's a hidden war on women being waged across America and the right wing's most radical zealots are winning. A shocking exposé as well as a passionate call to arms, *The War on Choice* lays out in frightening detail the right wing's thirty-year campaign to undermine the hard-won laws protecting a woman's freedoms. Did you know that there are:

- **335 new state laws restricting a woman's right to choose in just the last 8 years**
- **87 percent of U.S. counties with no safe abortion provider . . . and that number is *increasing***
- **24 states *so far* with mandatory delays and state-prepared anti-choice propaganda—despite the objection of the American Medical Association**

Gloria Feldt, the president of Planned Parenthood Federation of America, reveals how right-wing extremists are quietly plotting to snatch away our rights—and the rights of our sisters and daughters— while the vast majority of Americans assume our access to reproductive information and health care is protected. She describes:

- **Doctors prevented from giving accurate information about birth control and abortion to their patients**
- **Right-wing legislation that gives fertilized eggs more rights than women**
- **Anti-condom policies that result in unwanted pregnancies as well as an increase in STDs, including AIDS**

The War on Choice combines investigative research with the voices of those directly affected by this campaign, to reveal the extent of the damage already inflicted by the anti-choice right wing and its allies in the White House, Congress, and state legislatures. Most important, it also delivers a practical, realizable plan for victory—before it is too late.

ALSO BY GLORIA FELDT

Behind Every Choice is a Story

THE
WAR
ON
CHOICE

THE RIGHT-WING
ATTACK ON WOMEN'S RIGHTS
AND HOW TO FIGHT BACK

Gloria Feldt

President of Planned Parenthood® Federation of America

with Laura Fraser

Bantam Books

THE WAR ON CHOICE
A Bantam Book / May 2004

Published by
Bantam Dell
A Division of
Random House, Inc.
New York, New York

Library of Congress Cataloging in Publication Data
Feldt, Gloria, 1942–
The war on choice : the right-wing attack on women's rights and how to fight back /
by Gloria Feldt with Laura Fraser.
p.   cm.
ISBN 0-553-38292-6
1. Pro-life movement—United States. 2. Right-wing extremists—United States.
3. Abortion—United States. 4. Birth control—United States.
5. Women's rights—United States. I. Fraser, Laura. II. Title.
HQ767.5.U5F65 2004
363.46'0973—dc22   2004041097

Manufactured in the United States of America
Published simultaneously in Canada

10 9 8 7 6 5 4 3 2 1
BVG

To Alex

ACKNOWLEDGMENTS

My first acknowledgment goes to you, because if you have opened this book, it means you are already concerned about the threat to reproductive rights and health-care access. That's the first step toward fighting back and fighting forward to right the many wrongs you will read about herein.

But before you start reading the text, I want you to fix in your mind, or take out of your billfold and look at, a picture of a young woman you care deeply about. Maybe it is your daughter, your niece, your sister, your friend, your love. Keep that picture as the lens through which you read, because *The War on Choice* is about her, and for her—her dreams and aspirations for her life and her ability to realize those dreams. Too often we lose sight of that focus on the real lives of women, and on the people who care about them, in the increasingly vitriolic debate that surrounds the war on choice. Too often politicians and the media have reduced the rich complexity of some of life's most important decisions to one word—abortion—and reduced the intricate questions about individual rights under law to one issue—the future of *Roe v Wade*. Yet what's at stake is so much more, as these pages will attest.

I was so fortunate at the start that Paula Balzer and Sarah Lazin of Sarah Lazin Books believed that this book must be written, and that the amazing women of Bantam Dell—especially Nita Taublib, the associate publisher, Barbara Burg, the director of publicity, and my extraordinary editor, Beth Rashbaum—believed and convinced others that this book must be published. Beth worked as many weekends as I did to make sure the book was on time and on point. I was soon to understand why people told me she is one of the few "real editors." And she cajoled me into changes in the nicest way.

It has taken the proverbial village, and then some, to research and write this book. It was a pleasure to work with Laura Fraser, a talented writer with a passionate commitment to women's rights. I already miss our late-night conversations and shared outrage. To the incredibly committed, courageous, compassionate Planned Parenthood people everywhere, my profound appreciation is not nearly enough to express the full depth of my feelings for your contributions to this movement every day and to this book in particular. You are joined by the many sister and brother organizations that make up the larger movement devoted to women's human and civil rights. To all those heroes on the frontline every day making sure women have access to the services that make their rights meaningful, thank you.

I could fill an entire book with kudos to the many Planned Parenthood Federation of America staff whose passion for telling the important story of the war on choice led them to contribute way above and beyond the call of duty. They include Elizabeth Toledo, who was determined we would get this book published and doggedly pursued the myriad steps that are necessary on the path to publication; Mary Guidera, whose enthusiasm for the book kept my spirits up as she cheerfully did the impossible many times over; Gustavo Suarez, who was assigned the task of managing production of this book immediately upon joining the staff and did so admirably; Helena Clarke, who kept them all in line; Kate Rounds, whose journalistic skills were invaluable; our crackerjack editors, Barbara Snow and Jim Lubin, and researchers Jim Byrnes, Jennifer

Johnsen, Jon Knowles, Jessica Davis, Sarah Hill, Adina Wingate-Quijada, along with Rebecca Wind of the Alan Guttmacher Institute, and Vanessa Richardson, who assisted Laura Fraser. Page McCarley handled many and complex exchanges of information with grace and could miraculously always find just the thing I was looking for, Suellen Craig could pull things together when it looked like they were falling apart, and Traci Perry came aboard just in time to help get the final manuscript done while we were criss-crossing the country.

The brilliant Susanne Martinez and her equally stellar Washington staff responded with alacrity to my many questions about the facts and the politics and were so helpful with scheduling interviews with members of Congress: Jodie Leu, Jennifer Bolduc, Chris Korsmo, Deena Maerowitz, Dennis Poplin, Amy Taylor, David Broder, Shirine Mohagheghpour, Connie Watts, Corey Simmons, Abby Tibbs, Dresden McIntosh. Others who contributed content included Vanessa Cullins M.D., Ann Glazier, Mike McGee, Allie Stickney, Valerie De Fillipo, and Kirsten Sherk. Caren Spruch snagged some important interviews.

And then there are the lawyers, and ours are wonderful: Carole Chervin and Beth Otten, Dara Klassel (I hope that I have not given you grey hair), Roger Evans, Helene Krasnoff, and paralegal, Julie Strauss. Thank you for your patience and your precision in reviewing book drafts and contracts, and answering countless queries. Thanks also to Bantam Dell's lawyer, Matthew Martin, who contributed his own careful reading and helpful queries.

Many staff and volunteers from Planned Parenthood affiliates nationwide and the national board shared their stories of trial and triumph, action, political smarts, and courage. There were so many stories I did not have space for all of them in the book, but all of them informed me and I want to thank everyone who contributed: Christine Charbonneau, Audrey Bracey Deegan, Bob Lohrmann, Jamie Leonard, Scott Heyman, Betty Cockrum, Chris Funk, Jeanette Vargo, Chris Lalley, Tamara Carpenter, Carla Holeva, Karla Peterson,

Liz Accles, Elizabeth Snyder, Emily P. Goodstein, Lindsay Boyd, Linda Hahn, Pamela Smallwood, Rebecca Poedy, Barry Raff, Tony Thornton, Tomasina Chamberlain, David Nova, Jennifer Olenchek, Susan Flayer, and Bonnie Bolitho.

Thanks to LaDon Love for support and good advice; to Anita Perez-Ferguson for advocacy insight; to Marcia Gillespie for understanding. Hugs to Sally Blackmun for her warm and eloquent introduction. Last but not least, a special nod to the spirit of Sylvia Clark.

I am so very grateful to the elected officials and politically engaged folks who agreed to be interviewed and shared so freely of their wisdom, their hopes and fears about this war on choice. I'm not even going to try to name them all. While having coffee with one such person, I was introduced to Michel Foucault's observation, "The history which bears us and determines us has the form of a war rather than that of a language: relations of power, not relations of meaning." It resonated with my growing conviction about what is really going on when the anti-choice right launches yet another salvo against women's reproductive self-determination. Their fears are correct about one thing—we are changing the world. For the better, in my opinion, but in ways that are frightening to them because the expansion of justice for women changes the ancient balance of power between the genders so profoundly.

We delude ourselves if we believe the pundits who marginalize the pro-choice movement as though it were the polar opposite of anti-choice zealots, and claim that reproductive rights (read that as abortion, of course) are not an issue any more. And the recent spate of pronouncements that blame the pro-choice movement itself for the attacks upon women's rights to their bodies, their hopes, their dreams, point the finger in the wrong direction.

I thank my husband, Alex, for modeling action against injustice, and our collective children and grandchildren for being the picture in my head that gives me constant motivation to keep turning the spotlight onto those who would use the language of power in unjust ways.

I hope that this book will make you angry, angry enough to point your finger at the real culprits, the people of the anti-choice right who are bent on taking away reproductive rights and access to health care from those you love. And I hope above all that it will move you to action.

The status of legislation, lawsuits, and judicial nominations cited in the text is up to date as of January 2004.

CONTENTS

———◆———

INTRODUCTION

BY SALLY BLACKMUN, ESQ.

———➤◄———

In the fall of 1966, when I was a nineteen-year-old sophomore at Skidmore College, I received some shocking and extremely upsetting news. I learned I was pregnant. I was young and had thought I was being "careful," but I had no easy access to any kind of reproductive health care—it wouldn't be until 1972 that Planned Parenthood arrived in that part of New York State, a few years too late for me. Now I was faced with the painful truth that I had not properly protected myself. Who should I tell, and what should I do?

I confided in my older sister, who was living close by, and sought her advice about the best way to break this devastating news to our parents. My father always believed that, with a good education, my two sisters and I could be or do anything we wanted, so I knew he would be hugely disappointed if I had to quit college. There was no easy solution. I knew they would be heartbroken and disappointed in their "perfect" middle daughter.

I also sought out Skidmore's young chaplain, the Rev. Tom Davis, for his advice and support. Though he sympathized, he couldn't offer any good answers for me. In fact, it was cases like mine that later led him to help organize safe underground abortions for women, and to eventually serve as the head of Planned Parenthood's clergy board.

Once the shock wore off, I had to figure out what to do. My sister mentioned abortion as a possibility, but it was illegal in most states, and the fact that my father was a sitting federal judge made its illicit nature not only a risk to my health but a potential embarrassment to my family and his career. I came to the conclusion that I really had only two options: disappear and carry the baby to term, after which I would put it up for adoption (an option I did not feel was right for me), or marry the baby's father. Faced with such choices, I decided to do what so many young women of my era did: I quit college and married my twenty-year-old boyfriend. I thought I was in love and that having a baby would be wonderful.

I never discussed the decision with my parents, and never mentioned the possibility of abortion to them—I just told them what I wanted to do. Needless to say, they were not happy about the unplanned pregnancy, and worried about my marrying so young, but with reluctance, they supported my decision. Hard as it was for me to have gone to my parents with this news, I knew I could count on them to love me, no matter what. Other women of my generation who were not lucky enough to have such understanding parents felt that their only choice was a secret back-alley abortion, with all the attendant legal and physical risks.

I had a quiet, very small family wedding over the Christmas holidays and returned to Skidmore in January 1967 to take my semester exams and end my college education after only one and a half years. After I left Skidmore, I moved to Pennsylvania, where my new husband was completing his senior year in college. During one of my final semester exams, less than three weeks after the wedding, I suffered a miscarriage. It's some indication of the tenor of the times that as I ran across campus, trailing blood, my first impulse when I knocked on the infirmary door was to shout, "I'm married! I'm married!" because I was so concerned about how they were going to judge me for being pregnant. My young marriage ended six years later.

I returned to Skidmore only once, to attend the class of 1969's graduation ceremonies. Sadly, I was not one of the graduates, which was another painful memory for my parents and me. But later I was able to go back to college, and eventually on to law school, where I met and married my classmate—and soul mate— Michael. We have been married for twenty-seven years, and have two beautiful daughters, Lauren and Lisa, who have enriched our lives immeasurably.

Looking back on the hard choice I faced during what was probably the most difficult time of my life, I hope that my daughters and others their age will never be put in such a position. And if my hope is realized, it will be thanks in large part to organizations such as Planned Parenthood, which provide responsible sex education and family planning services for hundreds of thousands of American teenagers every day.

But today I fear that, as my father, U.S. Supreme Court justice Harry Blackmun, put it, "a chill wind blows," endangering women's reproductive freedoms, which are now under serious threat—far more than most of us realize. As Planned Parenthood president Gloria Feldt tells us in this important book, a war is being waged against those rights by an active, extremist minority, with frightening success on many fronts. Young women today don't understand the terrible choices—or lack of choices—women of Gloria's and my generation had to deal with. And unless those of us in the majority wake up to what is happening, we will face a crisis of immense proportions as a woman's reproductive choices are taken away and life in this country returns to the way it was before *Roe v. Wade*, the landmark decision that legalized abortion.

I have been privileged to have a front-row seat on the legal battle to win—and maintain—those most precious rights, courtesy of my father, who took the Supreme Court oath on June 9, 1970. In

1973, a mere seven years after my own unplanned pregnancy, he wrote the majority opinions in *Roe v. Wade* and *Doe v. Bolton,* two cases that legalized abortion by expanding the concept of a woman's right to privacy. These decisions did not, however, put an end to the battle being fought for and against a woman's right to choose, which has been and continues to be one of the most hotly debated and divisive issues this country has ever witnessed.

Two cases of critical importance to the outcome in *Roe* and *Doe* were on the books when the Supreme Court decided the first abortion rights cases. The first was *Griswold v. Connecticut,* decided in 1965, which involved a Connecticut statute that made the use of a contraceptive a crime. The executive director of a local Planned Parenthood group and its licensed medical director were convicted for giving married persons information about birth control and providing them with a contraceptive device. The Supreme Court found the Connecticut statute to be unconstitutional because it violated marital privacy, a right protected by the Bill of Rights.

The second case on the books was *Eisenstadt v. Baird,* decided in 1972. That case involved a Massachusetts statute that made it a felony to give a contraceptive drug or device to an unmarried person. Bill Baird was convicted for giving contraceptive foam to an unmarried university student. The Supreme Court ruled that dissimilar treatment for married and unmarried persons violated equal protection and that the right of privacy inheres in the individual, not in the marital relationship.

The *Roe* case was initially argued before the Court in December of 1971. In the summer of 1972, Dad spent two weeks in the medical library at the Mayo Clinic—where he had been general counsel during the 1950s—researching the medical and ethical aspects of the case.

As was his custom, Dad often discussed the broad issues involved in his cases around the dinner table. He really struggled with *Roe v. Wade.* At one point, over a meal, he asked all three of his daughters how we thought the case should be decided. One of my sisters recalls that the three of us gave him three different opinions—whereupon he announced he had developed a migraine headache and needed to go to bed. This was a typical scene in our family—it was always four women against Dad, and he felt outnumbered! I do think, though, that having three daughters and an outspoken, independent wife influenced his views about the choices women should be able to make in their lives.

Chief Justice Burger assigned Dad the majority opinion to write, probably because of his genuine interest in and knowledge of medical issues, thanks to his nine-year stint at Mayo. During his years at Mayo, Dad had seen firsthand the aftereffects of botched illegal abortions. The day the decision was announced was January 22, 1973. The courtroom was packed with spectators who had come in anticipation of the ruling. I was living in Washington and working on the White House staff at the time, so I was fortunate enough to be present. As usual, it was exciting to be in that chamber when a major opinion was issued, but it was particularly exciting for me that day because it was my father who was announcing it—and I didn't know what the outcome would be.

In the decision, Dad announced that the Court had reaffirmed that there is a right of personal privacy implicit in the Constitution, founded in the Fourteenth Amendment's concept of personal liberty and restrictions upon state action. This right of personal privacy includes a woman's decision to have an abortion during the first trimester of a pregnancy. But after the point of viability, he continued—when the fetus has a reasonable chance of surviving independently—the state may regulate and even prohibit abortion, except where it is necessary to save the life or health of the mother. I don't think anyone in the courtroom that day realized what a momentous decision it would turn out to be. At the time, Dad thought it was just one more logical step on the road to the full emancipation of women.

In the world outside the courtroom, the ruling was at first met with minimal commentary or reaction, because January 22, 1973, was also the day that President Lyndon Johnson died. The somber events of the day overshadowed the news of the Supreme Court decision. But the silence did not last long. There soon followed an outpouring of public reaction, pro and con. The mail the Court received in the ensuing two weeks was the greatest avalanche of communications it ever received before or since on any particular issue or series of cases.

Much to everyone's surprise, the decisions thrust my father into the kind of public spotlight few federal judges have had to endure. He personally received more than eighty thousand letters on the subject of women's rights and abortion between January of 1973 and his death in March of 1999. Some of the letters were critical or even hateful, and some were touching, sympathetic, and warm—but Dad insisted upon reading all eighty thousand of them. He often said that many of the most beautiful letters came from Catholic nursing nuns, who had seen and dealt with the many casualties of illegal and unsafe abortions and been as deeply disturbed by them as he had during his years at Mayo.

The abortion cases changed Dad's life. Although the decisions in 1973 were supported by seven of the nine sitting justices, it was he who became the primary recipient of both the pain and fame associated with them. He never anticipated that he would be the center of what has become a great and continuing controversy, and the object of cruel and personalized attacks. In addition to the ever-present hate mail, he was regularly picketed and demonstrated against at law schools he visited and speeches he gave. In 1989, a bullet came through my parents' living room window, narrowly missing my mother. The family was convinced someone was out to kill Dad, and thereafter always worried about his security and safety. In many ways his experiences paralleled the escalation of violence and harassment by anti-choice extremists against anyone associated with the advances in women's reproductive rights.

After the shooting incident, he received special protection and always traveled with the Supreme Court Police or U.S. Marshals. Needless to say, their constant presence in his life seriously eroded the privacy he and his family had always cherished. But Dad never complained. He accepted this heavy burden with grace and dignity.

A woman's right to choose has now been legal for over thirty years. It's difficult to imagine going back to the dark, dangerous days prior to 1973, but given how close the Supreme Court's pro-choice majority is, and the likelihood that one or more of those justices will retire while President George W. Bush is still in office, we may be there sooner than anyone would have believed possible just a few short years ago.

Of course, the assault on *Roe* didn't begin under the current Bush administration. In fact, it began almost immediately after the decision, both at the state legislative level and at the congressional level. Perhaps the worst blow came in 1986, in a Supreme Court decision (*Webster v. Reproductive Health Services*), which you'll be reading about in the pages that follow. This time my father was not in the majority, and wrote the dissenting opinion. It was there that he wrote the words that now seem so prophetic: "I fear for the liberty and equality of the millions of women who have lived and come of age in the sixteen years since *Roe* was decided. . . . For today, the women of this nation still retain the right to control their destinies. But the signs are ominous, and a chill wind blows." Since 1986, the wind has continued to blow ever harder—with each new legislative erosion of the right to choose, each federal judge that President Bush has appointed, each attempt to give rights to the fetus at the expense of the woman carrying it.

Today, I am a lawyer who volunteers as a court-appointed

guardian for abandoned, neglected, and abused children, primarily drug-addicted newborns, so I have had occasion to see what happens to unwanted children. One of these babies was born to a thirteen-year-old and tossed into a construction dumpster—fortunately he was found by construction workers and eventually adopted by his foster parents. Most of the kids I see are not so lucky, often placed in group homes or with relatives living in poverty. There are more than 30,000 children in Florida alone who are under the supervision of the Department of Children and Families, and nearly 3,400 awaiting adoption. It's easy for people to say "choose life," but when you see children who are abused, neglected, and living in poverty, you wonder about the quality of that life. Protecting the best interests of these children has made me realize, more than ever, how critical it is to have family planning and accurate sex education, to teach people how to prevent HIV/AIDS and sexually transmitted infections, and to provide women with choices and options. Ultimately, what is at stake, as my dad said, is a woman's right to control her own destiny.

Because of my dad's and others' lifetime commitment to the rights of women and the disadvantaged, women still have reproductive freedoms in this country. My daughters clearly have more options today than I had in 1966. And of course I hope they will continue to have those options, but, as Gloria points out in this book, we are on the verge of returning to the Dark Ages of the '50s and earlier. The younger generation cannot begin to understand and truly appreciate what it was like for women in this country before *Griswold, Eisenstadt,* and *Roe.*

At the time of Dad's retirement in 1994, Estelle Rogers made a wonderful tribute that focuses on the critical importance of *Roe:* "*Roe* irrevocably changed the lives of millions of American women: women who have babies, women who have abortions, and women who have both; women whose children are planned and women who make mistakes; women who have problem-free pregnancies and women for whom bearing children is the riskiest of propositions; and, perhaps, the most important, women whose tender years hardly qualify them as women at all."

It's imperative that my generation and your generation not be complacent about the continuing fight for reproductive freedoms— or we will lose them. We must not be silent or passive in confronting the war on choice. It's critical that the majority of U.S. citizens acknowledge the fight and engage in it. I hope you will join Gloria and me in that fight.

Sally Blackmun is senior associate general counsel at Darden Restaurants and is on the board of directors of Planned Parenthood of Greater Orlando. She is the daughter of the late U.S. Supreme Court Justice Harry Blackmun.

THE WAR ON CHOICE

ONE

GOOD OL' BOYS AND THE BAD OLD DAYS.

————◆————

THE RIGHT-WING WAR
TO TAKE AWAY OUR RIGHTS

I think contraception is disgusting—people using each other for pleasure . . . for those who say I can't impose my morality on others, I say watch me.

—Joseph Scheidler, executive director, Pro-Life Action League

I am outraged that [the abortion issue] is viewed from the perspective of the woman—a femme-centric perspective that condones the self-indulgent conduct of the woman who was damn careless in the first place.

—Dick Armey, former U.S. House Majority Leader (R–Texas)

I will do everything in my power to restrict abortion.

—George W. Bush

————◆————

On November 5, 2003, President George W. Bush took a giant step toward fulfilling his promise to restrict abortion. He signed a criminal ban on abortion procedures, the deceptively named "Partial Birth Abortion Act." Surrounded by a phalanx of gray-haired, self-congratulatory white men—and no women!—he signed away a great portion of women's power over their reproductive lives. This was an ominous milestone: for the first time in history, the two houses of Congress had passed, and a president had signed into law, a federal law criminalizing established medical procedures. With the House of Representatives, the Senate, and the White House now aligned in lockstep, ready to take away women's reproductive rights, the right wing's war on women and choice had scored a major victory.

> *Now we will begin to focus on the methods (of abortion) and declare them to be illegal.*
>
> —Rep. Chris Smith (R–New Jersey)

The law Bush signed that day is extraordinary: it is the only federal law *ever* enacted that criminally bans abortion procedures. And it is a law passed and signed in brazen defiance of the Supreme Court. For it was well known to policy makers that this abortion ban has the exact same constitutional deficiencies as the Nebraska law that the Supreme Court had struck down just three years before in *Stenberg v. Carhart:* it has no exception to save a woman's health, and only an inadequate exception to save her life, and the language of the law is so broad that it could ban techniques that doctors use regularly and safely even early in the second trimester. Besides placing the lives and health of women at risk, it puts doctors at risk of prosecution for providing safe, medically necessary care. In the Nebraska case, the court held that these restrictions are an "undue burden" on women. They are plainly bad policy, even if the law allowed them: who wants politicians telling our physicians what procedure to use on us for *any* surgery?

U.S. Attorney General John Ashcroft, for one. Immediately after the bill was signed, Ashcroft moved to assign enforcement of the law, which he said he intended to do vigorously. He directed the Justice Department's civil rights division to enforce the law, explaining that the law enlarges the civil rights of the fetus.

> *[The] partial-birth abortion ban is a political scam but a public relations gold mine. . . . This bill, if it becomes law, may not save one child's life. . . . The major benefit of this bill is the debate that surrounds it.*
>
> —Randall Terry, founder of Operation Rescue
> (a militant anti-choice group that conducts
> blockades of abortion provider facilities),
> September 15, 2003

The passage of the Partial-Birth Abortion Act was the culmination of a long-term strategy by right-wing extremists who have been working, ever since *Roe*, to take away a woman's right to control her reproductive destiny. The abortion ban seemed at first to prohibit only a small number of rare, late-term procedures (just which procedures those *are* is a matter of debate, since, as Randall Terry, one of its supporters, says, "partial-birth abortion" is a public relations term, not a medical one). But in reality, the ban uses sweeping language that the Supreme Court has already recognized would affect a wide range of abortions.

The entire debate about so-called "partial-birth abortion" is part of a larger campaign to make *all* abortions illegal. It is a right-wing public relations strategy to manipulate language in order to sensationalize the abortion debate, to make the public believe that abortions are performed willy-nilly through all nine months of pregnancy by reckless physicians in cahoots with mothers who are intent on murdering their viable babies, and thereby bring both the public and formerly pro-choice politicians over to the anti-abortion camp. The incendiary language was designed to deceive the American people, and it worked. Dr. Leroy Carhart, the plaintiff in the case that struck down the previous ban, calls it "partial-truth abortion."

And it is but one skirmish in a much larger war—the war on choice. The right to choose is not just about abortion, not by a long shot. It comprises the right to have full access to family planning information, health care, and products; the right to have children or not; sex education for young people that goes beyond the abstinence-only education being promoted by the right wing; and the right to medically accurate information about sexuality for the general public, too. Having the right to choose determines whether women will find an equal place at life's table, whether children will be truly valued, and whether everyone's personal liberties, privacy, and bodily integrity will be safeguarded against the ideology of the right.

Today's courts will almost certainly overrule the ban that President Bush signed into law. But the federal appeals courts are increasingly being filled with anti-choice ideologues, so who knows what will happen in the future? What those opposed to a woman's right to choose *hope* for is that by the time this law reaches the Supreme Court, there will be a different court, a court that, like the executive and legislative branches of the government, will be marching in lockstep with the anti-choice right.

THE ANTI-CHOICE, ANTI-WOMAN BACKLASH

The anti-choice minority in this country is taking full advantage of the pro-choice majority's complacent assumption that with

Roe v. Wade we won reproductive choice once and for all. Nothing could be further from the truth. In fact, *Roe v. Wade* so galvanized the anti-choice groups that almost as soon as the decision was handed down they began attacking reproductive rights on all fronts—in legislation, in the media, in the courts, in the state houses, in your hometown. This isn't an abortion war, it's a culture war, and its objective is to take away the economic, social, and political gains women have made since those years. Well funded and well organized, they are vocal, disciplined, and relentless in their assaults. They are creating a fearful atmosphere of sexual puritanism that hearkens back to the 1950s, and their goal is to return women to the position of powerlessness they occupied in that era.

To put it into its proper cultural and historical context, we must understand that the abortion ban—along with the many other attacks on women's reproductive rights—is part of a growing backlash against women's equality and freedom. Over the past fifty years, women have gained an astonishing amount of power, and *Roe v. Wade*, which gave women control over their fertility, was another major step toward empowerment. Not only did it legalize abortion but it became a symbol of our independence, because reproductive freedom is fundamental to a woman's aspirations—to education, financial stability, and self-determination. Reproductive freedom encompasses the right to freely and responsibly determine the number and spacing of our children. The simple ability to separate sex from childbearing gives women the power to control all other aspects of their lives. This is a profound shift in the gender power balance—a shift that most of us understand to be an advance in social justice, especially when we are thinking about ourselves and our own daughters. But it poses a threat to the status of the entrenched hierarchy.

That's why the right-wing extremists are so focused on taking away reproductive rights. And that's why they are using every weapon in their arsenals to ensure that politicians, judges, government appointees, and public health care agencies follow the anti-choice agenda. They are determined to take away not only the right to abortion but all reproductive rights.

That's right. *All* reproductive rights.

There is nothing new about this backlash. It's human nature that when the established order has been changed, there will be a reaction, and the magnitude of this reaction shouldn't surprise us. The advancement of women in the last fifty years has been breathtaking. There has been no comparable advancement in human history. There are victories along the way, but none of the victories is secure because of the pressures that undermine women's rights and advancement. Because reproductive rights are taken for granted, people who oppose them have been able to go on the offensive and make gains that do not reflect the will of the majority. So now, women who value their autonomy have to step up and take action.

—U.S. Senator Hillary Clinton (D—New York),
October 27, 2003

THE HIDDEN WAR ON WOMEN'S REPRODUCTIVE RIGHTS

You may have a hard time believing me when I say that it isn't just abortion rights that are threatened in this country—that the right wing is attacking our right to family planning and sex education, too. Slowly but surely, however, the right to make our own childbearing choices is disappearing. Having taken on the anti-choice agenda, the right wing has devised a multipronged battery of assaults—many so obscure or buried in bureaucracy that they go undetected by the media—to take away our reproductive freedoms. It's time for us to name those assaults, to connect the dots, and to realize that our rights to privacy and self-determination are on the line. Unless we do something now, it will be too late.

Here are just a few examples of what the anti-choice extremists are doing. Some are common knowledge; others have slipped beneath the radar.

- Taking away public funding for family planning services that reduce the need for abortion.
- Making abortion services so difficult to obtain that currently 87 percent of U.S. counties have no abortion providers, requiring people to travel long distances at a considerable, and sometimes prohibitive, expense of money and time.
- Turning laws intended to protect children from abuse into "sex police" laws, requiring that family planning providers file reports with state authorities about minors who have requested contraceptives, medical attention for sexually transmitted infections, or abortion.
- Replacing medically accurate sexuality education with "abstinence-only" education, which censors information about using contraceptives and fails to give useful information about much of anything else.
- Forcing health-care providers to give state-mandated anti-choice materials to patients seeking abortions.
- Passing laws to define "personhood" as beginning at the moment of fertilization, which threatens not only the right to abortion but many types of birth control, infertility treatments, and scientific research.
- Filling the lower federal courts with anti-choice judges.
- Packing scientific committees that oversee women's health and HIV/AIDS with ideological appointees, who are "experts" only in being against reproductive rights—and even condom use.
- Manipulating the media by harassing reporters and editors, and demanding that they always "balance" any story regarding

sexual or reproductive health with quotes from right-wing ideologues.
• Defunding family planning services in countries that depend
on U.S. foreign assistance for basic health care, birth control,
and HIV/AIDS prevention—resulting in unintended pregnancies, increased poverty, and the deaths of countless women in
developing countries.

When you add it all up, the picture is truly frightening. It's a hidden
war on women's reproductive rights. And of course the biggest
prize in this war, the one that could definitively end the right to
choose, is the Supreme Court. With a president who has committed
himself to restricting abortion and says that *Roe v. Wade* was wrongly
decided, and one or more justices on the Supreme Court likely to
retire in the next few years, the pro-choice balance could soon be
ended, and the already weakened *Roe v. Wade* overturned. The 2003
abortion ban law could be just the tipping point President Bush is
looking for when he says the country isn't ready "yet" to ban abortion entirely. If this law is allowed to stand, and the public, not understanding what it really comprises, rallies behind it, then the
president and the right-wing leadership in the Senate may be em-
boldened to nominate, and confirm, one or more additional anti-
choice judges to the Supreme Court.

WHILE YOU WERE OUT: A BRIEF HISTORY OF ANTI-CHOICE ASSAULTS

In order for us to defeat the anti-choice insurgency, we need to
wake up to the amount of damage they have already done. The recent passage of the abortion ban is only the latest in a long series of
legislative, judicial, and public relations victories revealing how or-

ganized and tenacious the anti-choice forces are, how well they can spin the media and the minds of Americans, and how far they have succeeded—already—in taking away women's reproductive freedoms.

Beginning in the late '70s, the anti-choice right engineered a series of actions on numerous fronts that resulted in severe restrictions on women's access to abortion. To recount only the highlights of this anti-choice juggernaut: in 1976, they passed the Hyde Amendment, which eliminated abortion from the health plans of the 23 million poor women who relied on Medicaid. Although many ostensibly pro-choice members of Congress chose not to fight the amendment because they believed that it would be overturned in the courts, later the same year the Supreme Court, in *Maher v. Roe*, held that states and localities were not required to pay for abortions, nor did hospitals have to perform them. Thus, low-income women lost their full right to choose long ago; the burden of this loss has fallen disproportionately on women of color.

The court also well knows its decisions will have the practical effect of preventing nearly all poor women from obtaining safe and legal abortions, and will brutally coerce them to bear children whom society will scorn for every day of their lives.

—Justice Thurgood Marshall,
in a dissent to *Maher v. Roe*

After the Hyde Amendment, the anti-choice right became ever more aggressive in trying to restrict not just abortion but family planning—in any way they could. They began by attacking birth control: cutting Title X funds for family planning, thus depriving poor women of access to contraception—and ensuring that, as a consequence, the number of women seeking abortions would rise. During the '70s and '80s, they bombarded state legislatures with bills to restrict abortion. They managed to pass bills requiring that women must have a husband's permission to get an abortion, that they must wait twenty-four hours before the procedure, and that they must have mandatory "counseling" during which they will be shown graphic anti-choice materials. They also voted to restrict second-term abortions to hospitals, and to restrict minors' access by requiring them to get parental consent before having an abortion.

THE RESULT OF HYDE

I grew up on welfare in the ghetto of South Philadelphia. For the women I come from, the women who brought me up, choice is basically a myth. Reproductive freedom comes with a big price tag and if you have no money, then you have no choice. In my neighborhood and in my family I watched women take pills, pitch themselves down flights of stairs, and drink and douche with all kinds of concoctions in attempts to force miscarriages on their bodies because those bodies go unprotected by the "right to choose." If you are too young, too poor, or a color other than white, then the coat hanger desperation everyone else left behind in the '70s is alive and well for you. That desperation was alive and well for my friends, my cousins, my own mother—right here in 2003, almost thirty-one years after *Roe*.

—Jenna McKean, age 23, co-organizer of the Smith
College Student Coalition for the
March for Women's Lives

In the late 1980s and early 1990s, anti-choice zealots ratcheted up their attacks on reproductive-health clinics. Going far beyond the routine harassment of clinic workers and of women seeking treatment, they moved into outright terrorism, bombing physicians and clinic workers. Those campaigns of terror did not succeed in deterring women from getting abortions. But they did alienate mainstream Americans, convincing them that anti-choice extremists are far outside the mainstream in their values and willing to go to any lengths—even murder—to impose those values on the rest of us. During this time, they also lost a number of ballot initiatives and referenda that attempted to outlaw or severely restrict abortion.

For once the right-wing public relations onslaught had stalled. It was clear to those who oppose choice that they could not win this fight by trying to outlaw abortion head-on, but that they could make incremental gains by chipping away at access until rights became meaningless. By 1995 the anti-choice right knew it needed to regain the sympathies of the American public, and they concocted the perfect vehicle with which to do that: the campaign against so-called partial-birth abortion. The phrase itself was made up by aides to former representative Charles Canady of Florida (who was subsequently appointed by Governor Jeb Bush to the Florida Second District Court of Appeals, where he now sits). Canady seized upon the idea of introducing a ban on specific abortion procedures as a way of refocusing the debate on the fetus rather than the woman, and he knew just which kind of procedure he wanted to put the spotlight on.

The National Right to Life Committee had obtained a copy of a paper by abortion provider Dr. Martin Haskell, in which he described a procedure he used in certain cases. Often those were very wanted pregnancies gone tragically wrong, so that the pregnancy was a serious risk to the woman's health, or the fetus had grave defects inconsistent with survival. The American College of Obstetricians and Gynecologists calls this technique intact dilation and extraction, or D and X, and estimates that it is used in less than one-fifth of 1 percent of all abortions performed in the U.S. While it is not pretty to contemplate, neither are the alternatives—for either the woman or the fetus. One of the main goals of physicians who employ it is to protect the woman's future fertility and health. Medicine is an art as well as a science, and physicians often develop new techniques or improve upon existing techniques and report their results to their peers. Canady used the paper Haskell had written as his ammunition to introduce a ban on abortion procedures in 1995. But he and his aides were unable to find a term in a medical textbook for what they wanted to ban. Although their public pronouncements centered on attacking Haskell's technique, in truth, they wanted a much broader prohibition that would fire a devastating shot at *Roe* and confuse the public about the issue of abortion. So they conferred with Douglas Johnson, legislative director for the National Right to Life Committee, and together they made up a new term. After rejecting "brain-suction abortion" and "partial-delivery abortion," they hit on the perfect media catchphrase: "partial-birth abortion."

The American College of Obstetricians and Gynecologists (ACOG), an organization of 44,000 physicians dedicated to women's health, immediately came out against the ban. " 'Partial-birth abortion' is a nonmedical term," the group stated, adding, "such legislation has the potential to outlaw other abortion techniques that are critical to the lives and health of American women." Nevertheless, much of the media began to use the term, and lawmakers across the country began supporting the ban.

The "partial-birth abortion" opponents portrayed the procedure as a third-trimester, postviability abortion elected by careless, immoral women who chose to arbitrarily kill their near-term babies. Upon signing the bill, Bush used that sensationalizing rhetoric, saying the procedure was "directed against children who are inches from birth." Publicly, the right-wingers argued that the ban only covered the D and X procedure. But the language of the ban is so deliberately vague that it would probably criminalize other procedures, including one called dilation and evacuation, which is used in most abortions done after twelve to thirteen weeks. The ban criminalizes abortions that are clearly protected under *Roe*—exactly as those who crafted the bill intended. And, as mentioned before, there is no provision in the ban for doctors to make exceptions if the health of the woman is at risk, and only an inadequate exception for the life of the woman. Sure enough, immediately after the bill was signed, some physicians began canceling appointments for all second-trimester abortions, fearing criminal charges.

The federal abortion ban was previously vetoed twice by President Clinton, in 1995 and 1997. He signed off on the veto surrounded by women whose lives and/or fertility had been saved by the procedures the ban would have outlawed—quite a different photo opportunity from the all-male group at the Bush signing. But the right, relentless, kept on introducing legislation with that bogus term. Anti-choice politicos introduced abortion-ban bills in nineteen states, and ballot initiatives in another two. The Wisconsin ban included mandatory life imprisonment for physicians performing the procedure. All of these were defeated in the courts, including the Nebraska ban, which the Supreme Court struck down in 2002.

Now Congress has passed the federal abortion ban again, and the president has signed it into law. In response to the most recent ban, ACOG issued a statement that called it an "inappropriate, ill-advised and dangerous intervention into medical decision making," and then pointed out that the best way to reduce the number of abortions is to prevent unwanted and unintended pregnancies. Exactly how ill-advised and dangerous it is can be seen from the stories of two women who had procedures that Congress and President Bush have just banned:

We were awaiting the arrival of a son. I'm diabetic, so I had more prenatal testing than most women. At twenty-five weeks I had an ultrasound and the doctor's exact words were, "Vick, you are disgustingly normal and so is the baby." At thirty-two weeks I went in for another ultrasound and my world came crashing down. They discovered that [the fetus] had not grown past twenty-five weeks, and further testing revealed that he had nine major anomalies, including a fluid-filled cranium with no brain tissue at all. He could never have survived outside my womb. My body was the only thing keeping him alive, and I chose to remove my son from life support. I'm a mom. I had three beautiful children, and in fact I have a new baby boy who's here with me now. Who are the people on the anti-choice side to judge me? They've never been in my shoes. I never in my wildest dreams thought something like this could happen, but it happened to me.

—Vicki Stella, who in 1996 had an abortion
now banned under the abortion ban law

I am not atypical—thirty-four years old and desperately wanting to have children. Tom and I have been married for four years, and trying to have a baby for two. After successfully fighting hormone-related infertility and experiencing the sadness of a miscarriage, we were thrilled to find ourselves pregnant. But at thirteen weeks, tests revealed the fetus had brain abnormalities and trisomy thirteen [a chromosomal abnormality]. Most fetuses with trisomy thirteen die in utero; of those that make it to birth, almost half do not survive past the first month. Long-term survival is one year, and theirs is a painful existence marked by periods of breathing cessation and seizures. We discussed our options with a genetic counselor. My husband and I felt strongly that it was in both the child's and our best interest to terminate as quickly as possible. The counselor said we could either have a D and E or have labor induced. My doctor described both procedures and we decided that a D and E was clearly best for me. The procedure was performed on the first day of my sixteenth week of pregnancy.

Upon arriving home from the hospital, a news story appeared describing legislation aimed at banning "partial-birth abortion." I don't think I really understood this issue emotionally or intellectually until I was in the position of having to terminate my much-desired pregnancy. Along with my sadness came the realization that if such legislation passed, the right to safe second-trimester termination of pregnancies might not remain available to those women who come after me. I don't know how these women will endure; I don't know how I would have endured.

—Audrey Eisen, testimony in
opposition to abortion-ban legislation

BACK[WARD] TO THE FUTURE

Thanks to the relentlessness of the right wing, we are returning to the days when young women who want control over their reproductive lives are being forced to make terrible, sometimes deadly, decisions. Anti-choice policies are undoing a century of progress, and they're not only cruel, they're completely unrealistic. Today, most women have thirty to forty fertile years. Gone are the days when we went directly from menarche to marriage, when we had one baby after another and few survived to adulthood. Gone are the days when women's main value was to bear children, often at the expense of their own lives. Gone are the days when women didn't contribute, as they do today, to the workforce because they weren't allowed to pursue careers and education. Most modern women spend a large portion of their fertile years trying to avoid pregnancy.

But without access to information and birth control, unintended pregnancies occur. In fact, accidents happen even under the best of circumstances. Not surprisingly, a third of American women choose to terminate their pregnancies at some point during their lives. Throughout history and all over the world, women who felt they could not carry a particular pregnancy to term have chosen to have abortions, whether legal or not. Still, the right-wing politicians who are in power and the anti-choice zealots behind them have done everything they can to strip women of their moral right and responsibility to plan their childbearing years. The right to abortion may be a matter of standing law, but its legal underpinnings are being hacked away at an alarming rate, so that many women in this country, particularly the young and poor, are having to resort to desperate measures we thought we'd never see again after abortion was made legal nationwide in 1973 by the U.S. Supreme Court decision in *Roe v. Wade*. In many ways we are back to where we were then, with a two-tiered system: women who had the means to travel to get a safe abortion could do so, and the others suffered illegal, unsafe abortions or unplanned pregnancies.

I can't overemphasize that this fight is about the full spectrum of women's reproductive and human rights—the fundamental rights of women to control their destinies by controlling their sexual and reproductive lives. How do I make that claim with such certainty? If the facts in the chapters that follow don't persuade you, then perhaps my personal experience will.

THE VIEW FROM OPPOSITE SIDES OF THE OIL PATCH

It's impossible to analyze the war on choice without looking at the record of its current commander in chief. George W. Bush and I both grew up in West Texas in the 1950s—although apparently we saw life from opposite sides of the oil patch. I have no personal animosity toward George W. Bush. I know all too well the West Texas good ol' boy culture that formed him. In spite of myself, I've always found good ol' boys as charming as the press and the public find George W. Bush. I don't doubt that he is a loving husband and father, nor do I doubt the sincerity of his belief system. What I do find shocking, and antithetical to the basic American values of re-spect, tolerance, and fair play, is his arrogance. Why do religious fundamentalists like Bush, Pat Robertson, Jerry Falwell, and their political operatives like Karl Rove, think that they are entitled to force their personal belief systems on the rest of us? And why are they so eager to take us back to the stifling culture of the 1950s?

I know how easy it is to romanticize the 1950s. Just last month, I bought a pair of pointy-toed black leather pumps with bows on them that looked almost identical to a pair I had in the summer of 1955. They're darling, but they still hurt my feet and crimp my ability to walk. Shoes are one thing, but larger cultural and social changes are another. In the same way those pointed-toe shoes bind the foot, nostalgia for a past era, stripped of the memories of their painful realities and pervasive injustices, can bind our thinking about the present.

The 1950s in West Texas were darned good times—if you were white, male, and privileged, that is. If you were anything else, America was at best stifling, and at worst oppressive. Racial segre-gation was the norm in public schools, hospitals, movie theaters, and elsewhere. Gays were either closeted or vilified. African-Americans had no hope of getting good jobs or holding public of-fice, they were discouraged from voting by poll taxes and violence, and the only way they could live in the Bushes' neighborhood was if they were the live-in maid or gardener.

Women fared only marginally better. What I remember is that a woman couldn't get a credit card without her husband's permis-sion, and if she wanted a loan to buy a car or start a business, a man had to co-sign. Life options were minimal. We could aspire to jobs that were listed in the "help wanted female" columns—secretary, clerk, nurse, teacher, housekeeper, seamstress—but only if we "had" to work because we didn't have a man to support us. And if we held jobs that men could also hold, the man was typically paid more because he was the "head of the household."

Back then, of course, abortion was illegal. Even birth control was illegal in some states, and inaccessible in most. In 1957, the U.S. experienced its highest teen pregnancy rate ever in its history, and that year, at the age of fifteen, I contributed to that number. Nobody had talked to me or any of my friends or classmates about sex or birth control. The few teen girls who got pregnant but didn't get married generally went to live with "Aunt Mary" for a year, and the resulting babies were never spoken of again, though the resulting pain and shame lasted a lifetime. Reproductive freedom was a nascent concept, though research on the birth control pill had already begun. In just a few short years, that new technology would begin to change the gender power balance in profound ways. Because once a woman has the ability to determine her reproductive destiny, she can aspire to control her destiny in every other area as well. Reproductive self-determination is the most fundamental civil and human right a woman can have. It's the key to enjoying full equality, liberty, and justice. And that's the very right that the right-wing extremists are fighting so hard to take away.

President Bush says that the *W* stands for "women." Then why is it that Bush and the right-wing constituency that supports him want to take women back to an era when we had less power, when we were less of a political threat? His administration has taken one action after another to deny women's reproductive freedoms, beginning with the nomination of an attorney general, John Ashcroft, who is vehemently anti-choice. Bush's anti-woman agenda is bolstered by a Congress that is now engaged in a full-scale attack on reproductive freedom with a vast array of anti-choice legislation. Since taking office, he has supported some fifty initiatives to curtail the reproductive rights of women and men, both in the U.S. and around the globe. (See Appendix A, page 267.)

Just as those pointy-toed shoes are back, so are attitudes and laws that threaten to take us back to the bad old days of high death

and injury rates from illegal abortion, lack of access to birth control programs that could have prevented the unintended pregnancies in the first place, and to sex education that in its dishonesty is
worse than the silence I experienced in the '50s.

Perhaps Bush and his allies are blinded by nostalgia for a seemingly simpler, more stable era. Selective memory may have caused
them to forget the injustices of those times—or, being one of the
privileged sons of that era, Bush may simply be unaware or indifferent. But unlike retro fashions in shoes, retro fashions in bedrock
human and civil rights can be devastating. The people of today's
America had better speak up or we will continue our trajectory
back to an unacceptable future, to a time when women were left out
of the mainstream, deprived of the opportunity to live lives as full
and rich as their fathers, brothers, husbands, and sons.

LOOKING FOR BARBARA AND LAURA

The Bush family's relationship to reproductive rights issues is a
cautionary tale for the country. The parents of former president
George Herbert Walker Bush helped found a chapter of Planned
Parenthood in Connecticut. As a congressman in the 1970s,
George H. W. Bush was a strong proponent of reproductive rights.
In fact, he was such an ardent supporter of international family
planning that his colleagues nicknamed him "Rubbers."

All that changed when he became Ronald Reagan's running
mate. Reagan needed a strong showing from the right flank of his
party in order to win, and they were adamant on curtailing choice, so
Bush Sr. had to make a choice: toe the hard line or lose his power
and position. Perhaps pro-choice Republicans—including women—
thought their position would resurface when their candidate was
safely elected; instead, it went underground for good. The radical

right had taken control of the Republican platform and it has remained in control until today, with Bush's son, George W., currently occupying the White House.

I can't imagine what Barbara Bush makes of some of her husband's or son's extreme positions. She herself has been perfectly straightforward about her pro-choice stance. "For me, abortion is a personal issue—between the mother, father, and doctor," she wrote in her memoir. "Abortion is not a presidential matter. Education is the answer. Morals cannot be legislated."

What's more, George W.'s wife, Laura Bush, has made it clear that she, too, thinks abortion should be a private decision. "No, I don't think [*Roe v. Wade*] should be overturned," she said on the *Today Show* in 2001, before she was silenced in the matter. And Bush is surrounded by other close advisors who are pro-choice. Condoleezza Rice has said that she's pro-choice, and believes "there's a lot of room in the middle [on abortion]." Secretary of State Colin Powell has been very clear on the issue: "I believe in a woman's right to choose."

Why, if his mother, his wife, and some of his closest advisors and confidants are pro-choice, is Bush so vehemently anti-choice? Why is he hell-bent on not only making abortion illegal but ensuring that women don't even have access to decent family planning services? Why are the policies of his administration decreeing that young people be brainwashed into thinking that sex is evil and there's nothing to be done to protect yourself from sexually transmitted infections and unintended pregnancies?

Maybe Bush truly believes that abortion is wrong. But if he does, why is he forcing that belief, against the American principles of tolerance for a diversity of religious beliefs, on the rest of us? And why in the world are Barbara, Laura, Condoleezza, Colin, and other pro-choice folks like former New Jersey governor and EPA director Christine Todd Whitman (who declined my request for an interview) going quietly along with him? Why are they mute when they should be screaming to be heard?

Politics, folks. The people who are attacking women's rights aren't engaged in a fight about religion or morality, though they may claim those lofty values: it's all about winning and keeping power. The reason the anti-choice minority has so much power is that it delivers a solid block of votes—and a big pile of cash—to whoever adopts its agenda. Politicians who might otherwise not be anti-choice—indeed, whose family members have quietly had abortions themselves—pander to anti-choice interests, because they want to win. Unfortunately, they're winning at the expense of American women and families, who'd better start fighting back now!

HOW DO THEY GET AWAY WITH IT?

With the majority of Americans believing in family planning, real sex education, and the right to choose, you have to wonder: How do the anti-choice politicians get away with it? How have we allowed our reproductive rights to be trampled by an extremist minority? Why have pro-choice Republicans rolled over and let these right-wing zealots take away our rights? Why have so many pro-choice Democrats been intimidated and failed to mount an effective challenge?

I asked some people with longtime political experience who should know: How did we get into this mess?

Jennifer Stockman, President of the Republican Pro-choice Coalition:
"My husband, David, was a Congressman from Michigan, and he was on the platform committee in 1980 when the anti-choice plank was put into the Republican party platform. That's where the anti-choice victories started. That should have been the alarm bell.

But a lot of people dismissed it as pure rhetoric. But that's when I became frightened.

"I was shocked that the pro-choice contingent didn't fight back as hard as they should have. I remember asking my husband how this could happen. All the men in leadership were patting us on the head, and saying, 'Don't worry, dear, it's just to appease the right wing.' I bought into it like everyone else. Well, not quite everyone else. Mary Crisp—who was the Republican party chair—resigned because of this plank in the platform. The men said, 'Good, get rid of her, she's a bitch.'

"What is so unfortunate is that the real core of the Republican party is in favor of privacy and keeping the government out of personal decisions. They [the anti-choice contingent] framed us as being cavalier about abortion—promoting promiscuous behavior. They cast a negative, threatening light on a lot of the good work Planned Parenthood is doing. That's one reason why Independents have grown so much—they've become a way station for disgruntled Republicans."

Congresswoman Eleanor Holmes Norton, (D–Washington, D.C.), and Longtime Civil Rights Activist:

"Winning *Roe v. Wade* created a backlash against women. The right wing was caught off guard, and they never got over it. They finally won in Congress in 1994.

"When people are successful at getting a long-sought-for goal, the fighting spirit goes away or is lowered. So part of the problem is that women have lost sight of who Congress responds to. Women are pro-choice, but we need to re-create our citizen's movement. I've just gone on the floor this very day to speak up against a late-term abortion bill, and it is going to become law anyhow. Part of the problem is that young women don't know what they could lose."

Senator Olympia Snowe (R–Maine):

"We know for a fact that those who oppose a woman's right to choose are both extremely organized and motivated. Those who would deny women this right have clearly recognized the fundamental rule of politics—all politics are local—and demonstrated the influence and power of a well-organized, highly motivated, effective grassroots. And they only grow stronger with time.

"In the first five years of the 1980s there were 30 roll call votes related to the issue of abortion. In the last five years of the 1990s, there were 144."

Ellie Smeal, President, Feminist Majority Foundation:

"We talk about being the greatest democracy, but we allow control by the very few. We have called this a moral issue, but it is a money issue—raw money and power. We must make reproductive rights a global issue. It is a social injustice domestically and globally. The Democrats' lackluster performance is part of the problem. None of this would be possible without the collusion of the Democrats."

Senator David Paterson, Democratic Leader of the
New York State Senate:

"What bothers me sometimes is the people who say they believe in choice have skepticism of conscience. They certainly recognize, based on their ideals and values, the right of a woman to make her own choice. But they are unwilling to say so decisively. Well, people respond to decisiveness. Anti-choice people don't acknowledge any moral conflict. It's such a clear point of view that others follow them because of their decisiveness. Yet their goal is really to control people. . . . There is a political vacuum when we don't stick to our point of view, and the anti-choice people exploit that vacuum."

Lynn Grefe, Former Executive Director, Republican Pro-choice Coalition:
"The troublemakers are small, active groups like the Christian Coalition and Focus on the Family. They're organized. They deliver money and they deliver votes."

Patricia Schroeder, Former Congresswoman (D–Colorado); President, Association of American Publishers:
"I honestly think *Roe* is in deep trouble. It's already been chopped up. One of the problems is that it's got to be young people leading the campaign—it can't be people with gray hair like me. On college campuses, young people laugh when you talk about the threat."

Tanya Melich, Author, The Republican War Against Women,
Political Consultant and Lifelong Republican Activist, Now an Independent:
"For many years, the Republicans have tried to pull in southern Democrats, and one of the ways you did that was by being against the big, bad feminist movement. In 1988, George H. W. Bush went through a very bad fight to get the nomination. Pat Robertson was running, and they had to cut deals along the way with him. When Dan Quayle was selected to be vice president, that was an indication that Bush was very aware of what he needed to do for his right flank, which had really become the base of the Republican party. The moderates left with John Anderson (Independent candidate for president) and never came back.

"George W. Bush has ideological attitudes that are very different from his father's and Ronald Reagan's. Reagan and Bush weren't ideologues on women's issues, they moved with whatever they needed to do to govern and hold the power. That's not the case with the present administration. And with 9/11, he's used the issue of security to circumvent everything else. If you are not secure in your home, the issue of whether or not you can buy birth control pills is not going to be important.

"But this is an administration that is going to take away the freedom that women have had to make choices of how they will live their lives, how many children they will have, all those things. They have consistently moved in the last three years to stop all that. To *stop* it."

Representative Loretta Sanchez (D–California):
"The biggest problem is that people don't know what's happening. . . . They don't even realize this movement is not just about abortion, it's about access to birth control and all reproductive health services. It's about choice."

Roselyn O'Connell, President, National Women's Political Caucus, and Republican Activist:
"The reason we're in this situation is that a lot of us have been asleep at the wheel. . . . We have to get a lot better at organizing. There are a lot more pro-choice Republican women than anyone believes. Why they're quiet, I don't know.

"I don't think a lot of people understand how fragile reproductive rights are. They can't quite make themselves believe that *Roe v. Wade* could actually go away."

Representative Louise Slaughter (D–New York),
Cochair of the House Bipartisan Pro-choice Caucus:
"For elected officials, there has been a lot of intimidation. So many of my colleagues say they don't really believe in the anti-choice position, but they are afraid. For example, one told me his bishop called him night and day to get him to vote for an anti-choice bill.

"The right-wing media, especially radio, have been spewing out a steady diet of right-wing propaganda. This is damaging not just to pro-choice beliefs but damaging to all kinds of issues in our democracy. The elimination of the Federal Communications Commission's Fairness Doctrine [which used to require equal time for political views] is to blame for much of this imbalance.

"Another basic mistake is having separate clinics for abortion services. They have become a target. Abortions should be a regular medical service, part of every hospital and health center."

Representative Nancy Johnson (R–Connecticut),
Cochair of the House Bipartisan Pro-choice Caucus:
"All the publicity for some years now has been about 'partial-birth abortion' or minors, where the issues are emotional and the factual basis is never addressed. There has been a decade of concentration on possible abuse or casualness of abortion based not on facts but emotional issues. We don't have families who have experienced the loss of a mother or daughter anymore. My husband, when he was in training, saw a woman die [from a self-induced abortion], and he never forgot that."

Representative Jim Greenwood (R–Pennsylvania),
Cochair of the House Bipartisan Pro-choice Caucus:
"Since *Roe*, Americans know they basically have the right to choose, even though those rights are constantly being chipped away. The anti-choice side knows that, so far, they remain on the losing side of the debate. So they say, 'I will not vote for anyone unless he or she is anti-choice.' If the polarities switch, the pro-choice people might become more doctrinaire. People become blasé until they lose [a right]."

Representative Diana DeGette (D–Colorado), Cochair of the House
Bipartisan Pro-choice Caucus:
"The anti-choice movement has mobilized at the local level to put terror into every congressman's heart. I think male members of Congress know that if they cast even one pro-choice vote they will be targeted for defeat by anti-choice groups. It's simply easier for them to vote anti-choice every time. Women pro-choice members seem to be more likely to stick to their guns. That's why we have to work even harder."

OPENING OUR EYES AND OUR MOUTHS—
BEFORE IT'S TOO LATE

Regardless of whether you see the beginnings of the right-wing anti-choice revolution as having begun in the fight to reverse *Roe v. Wade* after 1973, the passage of the Hyde Amendment in 1977, or the insertion of an anti-choice plank in the Republican party platform of 1980, and regardless of whether you attribute the right wing's success to the tactical brilliance of the anti-choice minority or the complacency of the pro-choice majority, the simple fact is that a handful of zealous, noisy, persistent extremists have convinced politicians that their political lives depend on being anti-choice.

Politicians only do what they can get away with! We must speak up about what is happening, and protest the fact that our country is being hijacked by the far right. This is not a partisan matter; it is a human matter that touches all of our lives. The first step is to understand what's going on—to realize how widespread, well-organized, and stealthy is the web of actions designed to take away our reproductive freedoms. That's what I hope to do in these pages—to open your eyes to the threats not only to family planning, education, health care, and reproductive choice, but to our democratic principles.

But what I most want to do is inspire you to take action. I didn't write this book simply to define the problems before us but to outline solutions. I don't just want to make you angry but motivate you to fight back. We not only need to keep what we have won but to restore what has been lost and right the injustices that remain today. I invite you to join me in the twenty-first-century battle to advance the cause of social justice and women's rights—for all women, for all time.

TWO

BAREFOOT AND PREGNANT

*There's a-gonna be some changes made . . .
'cause now I've got the Pill.*

—Loretta Lynn

The wife is to subordinate herself to her husband.

—James Leon Holmes, nominated to the
federal district court in Arkansas by President George W. Bush

Did you ever wonder where the phrase I've used as the title for this chapter came from? It's not part of some hillbilly folk saying but a phrase from remarks made by Paul Van Dalsem to a Rotary Club in 1963, when he was an Arkansas state representative: "[W]hen one of our women starts poking around in something she doesn't know anything about, we get her an extra milk cow. If that don't work, we give her a little more garden to tend to. And then if that's not enough, we get her pregnant and keep her barefoot."

When Paul Van Dalsem uttered that infamous formula for keeping women in their place, I was a young wife and mother of three in the neighboring state of Texas. His comments probably drew a big laugh, but they were only too accurate a reflection of a lot of people's attitudes in the 1950s and early '60s. But just three years before, a technological advance had come along that was going to rock the Van Dalsems of this country to their very souls: the birth control pill, approved by the FDA in 1960, made it possible for women to control their reproductive destiny.

When the Pill became widely available in the '60s, so many women all over America shared the experience of suddenly feeling free that Loretta Lynn made a hit song about it. Until the Pill came along, bringing reproductive self-determination along with it, most women didn't have many options. You were supposed to look pretty, attract a man, and stand by him—even when he left you home alone with a houseful of children, doing endless loads of dishes and laundry, watching your dreams go down the drain.

I was fifteen when I first got pregnant and married—in that order. It has taken me a lifetime to be able to say those words because there was such extraordinary silence and shame attached to the situation they describe. I was a child having a child, but at the time I felt grown-up. I truly believed that what would make me happiest in life was to marry my high school sweetheart, have his baby, and pack his lunch every day before he went off to work. I wanted a cute house, a cute baby, and cute clothes to wear. Of course, reality—for a lonesome, scared teenaged mother with no prospect of college—turned out to be not so cute. But no one had told me about reality. No one had explained anything about sexuality or how to prevent pregnancy. The sex education most of the girls of my generation received, if we heard anything at all, was couched in vague baseball metaphors, as in "don't let him get to second base," and we were left to imagine for ourselves what happened around that diamond. "Good girls" were told to say no, but we had no idea what the question was. I had no clue how to take control of my body—and therefore, my destiny, and my dreams. So when it finally came along, I felt that the Pill had saved my life.

People often ask me how I went from being a teen mom to president of PPFA, and I tell my story because it's an example of what a woman can do if she is free to make her own choices about childbearing. In the '50s, my story was the plight of so many women before all the advances in family planning that we take for granted today: the legalization of contraception and abortion, the wide availability of the Pill, and federal funding for birth control for those who could not otherwise afford it.

Like so many girls, I wanted to fit in, to be popular and accepted. My family had moved to a red-dirt farming town where being an outsider was odd but being a smart girl was downright peculiar. I hid my light under a bushel basket and set out to be popular instead. I was elected sophomore class favorite, junior class vice president, and cheerleader. I wanted nothing more than to be normal—the average, all-American girl. And so in 1957, I announced to my parents that I was married, pregnant, and moving to the larger town of Odessa, where my husband would find a job. I was average, all right: it turned out that 1957 was the record year for teen pregnancy in the United States. My parents'—and their entire generation's—silence around sex and young women's self-determination had come to its inevitable conclusion.

Six months into my marriage, I knew it had been a mistake, but I was too stubborn to admit that to myself. By the time I was twenty, I had three small children. My mental, physical, and emotional resources were stretched to the breaking point. I was panicked that at that rate, one every other year, I could end up with fifteen children. I had severe anemia with my pregnancies, and was so exhausted that I was shedding pounds involuntarily for the first and only time in my life. When the Pill reached Odessa, Texas, in 1962, I knew it would give me back my life. Another child would have put me over the brink and made it impossible for me to care for those I had and loved so dearly.

The Pill allowed me to reclaim the smart young woman I'd abandoned at fifteen, to go back to school, and eventually—after twelve years of taking courses when they were available and I could find the time and money to go—to finish my college degree. I worked part-time as a teacher for Head Start, too, and of course had primary responsibility for my three children. I was tired, but I was no longer trapped—I was learning, excited, and finally using my brain. I studied sociology and communications, and learned about the emerging civil rights movement. Although it was not a subject then being discussed, I realized that women were being denied many fundamental rights, too. The connection was clear to me: for women to have full civil rights, we must have reproductive rights. After I wrote a paper about global family planning, I became passionate about the issue, and applied to work at the Permian Basin Planned Parenthood, as executive director. I had no experience in health care or administration—just a stable West Texas address, which meant I might stay longer than the three previous executive directors, who each lasted a year. Just days after finishing my last college course, in 1974, I was hired. At the time I was only dimly aware of Margaret Sanger's struggles in the teens and twenties to provide birth control to poor women, or of TV personality Sherri Chessen Finkbine's trip to Sweden for an abortion because she'd taken thalidomide in the 1960s and knew she would risk giving birth to a severely deformed child, or of the 1973 *Roe v. Wade* decision legalizing abortion. But I did know how essential choice was to my life, and to the lives of all the women of my generation and generations to come, including, of course, my own children. In fact, I knew this to be our most fundamental human and civil right, the bedrock on which all the rest could become reality.

My experience as a young woman was common for the 1950s. I wish I could say that things are completely different today. Sure, girls are now more sophisticated about sex, and they understand a few things I didn't know. But I can't tell you how many letters I get from fifteen-year-old girls who are madly in love with their nineteen-year-old boyfriends and are sure that their love will last forever. They're at an age when their real, strong self goes underground, they feel a need to conform, and so they become spineless jelly women, doing everything they can to please everyone but themselves. Meanwhile, their hormones are running wild. It's an age when they not only need information about their powerful desires but they also need skills to make appropriate decisions, and support in learning how to stand up for themselves and take their future into their own hands. You can't tell a fifteen-year-old girl how to say no without giving her an idea about what yes means and how to protect herself.

You have to understand that for most of human history, menarche and marriage happened at about the same time, the midteens. There weren't many sexual decisions for a girl to make. But in the modern world, with good nutrition and health care, puberty starts early, at about twelve, and because of advances in women's education and careers, marriage is now delayed into the midtwenties or later. So for the vast majority of girls, there are a good number of years between the onset of puberty and marriage, and most of those girls are going to become sexually active sometime during that period, just as boys have always done.

I know from experience—and the data confirms—that sexuality education, reproductive health care, and access to contraceptives are the keys to helping young women through that vulnerable time in their lives when hormones are high and self-esteem is low.

Without access to good family planning, a teenage girl can end up in real trouble, convincing herself, as I did, that a dream of puppy love and domestic bliss is a good trade-off for education, independence, and self-growth. But if a young woman can control her fertility, she can control her future—set goals, meet challenges, and have a good shot at success and happiness.

It's hard to believe that there are people today who still oppose family planning, despite the fact that 90 percent of Americans believe in it, and 75 percent say the government should fund it for low-income women. But that's the plain truth: anti-choice zealots aren't just attacking abortion, they're attacking birth control programs. The government today is full of people like James Leon Holmes, people who are hostile to family planning—and to women in general—and would like to bring us back to where I was in the 1950s.

Plainly put, if women have reproductive freedom, they have more power. And that, of course, is what right-wing ideologues are so afraid of. That's why they're so obsessed with abortion, and that's why, in this day and age, they are even trying to discourage basic family planning. If you think those who oppose the right to choice are only against abortion, think again. Their goals are deeper, and more sinister. They're against women having the power to make any reproductive choices whatsoever, including the choice to use birth control. That's why they simultaneously refuse to fund poor women who need abortions, and then punish those who do give birth. If far-right politicos had their way, women would indeed be barefoot and pregnant—again. They want to return us to the era when father always knew best, and all mothers could think about was diapers, spit-up, and how to get the house clean and dinner on the table (even if there wasn't enough money for groceries) by the time our husbands got home.

THE ASSAULT ON FAMILY PLANNING

There is a highly effective right-wing campaign under way across the country—and around the globe, as I discuss in Chapter 7—to obliterate the family planning programs that have enabled so many low-income women to pull themselves and their families out of poverty, and replace these essential health care services with programs that teach abstinence as the only option to prevent pregnancies and sexually transmitted infection. On the face of it, of course, this strategy is ridiculous. If you want to prevent abortions, you *increase* access to family planning. But the anti-choice groups who are running this campaign, and strong-arming the government into going along with it, have views on family planning that are positively medieval. Many of them believe that all forms of contraception that are not barrier methods—in other words, anything besides the diaphragm and the condom—are abortifacients and should be banned, including the Pill. Others oppose condoms, too, spreading rumors and promoting policies that condoms are ineffective and even cause sexually transmitted infections. To them, the only solution to unplanned pregnancies and sexually transmitted infections, including HIV/AIDS, is total abstinence.

Many things denominated as "contraceptive" are truly abortifacient—the IUD, Norplant, RU-486, the so-called morning-after pill, and the so-called standard birth control pill.

—Robert C. Cetrulo, president of
Northern Kentucky Right to Life

As with all of the right-wing strategies to erode women's rights, the assault against family planning is unrelenting. Health care groups that are struggling to provide contraceptive services to people who can't afford to pay for them constantly have to fight efforts to take away their scraps of funding. When we succeed in staving off a threat in one arena, it comes back, redoubled, in another. The anti-choice right is like a punching clown: knock it down and it pops right back up again. The right-wing assault on family planning has been building for decades, and Planned Parenthood has been its main target. But make no mistake: they won't stop with our clinics—they'll take their attacks to your public health department and family doctor. Here are a few examples of their campaign against contraceptives:

- Right-wing extremists in our government have made several attempts to defeat contraceptive coverage by federal employee insurance plans. In 1998, Representative Chris Smith (R–New Jersey) attempted to exclude coverage of any contraceptive that might prevent implantation of a fertilized egg, claiming they were abortifacients, tantamount to abortion. Though that effort failed, similar proposals have popped up at the state level.
- In June 2002, Senator Bill Frist (R–Tennessee)—currently the majority leader of the Senate as well as a physician—circulated an amendment to the Safe Motherhood, Safe Babies Act (an act designed to reduce rates of maternal mortality and morbidity). Frist's amendment, which was part of an overarching campaign to reclassify birth control pills, emergency contraception, and IUDs as abortifacients, would have defined pregnancy as "the condition of a woman that begins at fertilization" as opposed to the medical definition, which holds that pregnancy begins at implantation.
- Anti-choice politicos have attempted to limit minors' access to family planning services in several states, by requiring parental consent for birth control and mandating reports to parents for very common sexually transmitted infections—for the specific purpose of undermining standard public health practices and getting around the law, which in all fifty states guarantees that

minors can get confidential testing and treatment for sexually transmitted infections.

- Representative David Vitter (R–Louisiana) has repeatedly advanced an amendment that would prohibit agencies that perform abortions with private dollars from receiving federal Title X family planning funds. That amendment has not yet been adopted, but right-wingers continue to try to get similar legislation through Congress, and have meanwhile succeeded in passing such gag rules in a number of states.

- Ever since the early 1980s, state legislatures have been attempting to cut funds to family planning programs that do abortion counseling or referrals. These efforts are becoming ever more numerous, and there could be an attempt to impose a similar gag rule at the federal level as well.

- Efforts are under way in some states to pervert important laws designed to protect children from abuse by using those laws to require family planning providers to file reports on minors seeking abortions. In Kansas, the attorney general has gone beyond that and issued an opinion in June 2003 stating that doctors must file a report with the Kansas Department of Social and Rehabilitation Services regarding minors requesting contraceptives or seeking medical attention for sexually transmitted infections. Similarly, the attorney general in Texas stated that anyone under the age of seventeen who is sexually active is by definition an abused child, possibly subject to the mandatory reporting law.

- Planned Parenthood has been specifically targeted in efforts to defund family planning programs. As the largest voluntary family planning service provider in the country, and the most trusted "brand name" in reproductive health care, Planned Parenthood is a crucial target for the far right.

In 2002, STOPP did an extensive research project to identify the name and location of every Planned Parenthood facility in the country. We identified a total of 846 facilities that PPFA operated around the United States (92 less than it did in 1993). Approximately 160 of these facilities killed preborn children on site, while the remainder offered various products for sale, including abortifacients such as the pill, the IUD, Norplant, Depo-Provera, and emergency contraception.

—STOPP (STOP Planned Parenthood) International

THE BUSH ADMINISTRATION AND CONGRESS TURN BACK THE CLOCK

For many years, family planning programs were supported by a broad bipartisan coalition. Richard Nixon was instrumental in making family planning available to poor women. George H. W. Bush supported family planning. But his son is much, much further to the right on the issue, pandering to an ultraright minority that has targeted family planning programs for years. As soon as he took office, George W. Bush, assisted by Congress, gave right-wing constituents a victory with cuts in family planning, here and around the globe, as well as potentially devastating changes in public policy concerning sex education and HIV/AIDS prevention efforts:

- In his first few months in office, Bush stripped contraceptive coverage for federal employees from the budget he proposed to Congress (which later restored the coverage).
- The Bush administration has appointed politicians who actually *oppose the use of condoms to prevent disease* to scientific advisory boards that oversee HIV/AIDS policies and international family planning programs (see Chapter 6).

- The administration has appointed "abstinence-only" proponents to oversee federal family planning programs, and they are using all the bureaucratic tools at their disposal to shift family planning funds into abstinence promotion (see Chapter 3).
- Funds for proven and effective family planning health-care programs, already inadequate to meet the need, have received little or no increase, while funding for unproven abstinence programs has soared.
- Words and information relating to homosexuality, abortion, and condoms have been censored from government Web sites and banned in government-funded programs (see Chapters 6 and 7).
- Organizations that go against the abstinence-only message of the government have been targeted for financial audits and threatening letters.
- The United Nations Population Fund has been defunded even after Congress passed legislation appropriating these funds.

In short, this is an all-out assault on federally funded family planning, making access to birth control difficult, particularly for poor women, and effectively turning back the clock on family planning to those pre-Pill, barefoot and pregnant 1950s days.

SNOOPING IN THE BEDROOM: THE GOVERNMENT AND THE RIGHT TO PRIVACY

The current puritanical climate, ushered in by religious zealots trying to make abortion illegal and family planning inaccessible, hearkens back to a much earlier time in this country, when Margaret Sanger, the founder of Planned Parenthood, was arrested for distributing information about birth control. Government-backed censorship and the attempt to criminalize birth control and abortion have always gone hand-in-hand in this country. We've seen this most recently in the gag rules the government has imposed both here and abroad on family planning programs, and in the deletion of basic information about condoms and contraception from government-funded Web sites and educational materials (see Chapters 6 and 7).

Sanger was charged under the Comstock Laws, passed in 1873, a broad federal obscenity statute prohibiting the transport of literature about birth control or abortion through the public mails. Anthony Comstock was a religious zealot—like many on the anti-choice right today—determined to root out "sin" wherever he could find it. And, like many of his ilk today, he equated birth control with promiscuity and prostitution, and not with sexually responsible people using birth control for legitimate and moral reasons. When Sanger was arrested in 1916 for violating the Comstock Laws, she described them as "designed to aid and abet both moral and religious prejudice and persecutions."

When the Comstock Laws were adopted, the criminalization of birth control information, contraceptives, and abortion was relatively new in the United States. The Puritans themselves weren't so puritanical. Neither birth control nor abortion was prohibited in colonial America. People had sex out of wedlock: in fact, one-third of the Pilgrim women were pregnant before they married. Recipes for abortifacients were openly traded and advertised. At the time the Constitution was ratified, abortion was common, usually performed by midwives.

In 1800, abortion was legal in every state in the union, but rarely discussed. It only became an issue over the next few decades, as women began making efforts to control their fertility. As Susan Faludi wrote in *Backlash*, "It was only after the mid-century rise of the women's rights movement that abortion became a battleground." Then as now, all of women's social aspirations—for work, education, and self-determination—rested on their ability to control when and whether they would have children. As women began to ask for some simple family planning measures—such as "voluntary motherhood," which proposed that wives be free to refuse sex sometimes for health reasons—doctors, legislators, and clergymen jumped in to deny them any measure of control over their childbearing whatsoever. Birth control suddenly became a hotly debated issue, and so did abortion. The American Medical Association, then a fledgling organization that used its new standards of professionalism to put midwives and female abortionists out of business, began a massive public relations campaign against abortion. Clergymen declared abortion a sin. "Purity" crusaders, not unlike clinic terrorists, stormed abortion clinics and dragged the women practitioners to court. By 1900, this backlash against reproductive rights resulted in a federal ban on all birth control distribution, and abortion was outlawed, except to save the life of the woman, in every state in the country.

LEGALIZING CONTRACEPTION
FOR MARRIED COUPLES: 1965

Incredibly, it wasn't until 1965 that the Supreme Court, in *Griswold v. Connecticut*, made it legal for married couples throughout the country to use contraception. Prior to that ruling, Connecticut had one of the most restrictive laws: anyone who used a contraceptive was guilty of a felony. Women had to go through the same kinds of hoops to obtain contraceptives that they did to get secret, illegal abortions. Condoms could only be purchased—by men, of course—for the prevention of disease. Women had to obtain contraceptives surreptitiously from sympathetic private physicians. Family planning groups couldn't legally give out contraceptives, and so Estelle Griswold, executive director of the Planned Parenthood League of Connecticut, organized station wagon shuttles to ferry women across state lines to be fitted for diaphragms.

To challenge the law, Griswold opened a clinic in New Haven and began openly dispensing contraceptives—anticipating her arrest, which came ten days later. Her case eventually made it to the Supreme Court, which struck down the Connecticut statute making contraceptives illegal, and recognized the right to privacy in reproductive matters, upon which the right to choose abortion now rests (see Chapter 5). One of the opinions in *Griswold* called the law against birth control an "uncommonly silly" law. Justice William O. Douglas, writing for the majority, asked, rhetorically, "Would we allow the police to search the sacred precincts of marital bedrooms for telltale signs of the use of contraceptives?" He answered, "The very idea is repulsive to the notions of privacy surrounding the marriage relationship." He held that the right to privacy was older than the Bill of Rights, older than America's political parties, and older than the school system. It was a right as ancient as marriage itself.

LEGALIZING CONTRACEPTION FOR UNMARRIED PEOPLE: 1972

Outside of marriage, though, contraceptives were still illegal in many states. It wasn't until 1972, in *Eisenstadt v. Baird*, that the Supreme Court declared that unmarried people had a constitutional right to use contraceptives, too. William Baird had been convicted of exhibiting contraceptives during a lecture to a group of students at Boston University, and of giving one of them a package of vaginal foam; he faced up to five years' imprisonment. Justice William J. Brennan, writing for the majority in the ruling that struck down that law, stated, "It would be plainly unreasonable to assume that Massachusetts has prescribed pregnancy and the birth of an unwanted child as punishment for fornication."

FAMILY PLANNING: "A PUBLIC HEALTH MATTER"

After the 1965 and 1972 decisions on contraception, all American women had the right to use contraceptives. Rates of unintended pregnancies went down, as did rates of maternal and child mortality. But women who couldn't afford contraceptives couldn't exercise their right to use them. It wasn't until the passage of Title X of the Public Health Service Act that the nation made a commitment to ensure access to family planning services. President Richard M. Nixon signed Title X into law in 1970, saying, "No American woman should be denied access to family planning assistance because of her economic condition." He made it a national goal to provide family planning services to "all who want but cannot afford them." Representative George H. W. Bush was one of the bill's sponsors.

We need to make population and family planning household words. We need to take the sensationalism out of this topic so that it can no longer be used by militants who have no real knowledge of the voluntary nature of the program but, [sic] rather are using it as a political stepping-stone. If family planning is anything, it is a public health matter.

—Congressman George H. W. Bush,
one of the Title X bill's sponsors, 1969

Title X was as revolutionary in its implications for the poor as the Pill had been for the middle class. Young, uninsured, and poor women now had access to contraceptives and counseling about how to use them. In 2002, nearly 5 million women received health care services at Title X–funded family planning clinics. Each year, publicly subsidized family planning services, of which Title X is the core, prevent an estimated 1,331,100 pregnancies, and 632,300 abortions. Among teenagers, the programs prevent an estimated 385,800 unintended pregnancies and 183,300 abortions. Each public dollar spent on family planning saves three dollars that would otherwise be spent in Medicaid costs for pregnancy-related care and medical services for newborns.

MATERNAL AND CHILD HEALTH ADVANCES AS BIRTH CONTROL AND LEGAL ABORTION BECOME AVAILABLE

Abortion Rates:
1950s and 1960s—as high as 25.8 per 1,000 women of reproductive age per year
2000—21.3 per 1,000 women of reproductive age per year
Infant Mortality Rates:
1960—26 per 1,000 live births per year
2001—6.8 per 1,000 live births per year
Maternal Mortality Rates:
1960—32.1 per 100,000 live births per year
2000—8.2 per 100,000 live births per year

But, since its inception, Title X has continuously faced threats from right-wing congressional opponents who intend to cut funding and attach harmful restrictions to what remains. Family planning funds were slashed during the 1980s' "Reagan Revolution," and while they increased during the Clinton administration, the total amount, adjusted for inflation, is currently 57 percent less than it was in 1980. This means that clinics are facing a major struggle to pay for the newer, more effective, but more costly methods of contraception, and for state-of-the-art diagnostic tests that would improve rates of detecting sexually transmitted infections and cervical cancer.

The current Bush administration has taken a stance on family planning that is far to the right of George Bush Sr.'s or even Ronald Reagan's. It has refused to seek any increases for the Title X program since it took office in 2001. Instead, it has asked for, and received from Congress, enormous increases in federal dollars for abstinence-only programs that prohibit discussion of contraception—except to mention failure rates—and provide no health care (see Chapter 3). And it is shifting existing family planning services into the faith-based abstinence-only programs it favors.

The policies of this administration are the most extreme right-wing in the history of the United States.

—Congressman Bernie Sanders (I–Vermont), 2003

The administration and its right-wing allies would take us all the way back to the days of the Comstock Laws. Today, those who are leading an assault on birth control again believe—contrary to Justice Brennan's ruling in *Eisenstadt*—that an unwanted pregnancy is indeed proper punishment for "fornication." The people who would take away the right to privacy that makes abortion a personal decision—one in which the government should not intrude—are also clearly eager to take away the right to the basic family planning services that prevent abortion.

GAG ME: THE THREAT TO FAMILY PLANNING PROGRAMS HERE AND ABROAD

In the 1920s, Margaret Sanger lectured to audiences around the country about the need for birth control—for the health, welfare, and personal rights of women and children, and for global peace and prosperity. While she was a popular speaker, some college campuses and religious institutions denied her the right to speak. She wasn't allowed on the radio, either, where discussion of birth control was banned on some stations until the mid-1930s. In 1929, when Sanger was going to give a speech in Boston, civil authorities intervened and cancelled her speech. Not to be deterred, she stood silent, her mouth taped shut to symbolize to the world that she had been gagged by the government. Harvard historian Arthur Schlesinger Sr. read her prepared statement: "As a pioneer fighting for a cause, I believe in free speech. As a propagandist, I see immense advantages in being gagged. It silences me, but it makes millions of others talk and think about the cause in which I live."

It seems amazing to think that all these years later, family planning providers are still being gagged, unable to tell women their reproductive options. But those of us in family planning are still wearing that gag. The administration started by imposing a global gag rule, to deny family planning to the world's most vulnerable women, because they couldn't get away with it in the United States. Successful at international censorship, they've started censoring speech about reproductive rights here at home. They've censored government Web sites that provide information on condoms. They've told scientists to censor words relating to sexuality from their grant applications or risk losing funding. And soon, if we're not careful, they will impose a gag rule on family planning health providers here in the United States, too.

George W. Bush's assault on family planning began on his first day in office. On that day, the twenty-eighth anniversary of *Roe v. Wade*, he issued an executive order reinstating the Reagan-era global gag rule, which had been removed by President Bill Clinton. Once again it was official government policy to deny all U.S. international family planning assistance to any programs around the world that provide abortion services, counseling, referrals, or engage in advocacy of or public discussion about abortion. The funding cutoff applies even when such abortion-related services are paid for *out of the organization's own funds* (see Chapter 7). Of course, any direct U.S. funding of abortions overseas had been prohibited ever since the Helms Amendment, passed in 1973. But the global gag rule goes much further than Helms, into the realm of pure censorship, preventing health care providers around the world from even *speaking* about abortion to their patients or to anyone else. This kind of censorship violates our principle of free speech, and destroys the trust inherent in a confidential doctor-patient relationship. It's a level of government intrusion into private matters that would be intolerable and unimaginable in this country.

Or would it? There is every chance that the Bush administration may yet seek to expand the global gag rule to Title X–funded family planning clinics back at home. This would mean that health care providers here, like their counterparts abroad, would be silenced, unable to provide counseling about abortion or make referrals. To understand the significance of such a restriction, it's important to realize that at the time Title X was implemented, it went only as far as saying that "None of the funds appropriated under this title shall be used in programs where abortion is a method of family planning." Now the right-wingers want to make sure people who take federal funds for family planning can't even *discuss,* much less perform, an abortion—despite the fact that abortion is a legal medical procedure. For a physician to deny information about reproductive options is a violation of medical ethics, and in cases where the pregnancy could harm the woman, would likely be considered malpractice but for the fact that it is being imposed by the government.

A domestic gag rule would not only make it more difficult for women to get abortions, it would mean an end to many family planning programs that receive government funds. Clinics that refused to comply with the rules, believing in their ethical obligation to provide medically accurate information about abortion as an option for women facing unintended or health-threatening pregnancies, would have to close or drastically reduce their services. Many poor women would be without not only abortion services but family planning and contraceptives, too. Most Title X funds go to public health departments. But Planned Parenthood affiliates alone could stand to lose $59 million in Title X funds if they failed to comply with such a rule, making it much more difficult to provide basic health care and contraceptive services to poor and uninsured clients.

> *If a statewide Planned Parenthood operated a string of ten separate family planning clinics, but offered abortions at only one of them, none of those clinics could receive Title X funds.*
>
> —Concerned Women for America, supporting
> an amendment to deny federal family planning funds
> to agencies that perform any abortions with
> their own funds, 2001

The Bush administration may very well be biding its time before trying to impose a domestic gag rule in a second term. This is exactly what Ronald Reagan did. After imposing the international gag rule in his first term, Reagan extended it to domestic family planning clinics in 1987, during his second term. Under Reagan's gag rule, Title X projects were prohibited by order of the Department of Health and Human Services from providing counseling or referrals concerning abortion. This was done even in the face of objections from the American College of Obstetricians and Gynecologists (ACOG), the American Medical Association (AMA), the American Psychological Association (APA), and the National Association of Social Workers (NASW):

- The AMA stated that it is its policy to "strongly condemn any interference by the government or any other third parties that causes a physician to compromise his or her medical judgment as to what information or treatment is in the best interests of the patient."
- The APA said it "deplores the effects of Title X regulations which prohibit providers, including psychologists, who receive Title X funds from informing women patients/clients of the availability of the alternative of abortion to terminate an unwanted pregnancy."
- The NASW said that the gag rule "not only deprived women of their reproductive rights but also denied health and human service workers their right of free speech."

The domestic gag rule also required that all Title X–funded services had to put their family planning facilities in a location separate from their abortion clinics, further marginalizing abortion providers, making them, among other things, easier targets for right-wing harassment and terrorism.

After the gag rule was issued, lawsuits were immediately filed in four states. Courts in Massachusetts, Colorado, and West Virginia struck down the rules, mainly on grounds that they were unconstitutional. But in New York, the appeals court upheld the regulations, saying the government has no obligation to subsidize an activity merely because the activity is constitutionally protected. This case reached the U.S. Supreme Court—*Rust v. Sullivan*.

Rust v. Sullivan (1991) is a chilling example of what can happen when the highest courts in the land are loaded with anti-choice conservatives (see Chapter 5). In a 5–4 decision, authored by Chief Justice Rehnquist, the Court upheld the regulations. The Court found that the gag rule's limits on speech were not unconstitutional, on the basis that when the government funds an activity, the government is free to define the limits of that activity, even when that activity is medical counseling and care. The majority ruled that "the Title X program regulations do not significantly impinge upon the doctor-patient relationship."

In his dissenting opinion, Justice Harry Blackmun argued that the gag rules violated constitutional principles of free speech and the right of a pregnant woman to be free from governmental interference in her private decisions, and that they did intrude on the doctor-patient relationship. He recognized that the rules were intended to coerce women to carry unwanted pregnancies to term. "Until today, the Court has allowed to stand only those restrictions upon reproductive freedom that, while limiting the availability of abortion, have left intact a woman's ability to decide without coercion whether she will continue her pregnancy to term. . . . Today's decision abandons that principle, and with disastrous results." The concept of liberty, he maintained, "if it means anything, must entail freedom from governmental domination in making the most intimate and personal of decisions."

After the decision, the fight continued: Planned Parenthood challenged the gag rule on many fronts—in Congress, in the Title X appropriations bill, and in new litigation. While lawsuits were pending, Bill Clinton was elected president. Immediately upon taking office, he suspended the Reagan-Bush gag rule, leaving family planning providers free to discuss all of a woman's options when she came to seek medical care and counseling.

That victory, of course, was secure only as long as the Clinton presidency lasted. Then the right-wingers came back with renewed vengeance, and with them, the gag rule. The gag rule, remember, was an executive branch regulation, not legislation. Ever since George W. Bush reinstated the global gag rule, U.S. family planning providers have been waiting for the other shoe to drop. While neither he nor Congress has reinstated the domestic gag rule as of this writing, most observers believe it is only a matter of time.

STATE GAG RULES

Thwarted at the federal level by Clinton's reversal of the gag rule, anti-choice extremists turned their attention to the states. Anti-choice legislators in the states have attempted for years to do what the Bush administration or Congress is likely to do on a federal level—take away funds for family planning programs that also provide abortion services, counseling, or referrals. In the late '70s and early '80s, several state legislatures debated the issue, and Arizona, Minnesota, and North Dakota enacted laws that defunded family planning agencies that provided abortion services with private dollars, regardless of whether the abortion activities were separate from the family planning activities.

I know the Arizona case well, because I was CEO of Planned Parenthood of Central and Northern Arizona at the time. The case is one of the best examples of the incredible persistence of the right. They never tire of finding new ways to accomplish their goals. In their first attempt to defund family planning programs, attaching restrictions to an appropriations bill, they actually named Planned Parenthood. That effort failed, because you can't single out an individual organization. But they came back, and in 1981 were able to block state funding of all agencies that "offer abortions, abortion procedures, counseling for abortion procedures or abortion referrals." This time the state appropriations bill included the restrictions they'd been lobbying for. But Planned Parenthood fought the bill, and the case, *Babbitt v. Planned Parenthood of Central and Northern Arizona,* eventually wound up before the Supreme Court.

You'd think, by the title of the case, that Governor Bruce Babbitt was anti-choice. But that's an indication of how cleverly the right can pit allies against each other. Babbitt was in fact pro-choice, but his administration had to fight Planned Parenthood because he would not veto the whole appropriations bill for the entire state. We argued that as long as we didn't use state funds for abortion, we could do what we wanted with our own money. The Federal Court of Appeals for the Ninth Circuit agreed, and ruled the law unconstitutional. The appeals court said the law would only be valid if the state could prove it was the only way to stop its money from being used to pay directly for abortions. The state couldn't prove that, so the law was struck down. In 1986, the Supreme Court affirmed the ninth circuit case without issuing an opinion. It's unlikely, of course, that if the administration is successful with its judicial nominations, the courts would rule in our favor today.

But anti-choice minions have become more clever about their language in drafting gag rules since then, and they have stepped up the state-by-state onslaught in recent years:

- Michigan: In 2002, a law was passed making it a priority to allocate funds to family planning programs that do not perform or refer for abortions or advocate for abortion rights.
- Missouri: A prohibition on family planning funding for entities that perform abortions has been repeatedly won and lost—every time we succeed in overturning it, the anti-choice extremists come right back with another piece of similar legislation. Finally, they just eliminated the whole program.

- Ohio: A 2001 budget measure was enacted requiring that family planning services funded by the state be "physically and financially separate from abortion-providing and abortion-promoting activities."
- Minnesota: Legislation has been introduced that would prohibit funding for organizations that refer, advocate for, display, or distribute marketing materials about abortion services or maintain a policy that abortion is considered part of a continuum of family planning services or reproductive health. Pending.
- New Jersey: Legislation was introduced to prohibit organizations that receive state funding for family planning from performing, assisting in, encouraging, or referring for abortions. Pending.
- Rhode Island: Legislation was introduced to prohibit the use of public funds for any organization that performs, assists, encourages, or counsels about abortion. Pending.
- Wisconsin: Introduced legislation similar to Rhode Island's. Pending.

Pro-choice forces have fought back, challenging every gag rule in court, ending or at least delaying their implementation. Planned Parenthood has recently had an important victory over a state gag rule in Texas. Texas had enacted a law that barred public funding to women's health clinics that provide abortion services with separate private funds. The law was passed despite the fact that 76 percent of all Texans surveyed believed that Planned Parenthood should continue to receive public funding to provide family planning services to low-income women. At stake was more than $78 million in annual funding, of which $12 million went to thirty-three Planned Parenthood clinics, serving 115,000 Texas women. Those women would have lost access to a wide range of reproductive health care services, including Pap smears, breast and cervical cancer screenings, sexually transmitted infection screenings, and contraception. In fact, abortion services represent only a tiny fraction—2.3 percent—of the total medical visits for services offered by Planned Parenthood in Texas. The gag rule was a blatant effort to target Planned Parenthood, and the result would have been that many women who needed family planning services would have lost their main and sometimes only source of health care as a result. As Peter Durkin, CEO of Planned Parenthood of Houston and Southeast Texas, put it, "some legislators care more about closing down Planned Parenthood than they care about preventing abortion."

In August 2003, Texas Planned Parenthood affiliates won a preliminary injunction from the District Court of Western Texas that blocked the enforcement of the law. The presiding judge noted that the law was unconstitutional because it penalizes family planning providers for engaging in the constitutionally protected activity of providing abortion services. The court noted that if the Planned Parenthood affiliates were forced to give up performing abortions in order to accept the family planning money, "patients seeking abortion services will be forced to travel long distances, travel to Mexico, delay obtaining an abortion, resort to unsafe methods of abortion or forgo their constitutionally protected right." The Texas affiliates are breathing a sigh of relief for now, but the state has appealed the ruling. "Women and families in Texas rely on us and we will not fail them, we will not be deterred," Durkin said.

With all the many restrictions on family planning cropping up, it's good to be reminded that abortion is still legal, and women do still have access to contraceptives. The question is, for how long? And meanwhile, how many resources will have to be drained away from providing services to paying the costs of litigation in order to keep our states and our country safe from egregious anti-women policies?

FUNDS FOR PREACHING ABSTINENCE, NOT PRACTICING FAMILY PLANNING

We renew our call for replacing "family planning" programs for teens with increased funding for abstinence education, which teaches abstinence until marriage as the responsible and expected standard of behavior.

—2000 Republican party platform

The biggest threats to family planning are stealthier than outright funding cuts. The newest strategy is to keep the programs but change their substance. Instead of health care, honest counseling, and contraceptives, right-wingers would like family planning clinics to dispense just one piece of advice: don't have sex if you don't want to get pregnant. The 2000 Republican party platform calls for replacing *all* family planning funds with abstinence education. In June 2003, the Bush administration announced new funding priorities for Title X that emphasize abstinence education and counseling. Piece by piece, the anti-choice right is attempting to dismantle effective family planning health-care programs and replace them with abstinence-only propaganda programs, which don't work and never will.

Already, abstinence-only programs are awash in funds. In 1996, Congress attached a provision to welfare legislation that established a federal program to fund abstinence-only education programs. These programs preach that abstaining from sexual activity is the only acceptable form of behavior outside of marriage, for people of any age. Programs that receive these funds are prohibited from discussing contraceptives in a positive way. Over the six-year period ending in 2002, approximately $700 million in federal and state matching funds were spent on abstinence-only education—despite the fact that there is no credible evidence that it works. In fact, the programs may actually have harmful health consequences by deterring the use of contraceptives when individuals become sexually active. Studies have shown that when they do—almost inevitably—break their "virginity pledge," they are more likely to have sex without using condoms or other contraceptives, putting them at higher risk for unintended pregnancies and sexually transmitted infections (see Chapter 3).

Not content with the bloated federal funds for these ineffective programs, the administration is now trying to increase those funds further, at the expense of the already scanty funding for the Title X program. And they have seen to it that the implementation of Title X will be under the control of an ideologically suitable appointee. In October 2002, the Bush administration named Dr. Alma Golden, a Texas-based pediatrician with a long record as an abstinence-only proponent, to the position of deputy assistant secretary of population affairs, overseeing the distribution of Title X funds. Soon after her appointment, predictably enough, Dr. Golden called for more emphasis on abstinence within the family planning program.

This new emphasis became evident in June 2003, when the Department of Health and Human Services (HHS) published an announcement regarding new priorities for Title X grants. It stated that to be successful, grant recipients "should include education to encourage abstinence outside a mutually monogamous marriage or union" and specified that priority for funding would go to projects that include "extramarital abstinence education and counseling." The administration specified that Title X–funded programs should promote condom use only for those individuals who engage in behavior that puts them at risk for HIV.

Meanwhile, the president's budget proposal for 2005 calls for almost doubling abstinence-only funding yet again, to $273 million!

> *We want to be sure that we really have not facilitated the early and intense involvement in sex and alcohol [of teens] by offering to pick 'em up when they're drunk or give them free condoms for their weekend party.*
>
> —Dr. Alma Golden, deputy assistant secretary of population affairs, who oversees the implementation of Title X family planning funds

Since there is no evidence showing that abstinence-only programs are successful, the administration has also been busy redefining "success." In late 2001, the Bush administration revised the performance measures for abstinence-only programs. The 2000 standards required that programs provide information on behavior changes in teens who participated—that is, how many really abstained from sex. The 2001 revisions allowed such factors as completion of programs and "commitment" to abstain from sexual activity to qualify as "success" instead—measuring attitudes instead of actual behavior or health outcomes for participants.

The administration's abstinence-only message, by the way, isn't aimed only at teens. It's for unmarried grown-ups, too.

WELFARE POLICIES TO PUNISH THE POOR: BAREFOOT AND PREGNANT, TWENTY-FIRST-CENTURY STYLE

The right-wing efforts to cut funds for family planning services have their main impact on the people who can't afford private health care—the poor. As with family planning funds, the administration has been diverting money from organizations that provide real services to economically disadvantaged women to programs that promulgate not a Father Knows Best but an Uncle Knows Best message—as in Uncle Sam! Right-wing efforts to control *women's* fertility through governmental policy can be seen in their starkest form in welfare law. Many provisions of the welfare law explicitly try to influence *women's* reproductive choices through penalties, bonuses, or incentives to states. The idea that the government has a role in determining when and under what circumstances women should have children is dangerous, and affects the rights of all *women*—not just those on welfare. I emphasize *women* because, notably, these policies apply only to mothers, not fathers.

The right wing has been trying to control welfare policy for years. In 1996, Congress enacted, and President Bill Clinton signed, the Personal Responsibility and Work Opportunity Reconciliation Act (PRWORA), which legislated a total invasion of privacy for Americans who receive welfare. Under the rubric of "personal responsibility," the PRWORA attempts to change social norms by influencing people's sexual behavior and reproductive choices. The first section of the act proclaims that "Marriage is the foundation of a successful society," and states that one purpose of the act is to promote childbirth only within marriage. Such language stigmatizes single mothers and divorced people everywhere, not to mention their children. Under this legislation, states may now use their Temporary Assistance for Needy Families (TANF) funds not only to promote jobs and provide assistance to needy families but to promote marriage and prevent and reduce the incidence of out-of-wedlock pregnancies.

In our society, there has been a long-standing tradition of scrutinizing and judging women's sexual lives, relationship choices, and reproductive decisions—especially if they are poor. The welfare debate is steeped in stereotypes—about welfare recipients' race, ethnicity, childbearing patterns, and willingness to work. The reality is that most welfare recipients, who receive an average of $351 a month, are between the ages of twenty and thirty, female, single, and have the same number of children as the average American family—two. But the stereotypes of irresponsible welfare queens, having one child after another to rip off the government, have been promoted by right-wingers in order to gain popular support for a series of invasive, irresponsible, and punitive welfare policies, including the following:

- **The Family Cap.** This policy allows states to deny the small incremental increase in benefits women receive for an additional child if the child is conceived and born while the mother is receiving welfare. In effect, this is a tax on childbirth, imposed only on poor women. Although Congress did not make this provision mandatory, twenty-three states have adopted some version of the family cap. As with policies that deny birth control or abortion choices, this one punishes women who want to make their own sexual and reproductive choices, and is, in real life, a form of coercion. It plays on the stereotype that women have children to get more money on welfare. In reality, incremental increases in benefits are so minimal that families actually plunge deeper into poverty when an additional child is born. Ironically, new data from New Jersey, which has a family cap, shows that the policy drives up rates of abortion.

- **The So-Called Illegitimacy Ratio.** This policy gives a bonus of $20 to $25 million to the top five states that decrease their ratio of out-of-wedlock births to all births in the state, while decreasing abortions below 1995 levels. This is a coercive intrusion of the government into matters that should remain strictly private, and privacy is further invaded by the data collecting the states will have to do. In order to get the bonus, states may require women on public assistance to answer personal questions, such as whether they have had an abortion, or else risk losing their benefits. To decrease the out-of-wedlock birthrate, states might also try to implement coercive family planning policies, such as giving financial incentives or tying welfare benefits to sterilization or long-term contraceptives, such as Norplant or Depo-Provera. Contraceptive methods should always be freely chosen, based on a patient's health history and preference.

- **Abstinence-Only Education.** The attempt to control poor women's childbearing leaves many right-wing policy makers in a dilemma. They don't want poor women to have more children, but they can't selectively call for them to have abortions. Diverting welfare funds from family support to abstinence-only initiatives, which are ineffective and unrealistic at best, and dangerous at worst, will only make the situation more dire.

- **Marriage Promotion Initiatives.** The federal welfare reauthorization proposal, passed by the House on February 13, 2002, would spend $300 million annually on programs promoting marriage. This money is being taken from funds that would otherwise be used to help people find jobs or provide them with basic support for food and shelter. The logic behind the diversion of funds is that children who grow up with married parents are less likely to live in poverty, but this sends a dangerous message to women in economically fragile situations—that marriage is the answer to poverty, and that even an abusive marriage is better than none. In January 2004, President Bush announced a new $1.5 billion—that's *billion*—marriage promotion initiative.

The common thread running through all of this welfare legislation is the denial of women's most basic human rights—the right to privacy, to economic equality, and to control over what happens with our own bodies. Enforcing such policies against women on welfare—the most vulnerable among us—sets the stage for similar abuses of power against women everywhere. If poor women can be denied sexual and reproductive freedom, so can all women. If the government can control poor women's sexuality, then it can control everyone's sexuality—men, women, gay, or straight.

I used to be a social worker. I worked with abused and neglected children. I know what can happen to children when they are brought into the world to parents who can't or won't care for them properly. The right to choose and contraceptive options protect against children being born in families that abuse them or can't care for them. I also believe in separation of church and state. The United States isn't Iraq, Iran, or Afghanistan. Fanatics are basically deadly to freedoms of all kinds.

—Representative Jim Greenwood (R–Pennsylvania)

We have come a long way since those days when the Pill made it possible for me, and millions of other American women, to embark on a new life, with new opportunities. And we aren't turning back. Women currently have control over their fertility, and control over the direction of their lives, careers, and families. Or I should amend that to say that women of economic means have those rights. But we are facing an anti-choice onslaught that will do anything to turn back the clock when it comes to women's reproductive freedom. Though their efforts to limit access to family planning have thus far mainly affected poor women, we need to open our eyes to the reality that we *all* risk losing the fundamental rights to make our own sexual and reproductive health choices, and to control the size of our own families. And we need to be clear about the fact that the fight over choice is not just about abortion, it's about the entire realm of reproductive freedom.

THREE

ABSTINENCE OF COMMON SENSE

———————◆————————

TEACHING KIDS "NO"— AND NOTHING MORE

Federally funded abstinence-only education:

- *has as its exclusive purpose, teaching the social, physiological, and health gains to be realized by abstaining from sexual activity;*
- *teaches that a mutually faithful monogamous relationship in the context of marriage is the expected standard of human sexual activity;*
- *teaches that sexual activity outside of the context of marriage is likely to have harmful psychological and physical effects.*

—1996 Welfare Law, U.S. Society Security Act, Sec. 510(b)(2)

The vows of abstinence break a lot more easily than latex condoms.

—Dr. M. Joycelyn Elders, former U.S. surgeon general

————————◆————————

The right wing is obsessed with sex—other people's sex lives, that is. I'll never understand this obsession and their need to control what the rest of us do. There's a small but very vocal minority in this country that believes that any sex outside of marriage is evil, and that it is their mission in life to force their view of morality on the rest of us. While they're not advocating the stoning of "adulterers" and "fornicators," right-wing extremists are doing everything they can to minimize and distort what people learn about sex. Their ideology is based on fear—fear that the ancient tradition of male-dominated marriage will come crumbling down, fear that women will have more power, fear that gay people will become more accepted. They are trying to instill those fears in others by force, teaching that sex is shameful and deadly, and silencing the voices that teach about how to prevent pregnancy and protect against disease. These extremists think that if they can keep young people in the dark about sexuality—by teaching them that virginity before marriage is the sum total of what should be known about reproduction, sexuality, relationships, and sexually transmitted infection—then sexuality will just go away until one's wedding day. And if it does not, anyone who engages in the sin of sexual intercourse outside of marriage will be rightly punished—by unplanned pregnancies, diseases, and death.

This is an appallingly backward, almost medieval view of the world. But it's a view they're forcing on the rest of us. One of their principal vehicles for promoting it is in the "abstinence-only" sexuality indoctrination that has become the norm in our schools, replacing real sex education with fundamentalist ideology. Fifty-eight percent of all schools in the U.S. have abstinence-only programs and those numbers are rapidly increasing. Right-wing ideologues have been so persistent and organized—starting small at the local school boards, and working their way up—that now the entire country is being held hostage to their policy of ignorance rather than information. Our children are particularly targeted, and vulnerable.

The United States is the only country in the world that requires government-funded sexuality education programs to limit their teachings to abstinence—and we've got the disease and pregnancy rates to show for it. Other industrialized countries teach comprehensive sex education, and they have far lower rates of teen pregnancy and sexually transmitted infections. Since 1996, our federal government has spent $700 million of taxpayers' money on abstinence-only education, and the annual expenditures are growing exponentially. Today, in order to get federal funding for sexuality education, schools must teach that having *no* sex is the *only* option for people of any age who aren't married. With no other acknowledged options, teachers can't even *mention* how young people can protect themselves from pregnancy or sexually transmitted infections, including HIV/AIDS; they can't say anything that would portray contraceptives or condoms in a positive light. Real sexuality education information is censored from textbooks. The religious right's belief that sex is inherently dirty and wrong has infected our education system, and is giving our young people dangerous, negative, frightening, homophobic, and misogynistic misinformation about sexuality.

What do you think your sixteen-year-old is learning in school? While 58 percent of all schools teach abstinence-only, a full 86 percent of the public school districts that teach sexuality education require that abstinence be promoted. And of those, more than a third require abstinence to be taught as the *only* option for unmarried people, and usually either prohibit any mention of contraceptives or limit discussion to their ineffectiveness. In the South, where teen pregnancy rates are significantly higher than in the rest of the country, abstinence-only classes are taught in more than half the schools.

"Control your urgin', stay a virgin," is typical of the messages students learn in abstinence-only classrooms. Students in these programs aren't getting the real information and skills they desperately need to develop a healthy understanding of their sexuality, make responsible decisions, and protect themselves from pregnancy and sometimes life-threatening sexually transmitted diseases. Imagine a driver's ed course where all they do is show students grisly photos of fatal traffic accidents, without ever teaching students to stop at red lights, use their turn signals, and buckle their seat belts. Abstinence-only sex ed is similar: it teaches only the negative consequences of sexuality, warning about the physical and psychological risks of sexual intercourse in exaggerated and alarmist tones.

Abstinence-only education is based on fear and ignorance. Here's what it does *not* teach young people but should:

- that sexuality is a natural, normal, healthy part of life
- responsible decision-making skills about relationships
- the facts about human growth and development
- positive messages about sexuality and sexual behavior, including the benefits of abstinence
- that consistent use of contraception can greatly reduce a couple's risk for unintended pregnancy
- accurate, factual information on abortion, masturbation, and sexual orientation
- factual information about sexually transmitted infections
- how to use condoms, and why—because they can significantly reduce the risk of unintended pregnancy, HIV, and other sexually transmitted infections
- interpersonal skills and relationships
- the full range of options for an unintended pregnancy, which include carrying the pregnancy to term and raising the baby or placing the baby for adoption, as well as ending the pregnancy with an abortion
- an opportunity to explore family, community, and religious values related to sexuality

In a country where six in ten women and seven in ten men have had sexual intercourse by their eighteenth birthday, most people don't get married until they're twenty-five, and the rate of unintended pregnancy is one of the highest in the Western world, abstinence-only programs are pathologically inadequate.

Abstinence-only programs do nothing to change the statistics cited above. Surveys of the programs have concluded that they are ineffective. In October 2002, reviewing all the available data on abstinence-only programs for a report for the National Campaign to Prevent Teen Pregnancy—a nonprofit, nonpartisan organization—researcher Douglas Kirby, Ph.D., found, "There do not currently exist any abstinence-only programs with strong evidence that they either delay sex or reduce teen pregnancy."

Such programs would be laughable if their results weren't so harmful—and sometimes even tragic. For example, young people who've had only abstinence education are less likely to use condoms or other contraceptives when they do have sex—and they *do* have sex!—than those who've had real sex education. In one study, Northern Kentucky University psychologist Dr. Angela Lipsitz surveyed 527 undergraduates who had taken virginity pledges, but found that 61 percent broke their vow to stay chaste until marriage. Of those who did keep their vows, many were confused about what constituted "sex." More than half of those who kept their pledges engaged in oral sex—as if oral sex isn't sex. But denial is rampant when people are not allowed to acknowledge their sexuality. The danger for them is that abstinence-only education doesn't tell students anything about how to protect themselves from infections that can be transmitted through oral sex.

Not long ago, I got a call from a bishop of the Evangelical Catholic denomination who wanted to become involved with Planned Parenthood. What prompted him to contact me was a tragedy. For the past year he had been counseling the parents of a fourteen-year-old girl who had died from a back-alley abortion. They were shocked and devastated, and couldn't believe what had happened. Adding to their pain was the fact that the priest at their home

church said the girl shouldn't be buried on church grounds because she'd had
an abortion. The minister, a bishop in his evangelical denomination, told me
he was moved to speak out—on the importance of compassion, and on the
need for young people to have good information about sexuality and contra-
ception in order to be safe and responsible. Sadly, this young woman had nei-
ther. Her death was the heartbreaking outcome of a set of cultural dictates
that keep young people ignorant about their sexuality, deprived of access to
contraception, and ashamed to discuss their pregnancy options and get the
help they need.

—Mike McGee, Vice President of Education and
Social Marketing, PPFA

We see the negative consequences of abstinence-only education all
the time at Planned Parenthood affiliates. We see teens who didn't
know how to protect themselves from unintended pregnancies and
sexually transmitted infections. Even worse, we see young people
victimized by sexual abuse because they do not know what inappropriate behavior is, or what to do about it. And we hear what young
people think of abstinence education. "The kids think abstinence-
only education is a joke—they come right out and tell us," says
Brenda Lee Green, vice president of education and training at
Planned Parenthood of Western Pennsylvania. "The abstinence-
only programs are so fear-based, overboard, and unrealistic, that the
kids think AIDS education is a conspiracy between parents and the
government to keep them from having sex, and they doubt what
we're telling them about sexually transmitted infections and pregnancy."

Despite the fact that a vocal minority has dictated what young
people in this country learn about sex, the vast majority of parents want their children to have real sex education in school, not
abstinence-only. Numerous surveys from around the country have
shown that parents want their children to have healthy attitudes

about sex, to know how to protect themselves, and they want them to have open access to medically accurate sexual health information:

- More than three-quarters of parents surveyed say that sexuality education should discuss, along with abstinence, condom use and other forms of birth control; abortion; sexual orientation; and psychological issues associated with having sex.
- Ninety-three percent of adults support sexuality education in high school, and 84 percent in junior high school.
- Sixty-six percent of American voters favor teaching age-appropriate sexuality education in elementary schools.
- Fifty-four percent of adults believe that eliminating sexuality education in schools would lead to more teenage pregnancies.
- Only 1 to 5 percent of parents remove their children from classes that provide comprehensive sexual information.
- Surveys of more than four thousand students, parents, teachers, and principals show that parents want schools to "go further" than they currently do on the topics of reproduction, HIV/AIDS and other sexually transmitted infections, and to "address issues often labeled controversial, like abortion and sexual orientation, as well as teach communication and coping skills."
- A majority of parents and teachers agree that schools should dedicate more time to sex education—half a semester or more.
- Of topics included in sex education curriculum, 85 percent of parents want students to learn how to use condoms; 84 percent, how to use other forms of birth control; 88 percent, how to talk about birth control with sexual partners; 94 percent, how to cope with pressure to have sex; 94 percent, the emotional consequences of becoming sexually active; 79 percent, abortion; 76 percent, sexual orientation; and 74 percent say controversial issues should be presented in a "balanced" way that describes society's diversity of views and values.

- Not only parents but many prominent health organizations, including the American Medical Society, the Institute of Medicine, the Society for Adolescent Medicine, the American Academy of Pediatrics, and over one hundred other medical and professional organizations are on record supporting comprehensive sexuality education programs.
- A wide variety of religious organizations support real sex education, including the American Jewish Congress, the National Council of Churches of Christ, and the Unitarian Universalist Association.
- Almost eight in ten conservative Christians support sexuality education in high school, and seven in ten support it in junior high.

Given these overwhelmingly favorable views of sex education, don't allow the shrill voices of the minority to silence the majority—and don't let them win elections or intimidate the school board, either. For it's not just parents but teachers, too, who believe in comprehensive sexuality education. Nine out of ten teachers say they believe students should be taught about contraception, but in this country, unlike every other industrialized nation, one in four teachers is prevented from doing so, in what amounts to censorship. One in five teachers say that the restrictions imposed on what they can say in the classroom are preventing them from meeting their students' needs. The proportion of sexuality education teachers who taught abstinence as the only way to prevent pregnancy and STIs increased from one in fifty in 1988 to one in four in 1999. Teachers across the country have been disciplined for doing what they're supposed to do: teach. In Belton, Missouri, a seventh-grade health teacher was suspended when she answered a student's question about oral sex. In Orlando, Florida, a teacher was suspended when he showed a student-made videotape about preventing AIDS transmission by using condoms.

Teenagers want and need real, medically accurate, comprehensive sexuality education. "Pet your dog, not your date" just doesn't cut it for them. They have questions about sexuality that they want answered. They're inundated with sexual images on television, in films, and on the Internet, and these sources are not going to give them the information they need about how to take care of themselves sexually. Many may be afraid to ask their parents, or may in fact be victims of parental or stepparental abuse. We get thousands of questions on-line at www.teenwire.com, and our affiliate clinicians and educators get thousands more during clinic visits and from anonymous question boxes in classrooms that make clear how much information teenagers want and need, and how much misinformation they have been exposed to. They want more than the "organ recital" or even the mechanics of contraception and condoms. They want help understanding relationships, making emotional connections, and developing social skills that will allow them to communicate effectively, assert personal boundaries, and negotiate dating relationships.

But they want the basics, too. Studies have shown that nearly half of high school students nationwide say they don't get enough information on birth control, HIV/AIDS, and other sexually transmitted infections. Forty-two percent of students would like more information on where to get contraception; 32 percent would like more information on how to use condoms; and 54 percent would like more information on where to go to get tested for HIV and sexually transmitted infections.

Sexuality education should certainly teach the benefits of not having sex too early, and the skills to say no, but it should also prepare young people to enjoy responsible, consensual sex, and prevent negative consequences at an appropriate time in life. After all, even those of us who want our kids to delay sex until marriage want them to know how to have healthy and positive sexual relationships at that time. We prepare young people for many experiences they will not have until after their school years—why would we want to deny them information about this one topic? Unlike abstinence-only programs, real sexuality programs work: studies show that school programs that promote *both* postponing sex *and* protecting yourself when you are sexually active are more effective than abstinence-only programs alone.

More effective at what, you may ask. Real sex education programs protect young people from unintended pregnancies and sexually transmitted infections. But unlike the claims of right-wing extremists, who say that sexuality education encourages young people to have sex, sexuality and AIDS education do not promote earlier or increased sexual activities in young people, as numerous studies have proven.

Few but the most ideologically driven extremists disagree with teaching young people the facts of life and love. Even President Bush's own surgeon general, Dr. Richard Carmona, has stated that in addition to abstinence, sex education programs need to teach about condoms and other forms of birth control. Secretary of State Colin Powell, too, is on record saying that he encourages the use of condoms to prevent disease. "Condoms are a way to prevent infection. Therefore, I not only support their use, I encourage their use among young people who are sexually active." But both of these officials were heavily criticized for their remarks by right-wingers who support abstinence-only programs.

A FEW FACTS ABOUT ABSTINENCE-ONLY VERSUS REAL SEX EDUCATION:

- A sexually active teenager who does not use contraception has a 90 percent chance of becoming pregnant within a year.
- The Netherlands, where sexuality education begins in pre-school and is integrated into all levels of school, has the lowest teen birthrate in the world—eight times lower than that of the U.S. The Dutch teenage abortion rate is three times lower than the U.S., and its AIDS case rate is eight times lower. In France, where sexuality education is mandated starting at age thirteen, the teenage birth rate is six times lower than the U.S., and the abortion rate is two times lower.
- A majority of North Carolina school districts teach abstinence-only sex education. Sixty-one percent of NC high school students are sexually active, and in 2001, the state's teen pregnancy rate was higher than the national rate—69.3 pregnancies per thousand girls, compared with 55 per thousand nationally.

INSIDE THE TEXTBOOKS: FEAR, SHAME, STEREOTYPES, AND MISINFORMATION

Most of the major abstinence-only programs are designed to spread fear. The main message is that having sex will result in deadly diseases, a terrible reputation, low self-esteem, embarrassment, ruined lives, and other calamities. It's not unlike the days when people were told that masturbation would make them go blind.

WHAT ABSTINENCE-ONLY EDUCATION TEACHES

Pregnancy, fear of pregnancy, AIDS, guilt, herpes, disappointing parents, chlamydia, inability to concentrate on school, syphilis, embarrassment, abortion, shotgun wedding, gonorrhea, selfishness, pelvic inflammatory disease, heartbreak, infertility, loneliness, cervical cancer, poverty, loss of self-esteem, loss of reputation, being used, suicide, substance abuse, melancholy, loss of faith, possessiveness, diminished ability to communicate, isolation, fewer friendships formed, rebellion against other familial standards, alienation, loss of self-mastery, distrust of complementary sex, viewing others as sex objects, difficulty with long-term commitments, various other sexually transmitted diseases, aggressions toward women, ectopic pregnancy, sexual violence, loss of a sense of responsibility toward others, loss of honesty, jealousy, depression, death.

—list of harmful consequences that should
be cited to students, from the *Facing Reality,
Parent/Teacher Guide* curriculum

What if I want to have sex before I get married? . . . Well, I guess you just have to be prepared to die. And you'll probably take your spouse and one or more of your children with you.

—*No Second Chance*, abstinence-only sex ed video

There is no way to have premarital sex without hurting someone.

—*Sex Respect*, student workbook

Conception, also known as fertilization, occurs when one sperm unites with one egg in the upper third of the fallopian tube. This is when life begins . . . even though he or she was only the size and appearance of a pencil dot, the baby was a separate, genetically unique individual.

—*FACTS*, middle-school teacher's guide

Using scare tactics to emphasize the negative results of pre-marital sex, abstinence-only teaching materials never mention that most of those potentially bad outcomes could easily be prevented. One federally funded student workbook, *Sex Respect,* says that AIDS and other sexually transmitted infections are simply the natural consequences of sex outside of marriage—"the same as getting sick from spoiled food." It tells students, "There is no way to have premarital sex without hurting someone." Another, *Facing Reality,* gives students a long list of the negative consequences of premarital sex, ranging from shotgun weddings to heartbreak to suicide.

Some of the abstinence courses have games students can play to illustrate the invariably dire outcomes of premarital sex. In a *FACTS* game, students roll a dice ten times—one for every year of sexual activity. When a certain number comes up, the student picks a card and reads their fate—and all the cards are negative. "You have an STD but are asymptomatic. Before it is diagnosed, it does permanent damage to your reproductive system, leaving you infertile," reads one card. "Do not pass Go!" "Your younger sister/ brother knows that you are sexually active and decides that if it is okay for you, it's okay for him/her. He/she contracts the AIDS virus," reads another. Some are a bit subtler: "Sex has been a way for you to feel good about yourself. Lately though, you noticed that you feel disgusted with yourself."

As part of their scare tactics, the guidebooks make numerous blatantly false claims about the risks of sexual activity and sexually transmitted infections. The books typically describe the worst-case scenarios of sexually transmitted infections, making it seem that easily curable infections, such as chlamydia, always result in infertility. *Choosing the Best* states, "over 100,000 new cases [of syphilis] are reported each year according to a CDC report." Well, if you try asking the CDC about that, you'll find that in fact there were only 6,657 cases of syphilis reported in the United States in 1999. *Choosing the Best* also describes how human papilloma virus (HPV) leads to vulvar cancer, requiring the "removal of the entire vulva area through major surgery." In truth, HPV is a common, and almost always benign, virus which in rare cases can lead to vulvar cancer—if undetected. However, a Pap smear can detect cell changes caused by HPV early enough to prevent cervical cancer—though the importance of *getting* Pap smears is never taught in abstinence-only curricula. In truth, vulvar cancer is rare, and if caught early, is 90 percent curable. Failing to inform people about how to prevent or treat HPV is what puts young people in danger.

Another scare tactic is to tell young people that condoms and contraception don't prevent pregnancy or infection. The fact is that, used correctly, condoms are 98 percent effective in preventing pregnancy, 99.9 percent effective in reducing sexually transmitted infections transmission, and ten thousand times more effective in preventing HIV than not using condoms. But the guidebooks are full of stories of condoms breaking, tearing, slipping off, and bursting. Teen-Aid's *Me, My World, My Future* abstinence-only text says that relying on condoms is like playing Russian roulette: "The first player spins the cylinder, points the gun to his/her head, and pulls the trigger. He/she has only one in six chances of being killed. But if one continues to perform this act, the chamber with the bullet will ultimately fall into position under the hammer, and the game ends as one of the players dies." The reality, of course, is that having sex without condoms is the real Russian roulette!

Not only do abstinence programs suggest that condoms won't protect students from unintended pregnancies or sexually transmitted infections, they convey the message that using them is extraordinarily difficult. The *Clue 2000* textbook says, "correct use requires self-control and discipline, special handling and proper storage, no foreplay . . ." *Choosing the Best* says that for condoms to be used properly, over ten specific steps must be followed every time. Now, it isn't hard to learn how to use a condom—practice once on a cucumber and you get the idea. But instead of teaching the very simple facts of condom use, these curricula actively warn students away from condoms, with the result that young people are putting themselves at needless risk for sexually transmitted infections and unintended pregnancies.

When the books aren't exaggerating the physical dangers of sex, they're concocting psychological ones. Teen-Aid's *Sexuality, Commitment & Family* tells teachers, "premarital sex, especially with more than one person, has been linked to the development of emotional illness." So, probably, has eating breakfast cereal.

Aside from fear, the abstinence-only guidebooks use shame and embarrassment to dissuade young people from having premarital sex. Many tell students that they'll lose their reputations if they engage in sex, or their families and peers will look down on them. They say that young people engage in sex for all negative reasons—low self-esteem, lack of self-control, peer pressure, and drugs. For students who have already had sex—that's more than a third of ninth graders already—these negative messages may themselves hurt their self-esteem.

Abstinence-only programs present a 1950s view of sexuality and gender relations, when guys were always trying to get to "third base," and girls were the ones who had to put the brakes on. Girls are warned against dressing in a sexually provocative way, making it seem that if they do, they deserve whatever they get—the kind of logic that suggests that female victims of rape are responsible for the crime committed against them because they were wearing shorts. In the books, boys are described as having uncontrollable sexual urges, while girls are only interested in intimacy. As the *WAIT Training* textbook says, "men sexually are like microwaves and women sexually are like crockpots." Apparently some girls, thanks to the "liberation" movement, have defied their basic nature and morphed from crockpots to microwaves, however: "The liberation movement has produced some aggressive girls today, and one of the tough challenges for guys who say no will be the questioning of their manliness," says the *Sex Respect* student workbook.

Homosexuality is rarely even mentioned in these books, as if by not talking about it, it will just go away. When it is mentioned, it's with the same old stereotypes of promiscuity and perversity that should long since have disappeared from any reputable publication. One guidebook equates homosexuality with incest and pedophilia. Another associates AIDS exclusively with homosexuality, telling students that the best way to avoid AIDS is to "avoid homosexual behavior," as if heterosexuals were immune to the disease. The books also promote shame about homosexuality. *Facing Reality* says, "many homosexual activists are frustrated and desperate over their own situation and those of loved ones. Many are dying, in part, due to ignorance. Educators who struggled to overcome ignorance and instill self-mastery in their students will inevitably lead them to recognize that some people with AIDS are now suffering because of the choices they made." Such statements make it seem that AIDS is punishment for nonheterosexual sexuality.

When it comes to the topic of abortion, abstinence-only messages of fear and shame are laid on thick, with a clear anti-choice bias. Students are told that life begins at conception, and the only possible way to deal with an unplanned pregnancy is by carrying it to term and placing the baby for adoption. "Is it fair to make the baby die because of a bad decision his parents made?" the *Sex Respect* workbook asks. The medical risks of abortion are wildly exaggerated and blatantly false. *Sex Respect* says, "If she is a young teen, pregnant for the first time, there's a chance the abortion will cause heavy damage to her reproductive organs. Heavy loss of blood, infection and puncturing of the uterus may all lead to future pregnancy problems." While all medical procedures involve some risk, in reality, abortion is one of the very safest—much safer than any other surgery and than childbirth—and that "chance" is practically nil.

All these fear-based messages are damaging to young people. They not only fail to provide medically accurate information but spread myths and stereotypes about gender, sexual orientation, pregnancy options, and sexually transmitted infections. They present a view that values one particular family structure and lifestyle over others, condemning those who do not fit into an idealized monogamous marriage. These programs don't respect the wide variety of religious and ethical beliefs that our pluralistic society is based on—which our Constitution should protect, and our education system should adhere to.

ABSTINENCE EDUCATION: AN AFFRONT TO THE CONSTITUTION

Abstinence-only programs teach students—and our society—that it is permissible to override the Constitution, for two key Constitutional principles are the separation of church and state, and freedom of speech.

Like efforts to discourage the teaching of evolution in favor of creationism, abstinence-only programs were created by fundamentalist groups that want to impose their beliefs on all students in public schools—despite the fact that their views on sex, sexual orientation, contraception, and abortion are not shared by the majority of people in our society.

Abstinence-only programs have been federally funded since 1981, when right-wing political groups encouraged Congress to pass the Adolescent Family Life Act, also known as the chastity law, which funded educational programs to "promote self-discipline and other prudent approaches" to adolescent sex. Right-wing fundamentalist groups began developing curricula to frighten young people away from sex, often with blatant misinformation, and to teach them to oppose abortion. These early programs had explicit religious content, such as, "Make Christ your chaperon." But the Constitution forbids the promotion or preference of any religious perspective in a public institution, so the American Civil Liberties Union immediately challenged the law, calling it an affront to the principle of the separation of church and state. More than a decade later, the U.S. Supreme Court held that the programs could not promote religion, but the underlying antisex, anticontraception message remained. Some of the biggest federal grant recipients, curriculum-creating groups such as Sex Respect and Teen-Aid, had already turned their curricula into robust businesses, building an infrastructure that remains in schools today.

Not only is public funding being used to support religion-based programs in the schools, some of it goes directly to religious institutions. In August 2003, Dr. Julie Gerberding, the Bush-appointed director of the Centers for Disease Control and Prevention (CDC), presented the Metro Atlanta Youth for Christ with a check for a federal grant of $363,936 to promote abstinence-only education. She was sending a message to the rest of the country that a right-wing, religious view of morality is trumping science. Of all people, the director of the CDC should be promoting condoms, not prayer, to prevent sexually transmitted infections. Your tax dollars are paying for this!

Youth for Christ is hardly the only religious organization to get public funding for abstinence-only education. It's happening at both the federal and state levels. In Montana, the Catholic diocese of Helena received $14,000 from the state's Department of Health and Human Services for classes in "Assets for Abstinence." In Louisiana, a network of pastors is bringing the abstinence-only message to religious congregations with public funds. In California,

Pennsylvania, Alabama, and many other states, schools regularly host chastity pledges and rallies on school premises during school hours, often organized by religious groups. During these rituals, students pledge "to God" that they will remain abstinent until they marry.

Publicly funded abstinence programs assault freedom of speech while silencing the truth. Materials on contraception, sexually transmitted infections, and sexual orientation have been razored out of textbooks. Articles about sexuality have been censored in student newspapers. Teachers are prevented from giving students facts about contraceptives and condoms, and have been threatened with dismissal, suspension, and lawsuits when they have answered students' questions with frank information. No discussion of homosexuality or other lifestyles outside the monogamous-marriage model is allowed.

Scientific information about comprehensive sexuality education is also being censored by the government. The CDC used to have information on its Web site called "Programs that Work," which identified sex education programs that have been found to be effective in scientific studies. In 2002, all five "Programs that Work" provided comprehensive sex education, and none were abstinence-only. But last year, without any scientific justification, the CDC erased all information about "Programs that Work" from its Web site. The censorship may have something to do with recent political appointees who support abstinence-only education. For example, the Bush administration appointed Dr. Joe McIlhaney, a prominent advocate of abstinence-only programs, to sit on the Advisory Committee to the CDC's director.

Meanwhile, those government officials who advocate real sex education have been dismissed or ignored. In June 2001, former surgeon general David Satcher, a Clinton appointee, unveiled a report on promoting sexual health and responsible sexual behavior.

While acknowledging the national debate over sexuality education, he was frank about the fact that abstinence-only programs have not been proven effective, and that real sex education is more effective. "Programs that typically emphasize abstinence, but also cover condoms and other methods of contraception, have a larger body of evaluation evidence that indicates either no effect on initiation of sexual activity or, in some cases, a delay in the initiation of sexual activity." His report suggested that good sexuality education is "thorough, wide-ranging, begins early, and continues throughout the lifespan." It should not only stress the value of remaining abstinent until involved in a committed, enduring, and mutually monogamous relationship, but assure awareness, for those who are sexually active, of optimal protection against sexually transmitted infections and unintended pregnancy.

There was a long delay before the Satcher report was published, and when it came out, its findings were promptly undermined by the Bush administration: "The president thinks abstinence education is important," said then-White House spokesman Ari Fleischer, who noted that "the surgeon general was not appointed by this administration." Satcher, who never expected to be appointed to a second term under Bush, commented, "We have created an environment where there's almost a conspiracy of silence when it comes to sexuality. It's talked about in the wrong places in the wrong ways."

When science is replaced by ideology, honest discussion is silenced, and students are denied potentially life-saving medical information, it's time to speak up.

SURGEONS GENERAL ON
SEXUALITY EDUCATION:

Dr. C. Everett Koop (under Ronald Reagan):
"There is no doubt that we need sex education in public schools and that it [should] include information on heterosexual and homosexual relationships . . . [starting] at the lowest grade possible."

Dr. Antonia Novella (under George H. W. Bush):
In a Surgeon General's Report to the American Public on HIV Infection and AIDS, Dr. Novella stressed the need for "scientific, dependable information about HIV and AIDS."

Dr. David Satcher (under Bill Clinton):
"We face a serious public health challenge regarding the sexual health of our nation. . . . This is a call to action. We cannot remain complacent. Doing nothing is unacceptable."

Dr. Joycelyn Elders (under Bill Clinton):
"Comprehensive health education should be taught to all children, starting in kindergarten and continuing through high school."

Dr. Richard Carmona (under George W. Bush):
Carmona stated that sex education programs should include discussion of condoms and other forms of birth control. "As part of comprehensive education, we should be talking about all of the issues."

FIGHTING FOR COMPREHENSIVE SEXUALITY EDUCATION

Abstinence-only education didn't make its way into our schools by accident. It was the result of a long-term campaign by members of the religious right, who lobbied school boards, stuffed envelopes, and wrote letters to change school curricula. The religious right has promoted candidates and won elections at every level of government, starting with the school boards. One of their tactics has been to wage "stealth campaigns" in which ultraconservatives get elected to school boards but don't reveal their right-wing agendas until after they're in office. Since school board elections are often poorly attended, right-wing campaigners have been able to win with few votes. The religious right wing has mapped out a coherent and extremely effective strategy to take over our school curricula—and our country. We need to organize just as effectively to take them back. This will require determined, committed citizen action.

The very first thing to do is to find out what children in your community are being taught about sex. Many parents may not even realize that their children are being indoctrinated into beliefs that they themselves do not subscribe to, or are being taught falsehoods masquerading as facts. (More typically, students are being taught nothing at all.)

To begin to bring comprehensive, reality-based sexuality education to your school system, you should gather together a group of concerned citizens, which may include parents, medical professionals, teachers, clergy, social service professionals, and school board members who share your views. Creating a broad coalition of like-minded supporters will make it clear to the community that you have to be taken seriously. You may have individuals in your group who belong to national organizations that promote real sexuality education, such as the American Medical Association, Boys and

Girls Clubs of America, Girls Incorporated, National Council of Churches, National Education Association, and Planned Parenthood. These organizations can provide assistance to your coalition.

Once you have a coalition, you can strategize the best way to meet your goal of comprehensive sexuality education. Depending on the situation in your community, you may want to take some legal action, you may want to put pressure on the school board, you may want to take the issue to the local media—or all of the above.

You'll need first to understand how your school board works, and what the legal requirements are for sexuality education in your state. A good place to start is to attend school board meetings and PTA meetings. The National Association of State Boards of Education, a nonprofit organization, can provide information on how school boards work. Then, contact the school district's curriculum staff and superintendent, and the state's board or department of education. Find out:

- Does the state have a law mandating or addressing sexuality, family life, or health education? If so, get a copy of the law(s).
- Are there state regulations regarding implementation of that law?
- Who makes sure that school districts comply with the state laws and regulations—the department of education, board of education, or local officials in the school district?
- Are there local rules regarding sexuality education, and who is in charge?
- How are schools' sexuality education programs funded? Is funding contingent upon approval of a proposed curriculum?

Once you've reviewed the laws, you can determine whether the educational materials in your school comply with them. You may be able to challenge the curriculum, as parent groups have done in many states. There have been successful lawsuits in which parent groups have argued that abstinence-only materials failed to meet the standards of comprehensive sexuality education that many states require. Other lawsuits have prevailed in getting abstinence-only materials rejected because of their overt religious content. In other cases, abstinence materials have been successfully challenged because they contained inaccurate medical information. But all of this requires determined citizen action.

Aside from legal challenges, a coalition should work to advance its agenda on several fronts:

- Monitor the school board. Make sure members of your coalition attend meetings on a regular basis, make their opinions heard, and track major issues in school curricula. Write letters to the local newspapers about school board decisions.
- Research the backgrounds of current school board members, and candidates who are running for office. Find out who supports each member, their political loyalties and leanings. Check their public statements and ask them at public forums about their stance on comprehensive sexuality education.
- Educate the current school board. Make information about the need for comprehensive sexuality education available to every school board member. Set up meetings and brief them on the issues.
- Inform the media. Announce the formation of your group, send out press releases, and keep in touch with local reporters about education issues.
- Lobby state legislators to introduce bills that mandate medically accurate or comprehensive sexuality education. Two states, California and Maine, have passed such bills.
- Write to your congresspeople as a group and object to using $273 million per year in federal funding for abstinence-

only programs that are ineffective and dangerous to young people.

Campaigns against abstinence-only programs and right-wing local politicians can make our cause stronger than ever. One example of what good organizing can do occurred in upstate New York, where Planned Parenthood was under attack by a group called STOPP (for Stop Planned Parenthood), which was formed in 1985 with the specific and only purpose of putting Planned Parenthood out of business. They started picketing Planned Parenthood clinics in Dutchess and Ulster counties. From the beginning, STOPP focused on sex education programs. Using misleading materials, STOPP suggested that Planned Parenthood was teaching students to become sexually active so that they would need Planned Parenthood services, get pregnant, and need abortions—all supposedly to fill our coffers! The guerrilla attack tactics that STOPP used then are used widely today—picketing, calling legislators late at night, boycotting businesses that deal with Planned Parenthood, annoying delivery people, and harassing staff. STOPP attempted to stop small grants for family planning, and soon county budget hearings were packed with people on both sides of the issue. The publicity was a boon to Planned Parenthood, because it made so many people aware that the pro-choice position is not just about abortion—that STOPP wanted to take away family planning, sexuality education, and basic health services. With the new supporters who rallied to their cause, Planned Parenthood of the Mid-Hudson Valley has been able to initiate new programs, expand its health service capacity, and open new centers in underserved areas. Meanwhile, the STOPP picketers have dwindled to a very few people, and almost no one takes their mission seriously.

With strong organization and willing activists, we can reverse the trend to presenting backward, abstinence-only programs in the classrooms. We can stop campaigns against sexuality education, family planning, and reproductive rights in their tracks—at the local level.

Meanwhile, if you know a student who attends a school where abstinence-only programs are taught, you can help make him or her aware of other good resources on sexuality, such as www.teenwire.com. If you're a parent of such a child, remember—you always have the option of taking your children out of abstinence-only classrooms.

Just say no to anti-sex programs!

FOUR

STATE OF THE UTERUS

◆——◆

FROM PETRI DISH TO PERSONHOOD

*One can make a pretty convincing argument, however, that
fetuses are persons. They are alive; their species is Homo sapiens.*

—Michael McConnell, Bush-appointed judge,
Tenth Circuit U.S. Court of Appeals, 1998

◆——◆

In Margaret Atwood's novel *The Handmaid's Tale*, set in the near future, the Republic of Gilead has been taken over by ultraconserva-
tive Christians. Though most of the women in Gilead are infertile
because they've been exposed to a toxic environment of nuclear
waste, pesticides, and chemical weapons, there are a few women
who can still bear children. They are taken to camps where they are
forced to become Handmaids, birth mothers for elite families. The
main character in the book is one of these Handmaids. Each
month during her fertile time she must lie on her back and pray—
in a Ceremony based on a Biblical verse in which Abraham has a
child with his wife's maid—that the head of the household makes

her pregnant. (Sarah's maid's child may have been the world's first recorded surrogate birth!)

In the Republic of Gilead, women are useful only as vessels to bear children.

Written in 1985, Atwood's novel now seems less like science fiction than prophecy. If that sounds like an exaggeration, it's time to open your eyes to the legislation and regulations the politicians currently in power are trying to pass, or have already passed, to give fertilized eggs, zygotes, embryos, and fetuses more power and rights than the "vessels" who carry them—women. If these initiatives succeed, and many already have, women in this country could have fewer rights than a six-celled blastocyst, which is smaller than the head of a pin. Such a change in the legal climate will be part of the most profound betrayal of our nation's fundamental principles of liberty and justice since the Constitution took the position that slaves counted as less than full human beings. This time, it's women who would count less than full human beings—and even less than fertilized eggs. No aspect of reproductive rights puts the debate into sharper focus than the fight over fetal personhood.

THE ELEVATION OF FETAL RIGHTS

As with many other anti-choice assaults, this one is taking place on many fronts, and it assumes many guises:

- In April 2001, the U.S. House of Representatives passed the so-called Unborn Victims of Violence Act. This bill would make harming an embryo or fetus—at any time from the moment of conception—a crime separate and equal to harming the woman, thus establishing the legal personhood of the fetus and elevating its value to that of the pregnant woman.

- In March 2002, the administration proposed regulations that would give health care coverage to fetuses—but not to pregnant women—under the Children's Health Insurance Program.
- In July 2002, President Bush announced federal funding for public awareness campaigns about embryo "adoptions."
- In October 2002, the government's Health and Human Services Advisory Committee on Human Research gave fertilized eggs new status, declaring them "human subjects."
- In December 2002, at a regional United Nations population conference in Bangkok, Thailand, U.S. government delegates advanced the position that life begins at conception, attempting to impose this ideological view—not even shared by the majority in the U.S.—on the rest of the world.
- In January 2003, Bush declared National Sanctity of Human Life Day, emphasizing *not* the sanctity of people who are already alive (that might require universal health care, among other things) but of human tissue.
- In May 2003, George Bush's brother, Florida governor Jeb Bush, tried to appoint a legal guardian for a fetus.
- In October 2003, when U.S. Attorney General John Ashcroft assigned prosecution of abortion under the abortion ban law, one day after President Bush signed it, to the Justice Department's Civil Rights Division, he delivered the clear message that this legislation created civil rights for the fetus.
- In January 2004, Governor Jeb Bush began looking into possible legislation to allow guardians to be appointed for fetuses, after the state courts ruled such appointments improper.

FETAL HOMICIDE LAWS

The following states have fetal homicide laws under which fetuses are considered victims at any stage of development:

Arizona	Nebraska
Idaho	North Dakota
Illinois	Ohio
Louisiana	Pennsylvania
Michigan	South Dakota
Minnesota	Utah
Missouri	Wisconsin

These states have fetal homicide laws under which fetuses are victims only at specific stages in development:

Arkansas	Nevada
California	Oklahoma
Florida	Rhode Island
Georgia	South Carolina
Massachusetts	Tennessee
Mississippi	Washington

The right-wing anti-choice strategy is clear: to elevate the status of a fetus—from the moment sperm and egg unite to form a zygote—to that of a person, for the specific purpose of eliminating women's reproductive rights. As Howard Phillips, chairman of the Conservative Caucus, so succinctly put it: "If personhood is declared and established, *Roe v. Wade* goes by the wayside, all of the other defenses of abortion go by the wayside." Which is why one of the chief goals of the Conservative Caucus (a right-wing public policy advocacy group founded by Phillips in 1974) is to pass the

Paramount Human Life Amendment, which would establish legal personhood from the moment of conception.

If no one knows when full humanness is attained, then we cannot prevent a Satan-worshipping neighbor, who believes that full humanness begins at the age of two, from sacrificing his one-and-a-half-year-old son to the unholy one.

—Christiananswers.net

ZYGOTES' RIGHTS

The notion that "life," meaning "personhood," begins at conception is extremely radical. Though much of this legislative and regulatory activity is being undertaken in the name of religion, in many religions, as I discuss below, the fetus is not considered a person until it has either "quickened"—developed to the stage where the woman could feel it moving—or grown to viability—the stage at which it could survive outside the woman's body. These views, steeped in centuries of tradition and moral philosophy, informed the *Roe v. Wade* decision, which holds that a woman has the right to an abortion any time before the third trimester, or viability, but that during the third trimester the state has the right to regulate or proscribe abortion—except where it is necessary for the preservation of the life or health of the woman.

Already, those who would like to push fetal rights back to conception have tilted the Supreme Court away from the viability standard set in *Roe*. With the *Planned Parenthood v. Casey* decision of 1992, the Court indicated that individual states could now decide to restrict abortions even before viability, as long as those restrictions did not place an "undue burden" on the woman. However, the Court did not define what an "undue burden" is, giving the states enormous leeway in how they choose to interpret the ruling. In the various opinions issued in *Casey*, a minority of justices argued that there was a "compelling state interest in the fetus *from the moment of conception*" [emphasis mine]. To understand how extreme that notion is, consider that it overrules the medical definition, which considers pregnancy to begin not at the time of fertilization but at the time of implantation. Defining a fertilized egg as a "pregnancy" has enormous implications for reproductive rights. Not only would abortion be a crime but by the same logic some common forms of contraception that prevent implantation, like the IUD, emergency contraception, and certain kinds of birth control pills, would be, too.

The Supreme Court rulings since *Roe* (including *Webster v. Reproductive Health Services*, 1989) have stopped short of granting a fetus full legal personhood, but abortion rights opponents in the states have been pushing for more and more fetal rights ever since. The effects of these fetal rights initiatives, which would give fertilized eggs—two-thirds of which are never even implanted in the natural course of events—the same legal standing as the woman whose body they inhabit, are chilling: women would be reduced to the status of incubators. Anti-choice zealots are offering up a vast array of policies to advance this goal.

WOMEN: THE <u>REAL</u> VICTIMS OF THE UNBORN VICTIMS OF VIOLENCE ACT

In 2001, the U.S. House of Representatives passed the Unborn Victims of Violence Act (UVVA). This act would amend the federal criminal code to create a new, separate offense if an individual kills or injures a "child in utero" during the course of another crime. This bill defines "child in utero" as "a member of the species Homo sapiens, at any stage of development, who is carried in the womb." This means that UVVA would be the first federal law to recognize a fertilized egg as a crime "victim," independent of the woman who suffers the physical injury. Penalties would differ with the crime, but harming the fetus would be counted as a separate crime that would earn offenders as much jail time as harming the woman. The bill is likely to pass the Senate and be signed by President Bush. It's been pushed along by the media attention given to the tragic murder of Laci Peterson, who was pregnant, and whose family wrote to lawmakers asking them to call it Laci and Connor's Law.

Let's make no mistake: I strongly condemn any act of violence that hurts a woman, or that interferes with a woman's choice to carry a pregnancy to term. I am a mother, a grandmother, and a great-grandmother. My heart goes out to Laci Peterson's family and to her loved ones who are grieving for their horrible loss. But Laci's murder has nothing—nothing—to do with fetal rights; it's unequivocally about violence against women. And it is cruel that this family has been exploited in their time of tragedy by people who would use them to advance an anti-choice agenda.

A woman suffers a uniquely terrible injury if a pregnancy is harmed or ended by an act of violence against her. It is appropriate that crimes where a fetus is injured or lost should carry additional penalties; in fact, in most states, they already do. But solutions should be genuine, not political. On the face of it, the UVVA is simply about creating additional penalties when a pregnant woman is victimized. But in reality, the sponsors of this bill don't care about the women who are the victims of these crimes. If they really cared about pregnant women, it would be the woman, rather than the embryo, who would be the focus of their bill. But in fact, nowhere in the bill is the harm to the woman resulting from an involuntary termination of her pregnancy even mentioned. It's all about the fetus. And when given a chance to vote for a substitute bill—

the Motherhood Protection Act—that would make the pregnant woman the victim of the crime, the bill's sponsors voted against it.

The real purpose of the (UVVA) law is to define a fetus at any stage of development as a person.

—Rep. Jerrold Nadler (D–New York)

They say it [the Unborn Victims of Violence Act] undermines abortion rights. It does. But that's irrelevant.

—Sen. Orrin Hatch (R-Utah) on CNN

As its title suggests, the UVVA legislation is not an attempt to protect women. Instead, it is a backdoor attempt to erode a woman's right to choose by making an embryo a distinct legal entity from the moment of conception. In fact, the wording of this act is a direct assault on the *Roe v. Wade* decision, in which the Court ruled that "the word 'person,' as used in the Fourteenth Amendment, does not include the unborn." During the committee consideration of this bill in the 106th Congress, the bill's advocates admitted that their true intent is to recognize the existence of a separate legal "person."

Laws like these don't help women. They harm women by creating a potentially adversarial relationship between the health needs of the woman and of the developing fetus: any dispute over whether to save the health or life of the woman by terminating a pregnancy could conceivably be won by the fetus. Moreover, it sets the stage for pregnancy police who could monitor women's behaviors and freedoms during their pregnancies. Anti-choice prosecutors have relied on similar state laws to prosecute pregnant women for behaviors—alcohol or drug use, suicide attempts—that are potentially harmful to the embryo or fetus. One woman was even prosecuted for failure to follow her doctor's orders to remain on bed rest during her pregnancy. These laws invariably come down hardest on the women who are most vulnerable—low-income and minority women.

In South Carolina, for instance—a state that has been a leader in the movement to establish rights for fetuses—pregnant indigent women who came to the Medical University of South Carolina (MUSC) in Charleston were tested for drugs starting in 1989. Some of those who tested positive were jailed for the duration of their pregnancies—which can hardly be considered in the interests of the health of the fetus. Others were jailed after giving birth, still in their hospital gowns. Of the women jailed under these circumstances in the state from 1989 to 2000 (at least thirty in 1992 alone), nearly all were African-American. The crimes these women were charged with—drug possession, child neglect, and distributing drugs to a minor—carried penalties of two to twenty years.

The "search and arrest" policy of MUSC was finally stopped in March 2001, when the U.S. Supreme Court ruled (*Ferguson v. City of Charleston*) that the drug testing scheme was in violation of the Fourth Amendment, which provides Americans with protection from unreasonable searches.

In other states where women can be prosecuted for fetal abuse, they've been held responsible for damage to the fetus caused by their battering husbands—while the husbands go scot-free. Sometimes it seems the authorities will go to any length to punish the woman. In Wyoming, a pregnant woman went to the hospital after being battered because she feared that the fetus might have been harmed. Instead of arresting the husband, the Wyoming police charged the woman with fetal endangerment because she had drunk a beer that day.

If the UVVA were really intended to protect pregnant women from violence, it would stand to reason that groups that work to prevent domestic violence—which is the main source of injury to pregnant women and their fetuses, just as it seems it might have been for Laci Peterson—would support this bill. Notably, they oppose it.

As Juley Fulcher, public policy director of the National Coalition Against Domestic Violence, testified to a House of Representatives subcommittee, the UVVA bill is not designed to protect battered women. "Instead the focus often will be shifted to the impact of that crime on the unborn embryo or fetus, once again diverting the attention of the legal system away from domestic violence or other forms of violence against women." Fulcher also pointed out that programs that work on the front lines to stop domestic violence are experiencing severe cuts in funding, passed by the same politicians who supported the UVVA.

Now, why wouldn't the people who support separate penalties for crimes that harm a fetus also give their support to funding that would help prevent the number one reason those fetuses are harmed—domestic violence? Because they know, as we should too, that this legislation is not about preventing violence. It's about preventing women from making their own reproductive choices. The assumption underlying the attempts to raise the legal status of a fetus to a person is that women can't be trusted to make moral decisions about their own pregnancies—a breathtakingly misogynistic notion. Legislation purportedly designed to protect the fetus is a slippery slope that eventually erodes women's rights to due process, privacy, bodily integrity, self-sovereignty, and equal protection.

Nearly all extensions of fetal rights are paid for by a curtailment of women's fundamental rights that extends far beyond the abortion context.

—Jean Reith Schroedel, political scientist, Claremont Graduate University

HEALTH INSURANCE FOR FETUSES—BUT NOT FOR THE WOMEN WHO CARRY THEM

If ever there was a clear indication of the present government's desire to make the point that embryos are more important than women, it's in their efforts to extend insurance benefits to fetuses, under the aegis of CHIP (the State Children's Health Insurance Program). CHIP was originally created to channel federal funds through the states in order to provide health insurance to children of low-income parents who are not eligible for coverage under Medicaid. By expanding the definition of "child" for purposes of this legislation such that it will refer to any income-eligible "individual under the age of nineteen *including the period from conception to birth*" [emphasis mine], the Bush administration has found yet another backdoor way to establish the principle of fetal personhood.

Though HHS secretary Tommy Thompson claimed that the change was made because he wanted to give states the flexibility to use some of their CHIP funding to expand prenatal care in order to improve child health, no additional money was provided to accompany this expanded definition of "child." Which means the same dollars are simply being stretched further, so that neither pregnant women nor their fetuses stand to benefit much. Moreover, Senators Jon Corzine and Jeff Bingaman had already proposed legislation to allow CHIP to cover prenatal care for women—*without* changing the definition of "child" to include zygotes. But their legislation was quickly a no-go (despite Secretary Thompson's initial support of it) and the change in the eligibility regulations of CHIP passed despite thousands of letters opposing it, including a letter signed by a number of U.S. senators.

Of course, even without additional dollars, who would not wholeheartedly support the goal of expanding access to pregnancy-related health care? The American Public Health Association, health provider organizations like Planned Parenthood, obstetrician/gynecologists, nurses, and pediatricians are all united in agreement that the best path to a healthy baby is a healthy pregnancy, in which the woman's health care needs are the foremost consideration. But under the CHIP regulations, it is very specifically the fetus, not the woman, whose health is covered, which in some areas may actually work against the best interest of the woman. For instance, more women may be encouraged to have unnecessary C-sections, in order to be covered for anesthesia. Why? Because, since the labor and delivery needs of the woman are not covered except as they benefit the fetus, and since in some states, such as Idaho, deadening the pain of childbirth isn't considered "necessary" for the fetus, having a C-section might be the only way a woman would be eligible for anesthesia.

Even worse than the fact that the interests of woman and fetus may not always coincide is that there are areas in which they may actually come into conflict. With advances in new reproductive technologies, regulations establishing the personhood of the fetus could mean that the woman would have to undergo in utero treatments for fetuses with life-threatening, or even nonlife-threatening but treatable, conditions. Who would give consent for such surgery? Who would decide whether or not a woman should undergo the knife in order that doctors may perform fetal surgery? The State? In the face of regulations created for the purpose of establishing fetal personhood, the health and well-being of the woman might not count for much.

Another problem with the legislation is that it puts the states into a bind. Since the expanded definition of who is covered under CHIP insurance was not backed up with an increase in federal funds, the states themselves may have to come up with the money, and might therefore choose not to go along with the plan to include fetuses in the CHIP program. However, only if they *do* agree to accept this new CHIP regulation can the states get federal matching dollars for benefits given to undocumented and newly arrived pregnant immigrant women, a population not covered by other programs. So women's health advocates have to choose between elevating the status of the fetus to a child, and walking away from the only opportunity the federal government offers to provide prenatal care to a population of women who were previously completely excluded. Talk about making a deal with the devil.

The change in the legal definition of "child," which does little to actually expand health care for pregnant women or protect children, was made for one purpose and one purpose only: it lays the groundwork for a multipronged assault on reproductive freedom by the courts, by congressional legislation, and by federal regulations. This is as good an example of the pernicious web woven by anti-choice hard-liners as I have seen, and it is critically important that we understand how these initiatives fit together. They are not isolated. The anti-choice zeal to eliminate women's reproductive rights leaves no stone unturned.

Over and over, laws and regulations that affect Americans' lives are being callously used to make a political point. And the politicians are dancing the two-step, like the governor in *The Best Little Whorehouse in Texas*, to lead the people on. The change in CHIP regulations was gratuitous, except insofar as it served to advance the political agenda of declaring a fetus a "person." Treating the fetus as a separate entity that is covered under insurance—giving the fetus health care, but not the woman—implies that the health of the fetus not only can but should be considered before the health of the woman. As in Gilead, women are relegated to the status of fetus-carrying vessels.

I believe that low-income women—and all women—deserve insurance coverage that provides for all of their actual pregnancy needs, not just the needs that are incidental to the health of the fetus. Why not simply expand CHIP to include pregnant women?

While we're at it, why not elevate the status of a *woman* to a person?

FEDERAL FUNDING FOR
EMBRYO "ADOPTIONS"

The federal government apparently doesn't have the funding to cover low-income pregnant women for basic prenatal care. But on July 25, 2002, the government announced the availability of $900,000 in tax dollars to support public awareness campaigns on embryo "adoption." The use of the "adoption" terminology for a six-celled blastocyst, and the campaign to position it as a "baby" to be put up for "adoption," is yet another attempt to turn the fetus into a person in the public consciousness.

Half of the federal funds went to a group called Nightlight Christian Adoption Agency, which has a program called Snow-flakes. "Like snowflakes," their literature proclaims, "each embryo is fragile, unique, and the most beautiful of God's creations." The agency matches infertile couples with "spare" embryos left over from other couples' in vitro fertility treatments. That's fine if the couple wishes to donate their embryos; most couples undergoing in vitro fertilizations as treatment for infertility do end up with spare embryos, after all, and what happens to them should be their decision. But there are other options. The moral value of embryo *adoption* is certainly no greater than an embryo *donation* for the purpose of humanitarian research. There are an estimated 200,000 IVF embryos stored in clinics throughout the U.S., many of which could be used for humanitarian stem cell research, if that option were available. But President Bush has severely limited government grants for research on stem cells, which could provide answers to cures for many diseases, including Parkinson's, diabetes, sickle-cell anemia, spinal cord injuries, and Alzheimer's.

Interestingly, some otherwise anti-choice politicians favor stem cell research, especially when it affects their self-interests. The late senator Strom Thurmond, who never saw an anti-choice bill he didn't like, supported stem cell research because his daughter was diabetic. But to the present administration, the interests of six-celled blastocysts take precedence over the millions of people alive who have diseases that could potentially be cured with embryonic stem cell research.

What's next? Legislation written that all unused sperm needs to be held because that's potential life?

—Lynn Grefe, former executive director for Republican
Pro-Choice Coalition

Funding the Snowflakes "embryo adoption" program is a PR snow job, yet another political strategy to emphasize the current government's position that an embryo is a person. The group has a clear faith-based anti-abortion view. "We believe in the dignity of every person, uniquely formed in the image of their Creator with the gift of life from the very start of their existence within the womb." A religious nonprofit group can take whatever stance it pleases. But our tax dollars shouldn't go to fund the political agenda of any religious group.

The truly frightening thing about this seemingly innocuous funding is that it reveals the extent to which we're experiencing a major governmental shift toward funding programs sponsored by ideologically driven, faith-based organizations. The wall between church and state is being trampled. The government isn't just allowing but *encouraging* these faith-based groups to impose their anti-choice religious beliefs on all. That's the mark of a theocracy, not a pluralistic democracy.

It's a private issue gone very public. It's a complex web of personal philosophy, religious orientation and social conscience about which everybody, and we mean everybody, has a strong opinion. But the fact is, and should be, what you do with the frozen embryos you don't use is your decision and yours alone.

—The American Infertility Association

APPOINTING A GUARDIAN FOR A FETUS, AND NEVER MIND THE WOMAN

In yet another attempt to set a precedent for courts to regard a fetus as a person, Florida governor Jeb Bush announced in June that the state would attempt to have a guardian appointed for a fetus. He took this action despite the fact that the U.S. Supreme Court has said that a fetus does not count as a person under the Fourteenth Amendment and the Florida Supreme Court has ruled that a fetus is not a person for purposes of the state's wrongful death statute. Meanwhile, the woman herself, a severely retarded twenty-two-year-old who was raped in a group home, had no guardian to protect her interests. It's a tragic case in which a disabled rape victim, a young woman who could not speak for herself, was used as a tool to promote an anti-choice agenda.

The woman is so mentally disabled that she needs help bathing and walking, and can barely speak. She has cerebral palsy and is autistic. She was raped at the state-licensed home where she lived, allegedly by the owner's husband. While Jeb Bush was busy sticking his nose—and his agenda—into the affair, very little was heard about the woman. How did she come to be raped in a state-supported facility in the first place? Why is it that when she turned eighteen, and was no longer in foster care, the state never named a guardian for her? Those questions will remain long after the woman gives birth. The court eventually appointed a guardian for the woman to make decisions about her health and pregnancy, but denied the request to appoint a guardian for the fetus. The judge did not arrive at his decision, however, until it was too late for abortion to be an option for the woman. Jeb Bush issued a statement saying, "I am disappointed by the decision not to address the issue of guardianship for the unborn child trapped in this tragedy." He said nothing about the young woman trapped in the tragedy.

The young woman never understood what was going on—that she was raped, that she was pregnant, or that the anti-choice movement was attempting to use her, and her body, as a political football. But against her knowledge, consent, or understanding, she was forced to have a baby. The state that declares so much interest in the fetus seems to have little interest at all in protecting women who can't protect themselves.

> *George Bush says he opposes abortions with exceptions. Acceptance of exceptions, allowing the killing of innocents fathered by rapists or close family members, surrenders the core principle that the first duty of civil government is to prevent the shedding of innocent blood.*
>
> —Howard Phillips, chairman, Conservative Caucus

PRO-CHOICE IS PRO-LIFE

I have spoken with and read letters from hundreds of women about their experiences with abortion, and one thing I know is that abortion is almost always a profoundly moral choice. Women and men plan their families because they have respect and reverence for human life. Women who choose abortions do so because they love children, and they want to care for them properly when they do have them. They believe that every child should come into the world a wanted child, not be forced into being by a government that believes women have no moral authority of their own—a government that does far too little to care for children once they're born.

People who oppose abortion call themselves "pro-life," but in truth, being pro-choice is much more authentically pro-life. What's important is that children come into the world wanted and loved, with the necessary resources to take care of them. "Every child a wanted child" is no mere motto for Planned Parenthood but an expression of our passionate belief that all human beings are entitled to what they need to achieve a decent life.

Anti-choice, conversely, is often anti-child. Just take a look at the correlation between the amount states spend on children's welfare and the restrictiveness of their abortion laws. One might expect that states with so-called pro-life policies that support fetal rights would adopt a range of policies designed to protect children's rights and welfare. Instead, the opposite is true. States with pro-choice policies are more likely to support adoption services and to provide aid to needy children than those with anti-choice policies. Anti-choice states spend less money per pupil on kindergarten through twelfth-grade education, and less on other social services for children. As public policy analyst Jean Reith Schroedel found in her study comparing these statistics, "Pro-life states make it difficult for women to have abortions, but they do not help these women provide for the children once born."

What's pro-life about that?

THE ETHICS OF THE MOTHERS: THE SACRED CHOICE OF ABORTION OR BIRTH

The anti-choice minority have not only laid claim to our bodies and our laws, they have laid claim to our morality. Many people believe, as a result of anti-choice propaganda, that abortion and even contraception are forbidden or certainly frowned upon by religions. But with all due respect, those who oppose women's rights to make their own childbearing decisions don't have a lock on religion, ethics, or morality.

I'm just trying to figure out how the sum total of morality in public life supposedly consists of anti-abortion and anti-gay positions. I guess those big Bibles were too heavy to carry around and consult all the time, so the religious right had to trim it down to the really, really condensed version: opposing the "big two."

—Sam Coppersmith, former congressman from Arizona

If you study the history of religions, it turns out that most of the world's religions are much more flexible on the topic of family planning and abortion than the fundamentalists would have us believe. Contraception and abortion are considered moral choices by many religions. In other religions, pro-choice and anti-choice traditions coexist, as I'll discuss below. Even in religions where abortion is generally forbidden, there are exceptions. So almost all are, to some extent, "pro-choice."

The fundamentalists' opposition to abortion certainly has no basis in the Bible. The closest the Bible gets to even discussing abortion is Exodus 21:22, which describes an accidental loss of a pregnancy, where a man who caused a woman to miscarry in the course of a "brawl" was required to pay a financial penalty. The penalty wasn't "an eye for an eye," as it would have been if a person had been killed. Instead, the issue was the father's right to progeny, and the fine was for depriving him of that right. As for the question of when life begins, again there's nothing in the Bible that speaks to that issue. According to Rabbi Balfour Brickner, senior rabbi emeritus at the Stephen F. Wise Free Synagogue in New York City, "Each

of the actions to make the fetus equivalent to a living, breathing human being is clearly unbiblical, un-Jewish, and if Christianity
claims to be based on biblical tradition, un-Christian."

Many religious traditions, from the Eastern religions to the
Greeks and up to and including Christianity, have a theory of "delayed ensoulment," which basically states that the spiritual human
soul doesn't arrive in a fetus until the point of "quickening," about
sixteen weeks. After that point, abortions may or may not be allowed, depending on the life or health of the woman.

Many religions go further and explicitly regard abortion as a
moral choice transcending even the law. When abortion was illegal
in the United States, it was often religious leaders and church group
members who helped women obtain safe, though illegal, abortions.
They recognized that compassion required them to act so that
women wouldn't be maimed or die from botched abortions. Church
groups led the way in the fight to legalize abortion. In 1967, a New
York City minister, the Reverend Howard Moody, founded the
Clergy Consultation Service on Abortion, in which ministers and
rabbis volunteered their time to counsel women about "problem
pregnancies," and help them arrange an abortion, if that was what
they wanted. Over the next few years, the network became national,
with over one thousand clergy risking arrest for helping women in
need get abortions. Today, many American denominations recognize the need for access to contraception and safe, legal abortion.
Planned Parenthood has a Clergy Network with thousands of
members from many denominations who support the mission to
prevent unintended pregnancies with good contraceptives and counseling, and to provide abortions if women believe they're necessary.
And the Religious Coalition for Reproductive Choice similarly involves clergy who are activists and spokespersons for the pro-choice
movement.

Finally, it should be noted that many religions today are much
more concerned about the health of the 6 billion people who

are already on this earth, 1 billion of whom are hungry and mal-
nourished, than about the righteousness of bringing any and every
fertilized egg to term. The health of the planet itself is also a matter of moral and religious concern, at a time when the needs of
these billions of people seem to be outstripping the planet's resources.

I believe in the freedom of Americans to believe what they
want to believe. If you believe abortion is against your religion, then
by all means don't have one. But here, for some perspective, are a variety of views on reproductive freedom from different religions:

PROTESTANTS

Protestants are among the most diverse of religions, disagreeing
among themselves on many basic tenets, including the issue of
choice. With 56 percent of Americans identifying themselves as
Protestants, it's no wonder there is so much dissension about contraception and abortion. What's important is that here in the
United States, we are free to disagree—without taking away the
rights of people with other beliefs. In fact, our country was
founded by Protestants who came here because they wanted the
freedom to worship as they chose.

However, in recent times Protestant anti-choice fundamentalists have made so much noise about their beliefs on the subject of
abortion that they have drowned out all other voices, to the point
where many people now believe that the anti-abortion position is
the only religious position. But Pat Robertson and Jerry Falwell do
not speak for all religions, for all Christians, or even for all
Protestants. Many Protestant church leaders and organizations, including the following, have made strong statements in support of
women's reproductive freedom—and also of the religious freedom
that allows a diversity of opinion on the subject:

- The General Board of American Baptist Churches said in 1988 that while their members differ on abortion, people on both sides of the issue can be good Baptists.

- The American Friends Service Committee (Quakers) has stated their support for "a woman's right to follow her own conscience concerning childbearing, abortion, and sterilization," and said "that choice must be made free of coercion, including the coercion of poverty, racial discrimination, and the availability of service to those who cannot pay."

- In 1988, the Episcopal Church General Convention defended "the legal right of every woman to have a medically safe abortion."

- The Lutheran Women's Caucus in 1990 acknowledged that their members hold diverse views on abortion, and "value the religious freedom that allows this diversity."

- The Presbyterian Church (USA), in five of its General Assembly meetings, approved of abortion until the fetus is viable. The public policy on abortion, it said, should be regulated by a health code, not criminal code. "Abortion should be a woman's right because, theologically speaking, making a decision about abortion is, above all, her responsibility."

- The Reorganized Church of Jesus Christ of Latter-day Saints (Mormons) affirmed in 1980 "the right of the woman to make her own decision regarding the continuation or termination of problem pregnancies."

- The Unitarian Universalist Association upholds "the personal right to choose in regard to contraception and abortion," which they say is grounded in "individual conscience."

- The United Church of Christ urges that alternatives to abortion should always be considered, but that "abortion is a social justice issue . . . [requiring access to] safe, legal abortions."

- The United Methodist Church General Conference in 1988 said, "We believe that a continuance of a pregnancy which endangers the life or health of the woman, or poses other serious problems concerning the life, health, or mental capability of the child to be, is not a moral necessity."

ROMAN CATHOLICISM

The Roman Catholic Church has never baptized miscarriages or stillborns, because it holds that the human soul doesn't develop until quickening, that time when the fetus can first be felt moving in the womb—around the fifth month. The early fetus does not have the status of a person in Catholic theology. In the fifteenth century, Antoninus, the archbishop of Florence, was the first Roman Catholic to do extensive work on the question of abortion. He approved of early abortions to save the life of the woman (and became the first pro-choice saint). In the sixteenth century, Antoninus de Corduba insisted that a woman could take an abortifacient if her health required it—she had a *"jus prius,"* or prior right over the life of the fetus. Most early Catholic theologians approved of early abortion to save the life of the woman. It wasn't until 1869 that the distinction between formed and unformed fetuses was eliminated by Pope Pius IX, and anyone who had an abortion was subject to the penalty of excommunication. After that time, the ban on abortions was absolute, until 1968, when Pope Paul VI held that there were two exceptions—to deal with an ectopic pregnancy and to treat a cancerous uterus—both of which were for the purpose of saving the life of the woman. Despite the fact that in recent times Catholic popes and bishops have spoken out often and strongly against abortion, 69 percent of Catholics in the U.S. believe a woman who has an abortion, even for reasons other than to save her own life, can still be a good Catholic.

Catholic women in the United States are as likely as women in the general population to have an abortion, and 29 percent more likely than Protestant women.

—Survey by The Alan Guttmacher Institute of 9,985
abortion patients, 1996

JUDAISM

Judaism has some of the oldest teachings on reproductive freedom. Most rabbis hold that the Jewish traditions of humanism and justice mean that there shouldn't be simply more human beings but more humane human beings—that quality of life is more important than the numbers of people born. The Talmud contains instructions for how to make a *mokh*, similar in concept to the contraceptive sponge. It also has recipes for birth control and abortifacients. Like some other religions, Judaism views the fetus as having a soul only after quickening. And even then, the fetus does not take precedence over the life of the woman. Abortion after quickening is forbidden if there is no reason for it, but considered necessary in certain cases, including rape, incest, adultery, and if a woman is too young or too old. Even late-term abortions are considered necessary at times. The Talmud says, "If a woman suffers hard labor in travail, the child must be cut up in her womb and brought out piecemeal, for her life takes precedence over its life" (Mishneh 6). The Jewish religion comes down firmly on the side of respecting the life of the woman over that of the embryo or fetus.

No woman is required to build the world by destroying herself.

—Rabbi Moshe Sofer, chief rabbi of Pressberg,
nineteenth century

ISLAM

In Islam, the need to plan births is becoming increasingly recognized as Muslim countries face population challenges. Women in Islamic countries, though, are often far behind men in equality of education and opportunity, and have little control over their reproductive lives. Still, contraception has a long history in Islam, justified on the basis of health, economics, and the common good. Though no text explicitly addresses the issue, some followers of Islam oppose all abortions, while others follow Islamic teachings allowing for abortion after four months if the continuation of the pregnancy would harm the woman. As with many other religions, the principle of the "lesser evil" often prevails.

BUDDHISM

Buddhism holds that an ideal existence would not include abortion. However, it also recognizes compassion in the face of necessity. Buddhists believe that life starts at conception, and oppose abortions done for self-indulgent reasons, such as sex selection. But they do acknowledge that there are times when abortion is necessary, as when the life of the woman is at stake, or when there is a likelihood that the baby would be born with conditions preventing it from enjoying a good quality of life. Buddhists celebrate sexuality, and do not condemn nonprocreative sex.

HINDUISM

Built into Hinduism is the idea of *dharma*, meaning whatever supports the highest good. Hindus see contraception and abortion as relative to the circumstances. Producing more children than you can support isn't a good, and can be harmful, so contraception might be the greatest good. However, most Hindu texts oppose abortion, while making exceptions, as with the case of protecting the life of the woman.

There is a great range of opinion among the world's religions, and even within individual religions, about the morality of birth control, abortion, and the question of when personhood begins. Often these beliefs are rooted in that particular religious tradition's views of sexuality as a good or evil force. They are also inevitably connected to the religion's views on women and women's place in the world. Many of our religious leaders recognize and value the sacred right of a woman to choose what happens to her body and the fetus she carries. They acknowledge that women are moral agents, and have the capacity to make difficult decisions themselves that are in the best interests of the fetus, their own lives, and the life of the community. They understand that while in a perfect world no one would have an unintended pregnancy or a life- or health-threatening pregnancy, we do not live in a perfect world, and in some cases abortion is the best, most moral choice. It's up to the woman who carries the fetus to make that choice. And it's up to all of us to see to it that the diversity of religious beliefs in this country is protected, so that we may all act on what we believe.

We live in a democracy that allows for freedom of beliefs. We do not live in a theocracy, controlled by the religious beliefs of a few extremists. To impose the beliefs of a few on the majority of citizens is against our nation's founding principles of freedom and pluralism, which permit and celebrate the existence of a diversity of moral, religious, and ethical beliefs.

Our nation's concept of liberty and our respect for religious diversity are fundamental to our democracy, and we must fight to maintain those freedoms. They are what separate us from the Taliban—and the Republic of Gilead.

FIVE

A CHILL WIND BLOWS

Webster v. Reproductive Health Services *"casts into darkness the hopes and visions of every woman in this country who had come to believe that the Constitution guaranteed her the right to exercise some control over her unique ability to bear children. The plurality does so either oblivious or insensitive to the fact that millions of women, and their families, have ordered their lives around the right to reproductive choice, and that this right has become vital to the full participation of women in the economic and political walks of American life."*

—Justice Harry Blackmun,
in *Webster v. Reproductive Health Services,* 1989

Roe continues to exist, but only in the way a storefront on a western movie set exists: a mere facade to give the illusion of reality.

—Chief Justice William Rehnquist, in *Planned Parenthood of Southeastern Pennsylvania v. Casey,* 1992

Recently, George W. Bush was quoted talking about his daughters. "Gosh," he said, "the thing I want most in life is for those girls to be able to grow up in a free world and prosper and realize their dreams."

Of course, that's what most parents want for their children. But I couldn't help thinking how ironic it was that those words came out of the president's mouth. Gosh . . . how in the world can any girl or woman be free and realize her dreams without reproductive freedom?

The anti-choice people, including those in the administration and their allies in Congress, have actually done everything in their power to limit women's freedoms, and to squash their dreams— unless, of course, those dreams involve living in a world where women have no self-determination, and no control over their reproductive lives. That's strikingly like the world of west Texas in the 1950s, where the president and I both spent our formative years—though our experiences of that world couldn't have been more different. Unlike overprivileged white men, we women, privileged or not, had very few choices in our lives. If we got pregnant, no matter the circumstances, we gave birth—with or without shotgun weddings. Or else we risked illegal abortions. Unmarried women were often forced to give up their children for adoption, and some African-American women were sterilized without their knowledge or consent. The freedoms and dream fulfillment possibilities that the president says he hopes his own daughters will enjoy were certainly not available to us.

The administration and the anti-abortion, anti–family planning, anti–sex education leadership that holds sway over Congress's agenda are engaging in a well-funded and well-organized strategy to dismantle not only *Roe v. Wade*, but many of our other basic human rights to reproductive self-determination and privacy, as well.

Let's be clear: the right to choose abortion is inextricably tied to other rights of bodily integrity and childbearing, whether it's the right to use birth control, the right to determine the number and spacing of our children, or the right to be free from the government nosing into our bedrooms and private lives. Lose one right to the freedom to make our own reproductive decisions, and we risk losing them all. Think Romania under Ceauşescu and China's one-child policy: the government that can tell you, you *must* have this child is the government that can tell you, you *can't* have this child.

AN END TO CHECKS AND BALANCES

One key building block in the anti-choice plan to outlaw reproductive freedoms is to stack the courts with judges who are not "conservative" but are in fact radical extremists—ideologues of the far right, whose views are at a great distance from the American mainstream. This is part of a deliberate strategy to achieve in the courts what the right wing has not been able to achieve through Constitutional means, since it has so far been unsuccessful in its attempt to add an amendment to the Constitution to ban abortion. What is particularly alarming about these judicial appointments is that they are for life. Judges appointed now will be serving for decades to come, long after Bush has left office, so the influence of the far right will be vastly more enduring than most voters realize.

Take Arkansas district court nominee James Leon Holmes as an example of the kind of people Bush would like to see on the federal bench: while supporting a constitutional amendment banning abortion, Holmes rejected a rape and incest exception as unnecessary, saying, "The concern for rape victims is a red herring because conceptions from rape occur with the same frequency as snowfall in Miami." Actually, 300,000 U.S. women are raped each year, resulting in 25,000 pregnancies.

If only that kind of thinking were merely stupid. But it's very, very dangerous. It's coming from the mouths and the minds of people whose views about women have a lot more in common with Afghan fundamentalists than with average, freedom-loving Americans. And the frightening truth is that more and more of these extremists are sitting on federal benches, dispensing their ideological brand of "justice," determining the last word on what we Americans can and cannot do with our lives.

By packing the courts with extremists, President Bush and the Senate, which advises and consents to his appointments, are undermining our very democracy. They are using the full force of the executive branch to muscle in on the judicial branch of government to an unprecedented degree, quietly pushing a reactionary agenda that the mainstream of America does not support.

Our government was meant to work by a system of checks and balances. The judicial, congressional, and executive branches each have separate powers that serve to protect the Constitution and offset the excesses of the other branches. But today's right-wing politicians and the religious political-extremist constituencies that support them aren't satisfied with having the White House and both houses of Congress securely in their hands. For the first time since *Roe*, they're aligned in perfect position to hijack the judicial branch, too, and one of their prize goals is to roll back women's reproductive rights.

Here's just one example of how the parts work together to create a stranglehold on reproductive freedom. Attorney General John Ashcroft, whose zealous anti-choice record is unbroken, has taken the unusual step of intervening at the federal appellate court level in an Ohio case (*Women's Medical Professional Corporation v. Taft*) regarding abortion. In 2002, the Department of Justice filed a brief with the Sixth Circuit Court of Appeals supporting the state and seeking to overturn the district court's decision that struck down the state's so-called "partial-birth abortion" law as unconstitutional. The Department of Justice did this even though the U.S. Supreme Court had declared a similar ban unconstitutional in *Stenberg v.*

Carhart in 2000. Despite having pledged at his confirmation hearing that he believes *Roe* to be "settled law" and intends to uphold it, the Justice Department under Ashcroft is invoking the power of the executive branch to build the platform to overturn *Roe*. "President Bush has expressed support for such legislation," said the first page of the Justice Department brief on the Ohio case, referring to the law the Court had struck down. This is precisely the situation that the framers of the Constitution were trying to protect us from by creating three distinct branches of government. That protection is now strained to the breaking point.

In December 2003, the Sixth Circuit Court of Appeals, by a vote of 2–1, *upheld* the Ohio abortion ban. Of the two judges who voted that the ban is constitutional, one was appointed by Ronald Reagan and one by George W. Bush. The dissenting judge was appointed by Bill Clinton.

Meanwhile, the president continues to nominate judges to the federal bench that will decide the case, and the Senate continues to confirm most of them. In the sixth circuit alone, the president either has or will be appointing eight judges to fill vacancies on the sixteen-seat court. If the Ohio abortion ban law, or the federal abortion ban that President Bush signed into law in October 2003, were to go to today's U.S. Supreme Court, it would almost certainly be found unconstitutional based on the Supreme Court's ruling in *Stenberg v. Carhart,* which affirmed once again the primacy of women's health. But the appointment of just one more anti-choice justice could change the balance, and that would change everything for American women. The anti-choice right persistently relitigates reproductive rights issues with the hope that when they reach the Supreme Court, there will be new judges—and new outcomes.

Despite the fact that the great majority of Americans favor the right to choose, reproductive freedoms are supported by only the slimmest majority in the current U.S. Supreme Court. President Bush has made it clear that when he has the opportunity he intends to appoint justices in the mold of Supreme Court justices Antonin Scalia and Clarence Thomas, both of whom have plainly stated that they oppose women's right to choose and that they believe *Roe v. Wade* should be flat-out overturned.

We believe that Roe *was wrongly decided, and that it can and should be overruled.*

—Supreme Court dissenting opinion in *Planned Parenthood of Southeastern Pennsylvania v. Casey,* joined by Justice Clarence Thomas, eight months after his confirmation hearing, in which he insisted he had an open mind on the right to choose

---

The right has long complained that Democrats and pro-choice Republicans have used *Roe* as a litmus test for court appointments. Well, *Roe* is the law of the land, and because it protects a fundamental human and civil right, it should be a litmus test. There's no way it would be acceptable to put someone on a court who said they were fundamentally opposed to *Brown v. Board of Education,* the decision that ended segregation in the schools. Why should we allow someone on the court who would take away a woman's civil right to have control over her own body? No one who opposes a fundamental right and is opposed to a core constitutional holding—privacy—can be impartial and fair-minded on the bench.

And yet, unnoticed by most Americans, the president has nominated and the Senate has confirmed reactionary jurists to fill the lower courts from top to bottom. I suspect the president is just as happy that he has not yet had to make an appointment to the Supreme Court. The public pays special attention to those appointments, and there is heightened media scrutiny. The lower federal courts are a different matter; as former senator Jesse Helms

(R–North Carolina) cynically, but accurately, observed: "You go out on the street of Raleigh, North Carolina, and ask a hundred people, 'Do you give a damn who is on the Fourth Circuit Court of Appeals?' They'll say, 'What's that?' "

Indifferent or uninformed as most people may be about them, federal judges, appointed for life, exercise enormous power in deciding cases that affect the lives of millions of American women and their families. With so many of the president's nominees set on turning back the clock on women's reproductive rights, workers' rights, civil rights, and other basic human freedoms, Americans need to wake up to the fact that the power to nominate judges is one the most effective ways for a president to advance his own cultural and ideological agenda. So far, Bush's strategy of packing the courts with ideologues has succeeded to a frightening degree. By the end of 2003, the Senate had confirmed 169 of the president's nominees, with only a handful facing filibusters aimed at blocking their confirmation. Contrast this to the 63 Clinton nominees who were either not given hearings or not confirmed. If Bush succeeds in filling every open seat, eleven of the thirteen Federal Circuit Courts of Appeals will be likely to have anti-choice majorities, some of them two-to-one. That's a sure-fire formula for a frightening and probably fatal assault on women's rights.

For the first time in modern history, the balance of powers sought by our Constitution is in mortal jeopardy. We the people have to take matters into our own hands.

_____

Simply put, complacency is not an option, as right now less than half of the U.S. Senate—or forty senators from both parties—could be considered solidly pro-choice. At the same time, the Supreme Court majority protecting a woman's right to choose is narrow. Yet this past June, according to an ABC news poll, 73 percent of those polled believed that the next person nominated to the Supreme Court should not only be questioned on his or her position on abortion, but be required to answer before being confirmed by the Senate. Rightfully, the public understands that anything less puts choice at risk.

—Senator Olympia Snowe (R–Maine)

TO BEAR OR BEGET: THE U.S. SUPREME COURT AND REPRODUCTIVE FREEDOMS

On January 22, 1973, the U.S. Supreme Court announced its decision in *Roe v. Wade*, striking down a Texas statute that made it a crime to perform an abortion unless a woman's life was at stake. In its ruling, the court recognized for the first time that the constitutional right to privacy is "broad enough to encompass a woman's decision whether or not to terminate her pregnancy." After a long fight, fueled by an activist pro-choice movement, abortion was finally explicitly decriminalized throughout the United States.

WHAT ROE GUARANTEED: A SENSIBLE BALANCE

Though anti-choice misrepresentations of *Roe* have tried to convince Americans that the ruling permits abortion for any reason during the full nine months of pregnancy, in truth *Roe* is a compromise, a delicate and sensible balance that took into careful consideration the religious and ethical, scientific, medical, legal, and social aspects of reproductive freedom.

- States cannot place any restrictions on abortion during the first trimester except to require that the abortion be performed by a physician.

- During the second trimester, the state's interest in the woman's health entitles it to regulate abortion only in ways necessary to protect maternal health.
- During the third trimester, after fetal viability, the state may regulate or proscribe abortion "except where it is necessary, in appropriate medical judgment, for the preservation of the life or health of the mother."

Together with earlier Supreme Court decisions legalizing contraception, *Roe* meant that women could choose their own reproductive futures without risking jail, humiliation, or even death. More than just legalizing abortion and validating our right to make our own childbearing decisions without government control, the decision was a sign that American women's civil and human freedoms had indeed come a long way. As Supreme Court Justice Harry Blackmun, who authored the decision, put it upon his retirement, "It's a step that had to be taken as we go down the road toward the full emancipation of women."

Thirty years later, it's hard for many to imagine what life was like when abortion was illegal. What we do know, though, is that making abortions illegal has never stopped women from having them, whenever they felt they could not bear and nurture children properly, for whatever reason. *Roe* did not invent abortion, nor did it promote abortion. In fact, the rate of abortion has hardly changed since the passage of *Roe*. Besides legality, the only other big difference between then and now is in the *safety* of abortions. Back then, women had to travel to other countries for safe abortions, if they could afford to, or risk their lives trying dangerous home remedies or having surgery at the hands of back-alley butchers, because very few doctors were willing to put themselves in legal jeopardy by performing clandestine abortions. Deaths from such abortions were tragically commonplace. In 1965, for example, 17 percent of all deaths due to pregnancy and childbirth were the result of unsafe, illegal abortions. Doctors who remember this time have told me that in some hospitals, the number of women recovering from complications due to unsafe abortions was so great that entire wings were devoted to them. In other hospitals, where no separate wing was provided, there were sometimes as many women in obstetrical wards recovering from abortion complications as from labor and delivery.

Today, death and injury from abortions are practically nonexistent in the U.S. Because abortion is legal, women can have the procedure performed by qualified practitioners, and with constantly improving technologies, abortions can be performed earlier and more safely. Today, abortion is eleven times safer than childbirth. The days when women were maimed or killed by crude abortion attempts are, thankfully, long-lost history to younger generations. In fact, most women under the age of thirty-five don't even recognize the meaning of a coat hanger as a symbol of unsafe abortions. Americans have come to take it for granted that abortion will always be safe and legal in this country. And they can't even imagine that access to abortion and birth control could be seriously threatened.

But believe it: the not-very-distant future may take us straight back to where we were in the past—to the days before *Roe*.

If *Roe* is overturned, the rights to other reproductive choices, even something as basic and taken for granted as birth control, may be dismantled as well. Amazing as it may seem, access to contraception, even for married couples, is a relatively recent "right," and it is grounded in the same principle that *Roe* is based on—the right to privacy and reproductive freedom. Two of the key decisions used as precedents for *Roe* were *Griswold v. Connecticut*, the 1965 Supreme Court ruling that struck down state laws that had made the use of birth control by married couples illegal, and *Eisenstadt v. Baird*, the 1972 decision that granted unmarried couples the right to contraception. *Eisenstadt* eloquently established that "if the right of privacy means anything, it is the right of the individual, married or single, to be free from unwarranted governmental intrusion into matters so fundamentally affecting a person as the decision whether to bear or beget a child."

"To bear or beget"—those two sides of the childbearing equation are always linked. If *Roe* is overturned, the entire edifice of reproductive privacy and self-determination could fall along with it, sending us back to the days when Margaret Sanger was prosecuted for distributing *information* about contraceptives.

In the almost forty years since *Griswold*, the resulting changes in the American social fabric have been profound and positive: women's freedom to control their fertility according to their own moral principles has not only resulted in dramatic improvements in maternal and infant health rates but has also allowed women to fulfill their increasingly diverse educational, social, political, and professional dreams. Moreover, the legal theories enshrined in *Griswold* and *Roe* protect not just reproductive rights but other basic human rights. For example, the July 2003 Supreme Court ruling (*Lawrence v. Texas*) that struck down anti-sodomy laws in Texas, making it no longer a crime to be a homosexual, is in a direct line with those earlier decisions, which protect our privacy in the bedroom. The link was made crystal clear by the extreme anti-choice and anti-gay-rights senator Rick Santorum (R–Pennsylvania), who was so outraged by *Lawrence v. Texas* that he was moved to declare that *Griswold* had established a "right to privacy that doesn't exist." Santorum has also stated that if *Roe* were overturned and abortion became illegal in some states, he would favor laws criminalizing women who cross state lines to get a legal abortion.

[If] the Supreme Court says that you have the right to consensual sex within your home, then you have the right to bigamy, you have the right to polygamy, you have the right to incest, you have the right to adultery. You have the right

> *to anything. Does that undermine the fabric of our society? I would argue*
> *yes, it does. It all comes from, I would argue, this right to privacy that doesn't*
> *exist in my opinion in the United States Constitution, this right that was*
> *created, it was created in* Griswold—Griswold *was the contraceptive*
> *case—and abortion.*
>
> —Senator Rick Santorum (R–Pennsylvania) on the right
> to privacy, as established by the landmark *Griswold* case

"AN UNDUE BURDEN"

From the moment *Roe* was decided in 1973, anti-choice groups began forming insurgencies across the country, plotting a strategy to once again make abortion illegal and diminish our rights to privacy and reproductive freedom. The *Roe* decision created a huge, well-funded, and well-organized backlash to the abortion rights and feminist movements. Justice Blackmun, who wrote the decision, began to get thousands of hate letters and death threats. The Right-to-Life Committee launched a campaign in Congress to amend the Constitution to undo the Supreme Court's decision. When they couldn't change the laws legitimately, they began to vilify, harass, and intimidate, to create a social climate where people would be afraid to support reproductive rights or provide reproductive health care. Anti-choice terrorists bombed health clinics, frightened patients and clinic staff, and even murdered physicians and health care workers who provided abortion services.

The multipronged attack is now on the verge of succeeding. Over the past three decades, the Supreme Court has been repeatedly called on to decide whether a wide range of abortion restrictions violate a woman's right to privacy. During this time, the legal bulwark protecting women's reproductive rights has become ever more fragile as the composition of the Court has shifted to the right.

The successful assaults on freedom of choice began with attempts to reduce access to abortion. Rights without access are meaningless, which is precisely the point of these assaults. Since the 1973 decision, the U.S. Supreme Court has handed down more than twenty major opinions regarding a woman's *access* to safe, legal abortion, many of them upholding various restrictions on abortion, gradually chipping away at *Roe*.

In several decisions—*Maher v. Roe,* 1977; *Poelker v. Doe,* 1977; *Harris v. McRae,* 1980; and others—the Court upheld bans on public funding for abortion services so that poor women could no longer have abortions covered by Medicaid. Then, requirements that young women obtain the consent of their parents were also upheld (*Planned Parenthood of Kansas City, Missouri v. Ashcroft,* 1983).

But other restrictions on abortion were held to be unconstitutional, such as those contained in Pennsylvania's 1982 Abortion Control Act. The Pennsylvania act required that women seeking abortions be given state-produced materials describing the fetus; that physicians performing postviability abortions use the method most likely to result in fetal survival; that a second physician be present at a postviability abortion; and that detailed reporting on all abortions be available for public inspection. In *Thornburgh v. American College of Obstetricians and Gynecologists* (1986), the Court held that most of the act was invalid.

By 1989, however, the composition of the U.S. Supreme Court had changed significantly. Three of the justices who had supported reproductive freedom in *Roe* had been replaced—by the solidly anti-*Roe* Justice Antonin Scalia, and by two swing votes, Justices Sandra Day O'Connor and Anthony Kennedy, both essentially leaning toward states' rights but also generally pro-privacy. Now the assault on *Roe* began in earnest. The Supreme Court announced it would hear *Webster v. Reproductive Health Services* and decide the constitutionality of a 1986 Missouri law that declared that life begins at conception, forbade the use of public funds to perform counseling or abortion services not necessary to save a woman's life, and required physicians to perform tests to determine the viability of fetuses after twenty weeks' gestational age. And who was the governor of Missouri who signed that law? None other than John Ashcroft, our current attorney general, and the same person named in the *Planned Parenthood of Missouri v. Ashcroft* decision of 1983.

Webster was a watershed decision, clearly a serious challenge to the integrity of *Roe*. It served as a kind of pro-choice Pearl Harbor. For the first time in more than a decade, people who had been complacent on the issue began to wake up to the threat, and there was a great upsurge in support for pro-choice organizations. The 1989 pro-choice march on Washington was the largest demonstration since the Vietnam War. Pro-choice groups such as PPFA, NARAL, NOW, and the American Civil Liberties Union spent about $2.5 million on advertising during the Court's deliberation. *Cosmopolitan* editor Helen Gurley Brown announced that the editors of sixteen women's magazines were going to increase their coverage of reproductive-rights issues.

However, the outcome of *Webster* was a blow to the integrity of the right to reproductive freedom. The Court:

- allowed the declaration that life begins at conception to go into effect because five justices agreed that there was insufficient evidence that it would be used to restrict protected activities such as choosing contraception or abortion, and that if it did, those restrictions could be challenged in the future;
- declined to address the constitutionality of the public funds provision;
- upheld the provision that barred the use of public facilities for abortions;
- upheld the requirement for viability tests.

While the Court did not overturn *Roe*, as anti-choice forces had urged them to do, for the first time a majority failed to uphold *Roe* in its entirety—particularly by allowing the declaration that life begins at conception. The constitutional status of the right to choose was dealt a blow. And it would soon be tested again.

Webster opened a new Pandora's box of opportunities to attack freedom of choice, virtually guaranteeing that legal challenges would escalate. *Roe*'s reach was now so narrowed that Justice Blackmun, delivering his dissent on *Webster* aloud from the bench, said, "I fear for the future." The nature of his fears, as he articulated them, demonstrated, once again, that the real issue isn't abortion but fundamental human rights. "I fear for the liberty and equality of the millions of women who have lived and come of age in the sixteen years since *Roe* was decided. I fear for the integrity of, and public esteem for, this Court."

Justice Blackmun's dissent was joined by Justices Thurgood Marshall and William Brennan, an alliance of the only three still-sitting justices out of the seven-justice majority that had decided *Roe v. Wade* sixteen years earlier. "For today, at least, the law of abortion stands undisturbed," Blackmun wrote. "For today, the women of this Nation still retain the liberty to control their destinies. But the signs are evident and very ominous, and a chill wind blows."

The lesson from *Webster* is clear: we can't be complacent in the face of a clear and present threat against our freedoms. Not ever. Eternal vigilance is indeed the price of liberty.

After *Webster*, anti-choice extremists were quick to draft state legislation intended to restrict abortion, introducing more than six hundred bills around the country in the next three years. Fewer than a dozen such bills passed, and the courts blocked most of those. But like waves crashing on the shore, the constant pounding of anti-choice onslaughts eventually reconfigured the shape of the law. For example, in Pennsylvania, the legislature once again passed a law called the Abortion Control Act, which amended the state's statutes with a number of anti-choice requirements designed to use the might of the state to influence a woman to choose childbearing over abortion. The Abortion Control Act requirements included measures that, except in narrowly defined medical emergencies, mandated that a woman requesting an abortion had to first receive counseling aimed at steering her toward continuing the pregnancy, and then had to wait twenty-four hours after the biased counseling before she could receive an abortion; that she be given state-authored materials on fetal development; that she inform her husband, if she is married, of her intent to have an abortion; and that a minor's abortion be conditional upon the consent of a parent or a judicial waiver. The Abortion Control Act was such an incursion on the rights affirmed by *Roe* that Planned Parenthood decided to challenge the new legislation in court. As Kathryn Kolbert, the ACLU lawyer arguing the case for Planned Parenthood of Southeastern Pennsylvania, put it, the law would "basically [eliminate] the procedure without having to ban abortions outright."

In 1992, when *Planned Parenthood of Southeastern Pennsylvania v. Casey* went to the U.S. Supreme Court, pro-choice supporters worried that the new majority on the Court might take the opportunity of using its review of the case to overturn *Roe*. And they had good reason to worry: then-president George Bush (who, you will recall, had been pro-choice until he decided he wanted to be Ronald Reagan's vice president in 1980) urged the Court to do just that. Although the Supreme Court ultimately upheld the core right of a woman to choose abortion before a fetus is viable and afterward if her life or health is at stake, and struck down the spousal notice provisions, its decision in *Casey* did pave the way for states to create many new obstacles to obtaining abortions, including enforced delays and biased counseling. The right to choose was no longer deemed "fundamental"; this means that future challenges to women's right to make their own childbearing choices would no longer be judged by a "strict constitutional scrutiny" standard. Now it was up to the courts to determine the limits of a vague new standard—"undue burden."

The undue burden standard means that to have a law restricting abortion overturned, one must prove either that it creates a "substantial" obstacle to women seeking abortion services or that it was intended to create such an obstacle. Under this standard, which allows broad interpretation, states and Congress can't outlaw abortion outright, but may do a great deal short of that to make access ever more difficult. Anti-choice legislators have followed suit, and so far the courts have found few burdens "undue."

MANDATORY DELAYS

Many states have passed laws requiring delays and state-directed biased counseling for women seeking an abortion. Often this "counseling" includes information designed to discourage a woman from choosing abortion, and requires two visits to a health care provider.

States requiring a delay following state-directed counseling:

Alabama	Michigan	Pennsylvania
Arkansas	Minnesota	South Carolina
Idaho	Mississippi	South Dakota
Indiana	Missouri	Utah
Kansas	Nebraska	Virginia
Kentucky	North Dakota	West Virginia
Louisiana	Ohio	Wisconsin

FROM CHIPPING AWAY TO CHOPPING DOWN

When Chief Justice William Rehnquist wrote, "*Roe* continues to exist, but only . . . [as] a mere facade to give the illusion of reality," he was so right. The full-scale right to choose that we thought *Roe* guaranteed has been reduced to the parsimonious "un-due burden" standard. As a result, women technically have the legal right to abortion, but because of the restrictions, often they have no way of making that right a "reality." Putting blockades in front of women trying to have abortions—whether by distance, expense, waiting periods, consent, or mandatory biased counseling—is the same in practice as denying them their rights. Rights without access are no rights at all. This is no longer about chipping away small pieces. Now we are seeing whole trees chopped down.

Over the past decade, since the Supreme Court gave legislative bodies more authority to limit reproductive rights and access, states have enacted well over three hundred anti-choice laws. Today, forty-four states have laws restricting minors' access to abortion, and in thirty-three of those states the laws are being enforced. Anti-choice lawmakers are seeking to make it more and more difficult for mi-nors to get services, by prohibiting the transportation of minors across state lines to seek abortions. Abortion services are not even available in 87 percent of U.S. counties, making it difficult to im-possible for many women to get the medical services they need. There is no U.S. government funding for abortion (except, if states choose, for Medicaid recipients in cases of rape, incest, or life en-dangerment) and only seventeen states have chosen to fund abor-tion to preserve the woman's health. Gag rules, hospital rules against providing abortion, and physician training programs that do not include abortion training, or even training in how to counsel patients about birth control or pregnancy options, further reduce access to care. And women have begun to die again.

We face the bleakest political landscape for women's reproduc-tive freedoms in a generation. And it is always the most vulnerable women for whom the burdens are the greatest: the young, the poor, the geographically isolated, the uneducated, and all those without support systems to help them through the maze of obstacles.

Even more alarming, the balance of the Supreme Court may

soon be tipped by the efforts of the administration. The makeup of the current Supreme Court has been in place for nearly a decade, since President Clinton nominated Stephen Breyer, who took the bench on August 3, 1994. When *Roe v. Wade* was decided, seven justices supported the ruling, and two did not (including current chief justice William Rehnquist).

> *Would you join with me and many others in crying out to our Lord to change the Court? If we fast and pray and earnestly seek God's face, then He will hear our prayer and give us relief. One justice is eighty-three years old, another has cancer, and another has a heart condition. Would it not be possible for God to put it in the minds of these three judges that the time has come to retire? With their retirement and the appointment of conservative judges, a massive change in federal jurisprudence can take place.*
>
> —Pat Robertson, founder of
> the Christian Coalition

Here is the current makeup of the Supreme Court:

Three justices are clearly opposed to the constitutional right to choose: Chief Justice William H. Rehnquist (b. 1924), Justice Antonin Scalia (b. 1936), and Justice Clarence Thomas (b. 1948). If one of these retired, the replacement couldn't be much worse for women's rights than the sitting justices.

Three justices clearly support the constitutional right to choose: Justice John Paul Stevens (b. 1920, the oldest on the court), Justice Ruth Bader Ginsburg (b. 1933), and Justice Stephen G. Breyer (b. 1938). The retirement of any of these justices could be disastrous for reproductive rights.

Three justices are "swing" votes: Justices Sandra Day O'Connor (b. 1930), Anthony M. Kennedy (b. 1936), and David H. Souter (b. 1939). The loss of any of these justices could shift the balance of the Court toward the right, but the loss of O'Connor or Souter, who have been more consistent in supporting a woman's right to choose, would be worse than a Kennedy retirement.

The most recent abortion-related case to test the durability of *Roe* in the Supreme Court was *Stenberg v. Carhart* in 2000. The Court declared, by a vote of five to four, that Nebraska's ban on so-called partial-birth abortion was unconstitutional. The justices in the middle—Souter, O'Connor, and Kennedy—disagreed with each other this time. Justices O'Connor and Souter took a position more supportive of *Roe* and the right to choose, holding firm on the issue of a woman's health being a paramount concern. They voted to strike down the Nebraska law. Justice Kennedy was prepared to retreat further from *Roe*, and voted to uphold the Nebraska law even though it lacked an exception for when a woman's health was threatened.

That was the landscape in the fall of 2003, when Congress voted to approve the first ever federal law criminalizing some abortion procedures, and the president signed it into law. With lawsuits already filed, the fight has moved to the courts. If and when the federal abortion ban reaches the Supreme Court, *Roe* will be tested once again, and we'll see what shreds remain of that law, which, for a time, guaranteed women full civil rights.

We can't predict what the Supreme Court will do. But already we can see a striking contrast between the present stance of the Attorney General of the United States and the position of states' attorneys general in previous cases. The language in the abortion ban statutes is sweeping and, as the Supreme Court recognized in *Stenberg*, could be used to prosecute doctors for providing a wide range of common and safe pre-viability procedures. When legal challenges were mounted to individual state laws, state attorneys general defending the laws tried to blunt this concern by insisting that the laws were meant to apply only to a very small number of procedures. Indeed, in some instances, the states' attorneys general argued for interpretations of their laws so narrow that they may not even have banned a single procedure. The Ashcroft Justice Department, however, has taken a dramatically different and troubling approach. It is boldly defending the federal law's broad language, and making no effort to save it from judicial invalidation by asserting a narrow interpretation. This fits neatly into the right-wing agenda because, if the federal law is eventually upheld by a changed Supreme Court—as is their plan—then an ideologically committed Justice Department will be armed with a broadly worded statute that it can use to prosecute doctors for a dangerously wide range of pre-viability abortions, whether or not *Roe* is overturned.

> *We just hope that by the time [the Partial-Birth Abortion Bill] gets up to the U.S. Supreme Court, there will be at least five justices there who will abandon the extreme position they took in the Nebraska case in 2000.*
>
> —Douglas Johnson, legislative director for the National Right to Life Committee (NRTL), June 4, 2003

It's clear that *Roe* is in severe jeopardy, and that the current anti-choice administration will, if given the opportunity, nominate one or more justices who would deliver the final blow. It's up to us to mobilize, to remind the Senate and the country that a woman's right to choose is a fundamental freedom, and to make sure that any nominee to the federal courts—and especially the Supreme Court—will support that freedom.

THE LOWER FEDERAL COURTS: HAZARDOUS TO WOMEN'S HEALTH

As devastating as a rightward ideological shift in the Supreme Court could be, most decisions that affect Americans' lives happen in the lower courts, especially in the thirteen U.S. circuit courts of appeals. These courts have a tremendous say over the laws that shape the direction of our country. There are currently 862 federal benches. The vast majority, 665, are district, or trial level, courts. Cases from those courts can be appealed in one of the thirteen circuits of the courts of appeal. The court of last resort is, of course, the Supreme Court. The Supreme Court decides only about eighty-five cases a year. In nearly thirty thousand other cases, the lower courts are the last word on our rights as Americans. For example, South Carolina enacted very burdensome and medically unnecessary regulations that target only abortion clinics—allowing the state to inspect and copy patient records at abortion clinics, and requiring clinics to give clergy referrals. The case went to the U.S. Court of Appeals for the Fourth Circuit twice and, both times, the fourth circuit upheld those requirements. Both times, the plaintiffs tried to bring their case to the Supreme Court, but the Court refused to hear it. Thus, the fourth circuit was the last word.

It isn't only that so many cases are decided in the lower courts but that they also set up the legal framework and precedents for the higher courts. The "undue burden" standard is subjective and remains to be defined. With the seizure of control of the lower courts, these determinations will be made by ideologically driven judges, most of whom, never having recognized any burden on a woman's right to choose as "undue," will generally find all proposed restrictions on abortion acceptable.

Such scenarios are likely only to proliferate, as the president systematically submits to Congress the names of anti-choice candidates who, if confirmed by the Senate, will hold lifetime jobs in the federal judiciary. These nominees, far from being impartial jurists, should come with a warning label: Beware: May Be Hazardous to Women's Health. Indeed, the warning label should be even broader, since most of these individuals are opposed to other basic civil rights, too.

All of us are hoping and praying that the day will come under the leadership of George Bush that we'll have a Supreme Court in the future with justices who will leave it to the states to decide the legality of [abortion] by overturning Roe v. Wade.

—Michael Fisher, nominee,
Third Circuit U.S. Court of Appeals

Federal judgeships have been the administration's prize payback to its far-right supporters. As Nan Aron from the Alliance for Justice wrote in the *Los Angeles Times,* lawyers who have worked for right-wing senators such as Strom Thurmond and Orrin Hatch have been on a fast track to judgeships. Thurmond staffer Terry Wooten became a judge despite claims that he leaked an FBI file to discredit Anita Hill's allegations against Clarence Thomas. (Wooten denied those claims.) Sharon Prost, former counsel to Judiciary Committee chairman Hatch, was nominated to the federal circuit despite a lack of trial experience. John Bates, now a judge in district court in Washington, was rewarded with his job after helping Ken Starr investigate President Clinton. Others have been nominated for their right-wing opinions, including opposition to gay rights. Fourth circuit nominee Claude Allen, while campaigning for his former boss Jesse Helms, said that Helms's opponent had links "with the queers."

The vast majority of these nominations have been speedily confirmed by the Senate, with only the most extreme ideologues coming under scrutiny. Further, in a stroke of arrogance seldom seen even in Washington, once the 2002 elections created a more anti-choice Congress and returned the chairmanship of the Senate Judiciary Committee to anti-choice senator Orrin Hatch (R–Utah), the president renominated some of the few judges that the previous Senate had rejected. For example:

- Charles Pickering, twice nominated to the U.S. Court of Appeals for the Fifth Circuit and twice rejected by the Senate, chaired the 1976 subcommittee of the Republican party's Platform Committee that called for a constitutional amendment to over-rule *Roe v. Wade*. In 1979, as a Mississippi state senator, he called for a constitutional convention to propose an amendment to ban abortion. As a state senator, he repeatedly voted against state funding for family planning programs. And in 1984, as president of the Mississippi Baptist Convention, he presided over a meeting adopting a resolution calling for legislation to outlaw abortion. In 1994, he lobbied the Justice Department for a lighter sentence against a man accused of burning a cross in front of the home of a mixed-race couple. In January 2004, President Bush overrode the Senate and appointed Pickering to the court, using rarely invoked recess appointment powers.

- Texas Supreme Court justice Priscilla Owen, renominated to the U.S. Court of Appeals for the Fifth Circuit, has consistently used a Texas law requiring parental notice before a minor may have an abortion as a roadblock to minors' access to the service. Under the law, minors who do not have parental consent must undergo a judicial bypass, which Owen has refused in most cases. Her record demonstrates insensitivity bordering on hostility to the plight of young women. Her opinions were so far outside the legal mainstream that one of her conservative colleagues on the Texas Supreme Court, current White House counsel Alberto Gonzales, once accused her, when she voted to deny a minor access to abortion, of an "unconscionable act of judicial activism" and of "create[ing] hurdles that simply are not to be found in the words of the statute." But Gonzales's choice for the post, Deborah Hankinson, lost out to Owen after presidential pal Karl Rove put in a good word for his former client Owen (who had paid him $250,000 for consulting during her 1994 Texas Supreme Court campaign). Confirmation pending.

Consider the extremist positions of some of the other nominees to the federal bench:

- William H. Pryor Jr., Alabama attorney general, nominated to the U.S. Court of Appeals for the Eleventh Circuit, besides having called *Roe v. Wade* "the worst abomination of the history of constitutional law," has also fought strenuously against legal protections for gays and lesbians, once comparing homosexuality to necrophilia and bestiality. Recess appointment.

- James Leon Holmes, nominated to a federal district court judgeship in Arkansas, has said that "the abortion issue is the simplest issue this country has faced since slavery was made unconstitutional." We are in complete agreement on that, while falling on opposite sides of the debate on how that "issue" should be decided. Holmes has also written that "the wife is to subordinate herself to her husband," and that her job "is to place herself under the authority of the man." Holmes's positions on a woman's place in the world and a woman's right to control her own body make the connection between equality and reproductive freedom perfectly clear. Confirmation pending.

- Carolyn Kuhl, nominated to the U.S. Court of Appeals for the Ninth Circuit, urged the Justice Department not only to support several Pennsylvania abortion restrictions but also to call for outright reversal of *Roe v. Wade*. The Justice Department took her recommendation and argued, "The textual, doctrinal and historical basis for *Roe v. Wade* is so far flawed, and . . . is a source of such instability in the law that this court should reconsider that decision and on reconsideration abandon it." In private practice, Kuhl wrote a brief backing the "gag rule" imposed on doctors in federally funded clinics, preventing them from discussing the legal option of abortion with patients. Confirmation pending.

- Michael McConnell, confirmed in November 2002 to the U.S.

Court of Appeals for the Tenth Circuit, wrote in the *Wall Street Journal* in 1998 that "[t]he reasoning of *Roe v. Wade* is an embarrassment to those who take constitutional law seriously." McConnell has also called *Roe* a "gross misinterpretation of the Constitution" and a "mistake."

- Miguel Estrada, nominated to the District of Columbia Circuit Court of Appeals, has a reputation for having an unusually conservative agenda. At his hearing before the Senate Judiciary Committee, when he was asked about his views on privacy and reproductive rights, Estrada dodged and replied that he had not given the issue enough thought. After a lengthy filibuster, Estrada removed himself from consideration in September 2003.

- Janice Rogers Brown, nominated to the U.S. Court of Appeals for the District of Columbia, has written opinions while on the California Supreme Court that are in line with Supreme Court justice Antonin Scalia's reasoning that the Constitution does not encompass a woman's right to choose. When the California court struck down a law requiring that a minor seek parental consent prior to having an abortion, Brown dissented, criticizing her colleagues for allowing the courts to "topple every cultural icon, to dismiss all societal values, and to become the final arbiters of traditional morality." Confirmation pending.

- Pennsylvania attorney general D. Michael Fisher, nominated to the Third Circuit Court of Appeals, has been clear on his opposition to choice. It was in an address to the National Right to Life Convention in June 2002 that Fisher anticipated the day that would come "under the leadership of George Bush [when] we'll have a Supreme Court . . . with justices who will leave it to the states to decide the legality of this issue by overturning *Roe v. Wade*." Confirmation pending.

NO "SINGLE ISSUE"

These are just a few examples of the kinds of extremists who have been nominated to hold lifelong appointments on the federal bench. The scales of justice are tipping against women's reproductive rights, positioned to take away our freedoms. We must not buy into the argument advanced by some members of both political parties that reproductive freedom is merely *one* isolated philosophical issue with no bearing on a nominee's qualifications, so therefore not a matter for scrutiny by the Senate. Quite the contrary—reproductive freedom, a basic human right, is a bedrock principle. It is our duty as citizens to bring into the light those who want to eliminate our freedoms. We must insist that all judicial nominees positively affirm their commitment to Americans' fundamental civil and human rights, including a woman's right to make her own childbearing choices. At stake is our country's most precious value: our freedom.

NEXT ON THE DOCKET

We are clearly at a point where we can no longer rely solely on the courts to protect the freedoms guaranteed by the *Griswold, Eisenstadt,* and *Roe* decisions. We must mobilize to let our senators know that we expect them to reject any judicial nominees who do not uphold fundamental human and civil rights, including the right to choose. We must demand that senators not act like rubber stamps with court nominees. Our system of government requires an independent judiciary. The Senate must make independent judgments about court nominees, and use all the tools at their disposal to prevent lifetime appointments of judges whose ideology overrides the Constitution, including filibusters if necessary. Our civil rights demand no less devotion from our senators.

But as important as it is to preserve and protect *Roe* and its principle of reproductive privacy, upholding *Roe* alone is not enough. *Roe* is only a shell of what it was thirty years ago. The fabric of reproductive rights has been worn threadbare by years of attempts to shred it. It's time to weave a new and stronger cloth that will explicitly secure the right to make childbearing choices. We won reproductive freedom from the top down the first time. We must win again, this time from the bottom up. We need to take the struggle to the local level, working to make sure state legislatures and governors block anti-choice laws from ever getting to the courts in the first place. We must also press bar associations and legal groups to join in the fight for fair and independent judiciary, and work with other civil rights groups and environmental groups that have a shared agenda of seeking judicial nominees committed to fundamental, constitutional rights.

Since fighting to save what's left of *Roe* won't fully protect us from the judicial siege being waged against women's rights, we must introduce and pass legislation such as the proposed federal Freedom of Choice Act, which would codify the principles of reproductive freedom. Such legislation will state in very simple but clear terms that no government can deny a woman's right to choose whether or not to use birth control, whether or not to become pregnant, and whether or not to carry a pregnancy to term, nor may the government in any way discriminate against a woman because of her choices. A similar act with the same name failed to pass in the early 1990s. Now we must gather more support and see to it that Congress passes it this time around, because once it becomes the law of the land, it will make women's reproductive self-determination impervious to the vagaries of judicial activism—even if *Roe v. Wade* is overturned. Meanwhile, to demonstrate public support for the measure, we must also work at the grassroots level, pressuring state legislatures to pass laws assuring our freedoms. California passed such an act in 2002, and six other states already have a similar law on the books.

Getting Congress to pass the Freedom of Choice Act will be the hardest political battle we have ever fought. But it will be, by far, the most important.

THE COURT NETWORK

The Court Network is a coalition of organizations engaged in educating people about the ways an unbalanced judiciary threatens our reproductive and civil rights. If you belong to any of the groups listed below, you are already part of an important collaborative project of coalition building, grassroots organizing, and public education to raise awareness of the importance of the Supreme Court and lower federal court nominees to protecting our rights. By working together, we are able to amplify our voices and exert the power of collective action, a hallmark of our democracy. I encourage you to join any of these groups, and get more involved.

The Court Network includes:
Alliance for Justice
Black Women's Health Imperative
National Council of Jewish Women
National Council of Negro Women
People for the American Way Foundation
PFLAG (Parents, Family, and Friends of Lesbians and Gays)
Planned Parenthood Federation of America
Sierra Club Foundation

For more information on the Court Network, visit www.saveroe.com/facts/coalition/index.asp.

SIX

ANTI-CHOICE, ANTI-SCIENCE

REPLACING FACTS WITH
RIGHT-WING IDEOLOGY

Imagine a country where:

- the government promotes the myth that a safe medical procedure causes a deadly disease
- laws require physicians to give false, ideologically based information to trusting patients
- the government's largest and best-known public health organization censors its own publications under pressure from the administration
- appointees to scientific advisory committees claim condoms are ineffective and can cause promiscuity and disease
- leaders ban promising scientific research into a range of diseases because of fundamentalist religious beliefs
- government "experts" are appointed to health committees because of their right-wing ideology, not their knowledge

Now guess what country this is:

Answer:
the U.S.A.

Yes, it's hard to imagine a government that would deliberately ignore legitimate scientific data and tell lies to its citizens in order to promote a fundamentalist religious worldview. And it's even harder to believe that the time and place described above are the United States in the twenty-first century—not the Dark Ages, the Inquisition, or Afghanistan under the Taliban. But this is how the current government operates in the most technologically and scientifically advanced country in the world. Our leaders are so ideologically driven that they are running roughshod over scientific principles and sound medical research. Forget about science, reason, and enlightenment—this administration has a worldview that is positively medieval.

Of course, it's true that throughout history, governments have punished citizens when their scientific findings ran afoul of the ideology of the day. In 1600, Giordano Bruno, an Italian friar, was burned at the stake for asserting that the earth revolved around the sun. Later that century, Galileo Galilei was convicted of heresy by the Inquisition and sentenced to lifelong imprisonment for publishing similar conclusions. In those days, theocratic governments could reject any science that conflicted with their worldview and consign their citizens to the darkness of ignorance. But the Age of Reason was supposed to have put an end to that kind of willful repudiation of scientific thinking.

Our country was founded partly on the principle of religious tolerance, and separation of church and state. And so far no one in the U.S. is being burned at the stake or imprisoned for their scientific beliefs. But citizens are being punished nonetheless: medical disinformation is being spread to frighten women about nonexistent dangers of abortion; policies aimed at preventing people from using condoms and other forms of contraception are putting lives in real danger; and physicians and researchers are being prevented from providing care and doing their work. Moreover, the administration monitors the scientific information on its Web sites in order to censor anything that doesn't conform to its ideological agenda; appoints experts to scientific advisory boards on the basis of their right-wing political resumes, not their professional expertise; and punishes organizations that disagree with the administration's puritanical and unrealistic abstinence-only stance with unusual financial audits and other forms of monitoring and interference.

If you imagine that the anti-choice zealots who are in power in the United States today have any respect for science, then you might as well start believing that the earth is flat.

LACK OF CONDOM SENSE

Anyone who understands the first thing about public health knows that condoms can be an essential tool for preventing pregnancy, HIV/AIDS, and other sexually transmitted infections. While the only 100 percent sure way to prevent sexually transmitted infections and pregnancy is to have no sex at all, let's be real: people have sex. People *like* having sex. Having sex is natural and normal, and so is wanting to prevent pregnancy and sexually transmitted infections. Having safer sex prevents disease and saves lives, and using condoms is how you have safer sex. It's simple, and most people these days can understand the basic rule of how to protect themselves: no condoms, no sex.

Yet the present administration, at the behest of its anti-choice constituents, is doing everything it can to discourage condom use! It believes that any mention of preventing pregnancy, HIV/AIDS, and other sexually transmitted infections with condoms goes against the anti-sex, anti-pleasure (especially anti-women's pleasure), abstinence-only ideology that has infected the government. It has pulled scientifically accurate information about condoms off government Web sites, it has harassed AIDS prevention groups with unwarranted audits, and it has appointed people who oppose condom use to key administrative posts in family planning. The underlying message seems to be that anyone who has sex outside of marriage deserves to get a disease or die, and that the only purpose of sex in marriage is procreation.

> *In [the Bible, God] tells us not to have sex until we are married; not to have sex with anybody other than the one man or one woman to whom we are married; and to stay married the rest of our lives. That's the one and only prescription for safe sex.*
>
> —Dr. Joe McIlhaney, appointed to a
> CDC advisory committee

The last time this country saw such rigid ideology in direct opposition to a proven public health approach was nearly a hundred years ago, when the American Social Hygiene Association fought hard to prohibit condom use. "Social hygienists" believed that anyone who risked getting venereal diseases should suffer the consequences. It's no wonder that by the end of World War I, American troops had very high rates of sexually transmitted infections, while our British allies, who had condoms, did not. The Secretary of the Navy at the time believed that condoms and other prophylactics "were not Christian." But when he was out of the office, his more astute assistant, Franklin Delano Roosevelt, ordered that prophylactic kits be distributed to sailors. By World War II, military leaders were more realistic, promoting the use of condoms with training films that urged soldiers, "Don't forget—put it on before you put it in." Today, General Colin Powell has made his views about the importance of condom use clear, despite administration policy to the contrary.

Condoms save lives, which became clearer than ever when AIDS hit the United States in the 1980s, and public health officials promoted condom use to stem the epidemic. Used correctly, condoms are 99 percent effective against HIV/AIDS. In a 1991 study of couples in which one partner had HIV, all 123 couples that used condoms every time for four years prevented transmission of the virus. In 122 couples that did not use condoms every time, 12 partners became infected. In the U.S., nearly 800,000 cases of AIDS have been reported to the Centers for Disease Control and Prevention (CDC), and there are nearly 40,000 new cases in the U.S. per year. Many such cases could have been prevented by condoms.

It's almost unfathomable that the government of the United States of America is discouraging condom use at a time when we are still seeing so many new cases of AIDS, but that is indeed the goal of the ideological right. In fact, the administration has gone so far as to censor health information on a Centers for Disease Control and Prevention Web site. Under threat of losing funds, the CDC was forced to remove a Web site fact sheet that described accurate condom use and discussed the effectiveness of condoms in preventing HIV/AIDS transmission. Our public health information is becoming infected with policies that are threatening the health of our citizens, young and old.

The CDC is the leading federal agency charged with protecting the health and safety of Americans, and "providing credible information to enhance health decisions"; it is responsible for developing and applying disease prevention and control, and health promotion and education. Given the CDC's key role in public health, it is nothing short of astonishing that the administration would try to exercise censorship over a CDC informational Web site. It is even more astonishing that CDC officials acquiesced. The original comprehensive fact sheet about condoms, which made reference to research showing that educating people about condom use does not promote sexual activity, has now been replaced by a new fact sheet, which emphasizes condom failure rates and the effectiveness of abstinence. It no longer describes how to use condoms, nor which types of condoms are most effective. It also fails to mention the evidence that neither sex education nor condom availability leads to more sex.

"The threat came from high up in the administration that if we did not pull information on condoms off the Web site, the CDC would not get their money, period," says one CDC insider, who, like many CDC colleagues, was appalled at the changes but afraid to be quoted by name. Several CDC scientists have left the organization because, as the insider put it, they can't stand "constantly having to compromise their science with the politics."

In February [2003], a hundred CDC researchers on sexually transmitted infections were summoned to Washington, by HHS deputy Claude Allen, for a day-long seminar consisting entirely of speakers extolling abstinence until marriage. There were no panels or workshops, just endless testimonials, including one by a young woman calling herself a "born-again virgin."

—from "Science Gets Sacked," by Jennifer Block,
The Nation, September 1, 2003, pp. 5–6

The administration's misguided and potentially deadly position that information about condom use leads to increased sexual activity is affecting sex education not just at the CDC, but at the State Department's Agency for International Development (USAID), which has also removed information on the effectiveness of condoms from its Web site.

Administration-mandated censorship now extends to scientific grants as well. *The New York Times* reported that a researcher at the University of California said he had been advised by a National Institutes of Health project officer that the abstract of a grant application should be "cleansed" and should not contain any inflammatory wording like "gay," "homosexual," or "transgender." The researcher, whose grant proposal dealt with a study of gay men and HIV testing, said it was difficult not to use those terms in his abstract.

That sort of censorship goes against every principle of scientific ethics. "Funding officials are suggesting that areas of science are so taboo that the very mention of these words becomes reason for not funding," says University of Pennsylvania bioethics expert Paul R. Wolpe, Ph.D. "That is destructive to science as a process, as well as to academic freedom." Even more important, he says, it closes the door on scientific inquiry into very important research areas. "Everything from AIDS to abortion rates to teenage pregnancy becomes decided in public policy by ideological positioning rather than through scientific rigor. That is a very dangerous posture for a society that is used to making decisions based on scientific evidence."

Meanwhile, at the direction of Tommy Thompson, secretary of the Department of Health and Human Services, the HHS has started targeting AIDS prevention groups for financial audits and content reviews. The HHS inspector general investigated at least eight AIDS groups that receive federal funding to see if their content was too sexually explicit or promoted sexual activity. In the case of the Stop AIDS group in San Francisco, which focuses on teaching gay men how to stop the spread of AIDS by having safe sex, the verdict was guilty on both counts. Another group, the Washington, D.C., Advocates for Youth, which trains sex-education professionals, was audited three times in one year. And the Alan Guttmacher Institute, a highly respected reproductive and sexual health research organization, was also audited.

Shana Krochmal, of the Stop AIDS Project, which does HIV prevention for gay and bisexual men in San Francisco and receives some funding from the CDC, says they've not only been subjected to two HHS audits, with teams of evaluation experts scrutinizing their work, they have to answer constant questions from government officials. "We're routinely harassed by project officers at CDC and HHS, which often start with a call from a congressional office." She says they've spent hundreds of staff hours on the issue. "The witch hunt has hurt our ability to be as effective as possible. To have to spend all this time squabbling about politics rather than improving public health is outrageous." In response to the harassment, Stop AIDS has toned down its sexual content somewhat, she says, but not much. "It's important for anyone working with gay, STD, HIV, and teen pregnancy issues to speak openly and honestly about the activities they've been participating in."

Right-wing ideologues are not only censoring information they don't like, they're spreading misinformation. The politicos who want to mandate sexual abstinence until marriage for all Americans have also characterized public health messages advocating condom use as a "conspiracy." Moreover, they have started a campaign to spread myths that condoms increase the risk of getting human papilloma virus (HPV)—a claim that is patently untrue. Former U.S. representative Tom Coburn (R–Oklahoma) and current representative Mark Souder (R–Indiana) are on a misguided crusade to add warning language to existing condom packaging, stating that condoms do not prevent HPV. Although the condom-labeling amendment Coburn attempted to attach to several pieces of legislation while he was in Congress ultimately failed to pass, he did succeed in forcing it into the Labor HHS Appropriations Bill. Many health organizations and public health officials decried the measure for its potential to discourage condom use.

The undeniable truth is that condom use is a major deterrent to the spread of HPV, and in any case, HPV is *not*, contrary to the alarmist tone of these warnings, a dire problem. Most people have had some form of HPV without even being aware of it, and it usually clears up on its own. While there *are* a handful of specific subtypes of HPV that *can* cause a variety of conditions that in turn *can* lead to dangerous cancers if they remain untreated, it is a gross and egregious exaggeration to characterize HPV, as right-wing propaganda has done, as a "dreaded virus." In fact, some 75 percent of sexually active women aged eighteen to forty-four have or will have HPV. The best way for women to protect themselves from serious complications with HPV is to have a regular Pap smear.

The worst that can be said about condom use in the context of HPV is that condoms do not completely eliminate the risk of transmitting the virus, since some virus-infected skin may shed outside the condom-protected area. But condoms do greatly reduce the risk of infection, which is why the CDC recommends them as preventative for HPV, even though this information is no longer allowed to appear on the CDC Web site. In other words, a condom is vastly better than no condom for preventing HPV—and all other sexually transmitted infections. What people need to make responsible decisions and protect themselves from sexually transmitted infections like HPV or HIV/AIDS is not misinformation but good information and accessible health care. And condoms.

SCARE TACTICS: THE CREATION OF AN ABORTION/BREAST CANCER MYTH

Another favorite tactic of anti-choice extremists is to scare women away from having abortions by telling them that the procedure causes breast cancer. In other words, when they don't have law or truth on their side, they just lie. The link between abortion and breast cancer is about as medically sound as the link between root canals and mouth cancer, but the right-wingers have spread this lie far and wide. Women who ride buses in Philadelphia are exposed to completely inaccurate ads sponsored by Christ's Bride Ministries warning them that "women who choose abortion suffer more and deadlier breast cancer." An anti-choice organization that misleadingly calls itself the Breast Cancer Prevention Institute has sponsored similarly inaccurate TV commercials saying, "Studies show that the increased risk of breast cancer [after abortion] can be fifty percent or more." The few studies cited by proponents of the link between breast cancer and abortion have all been old, small, and flawed. Put their claims up against the conclusion of a study of *1.5 million women* that appeared in the *New England Journal of Medicine* in 1997: "Induced abortions have no overall effect on the risk of breast cancer."

And, in case there is any question about the validity of this conclusion, in 2001 the prestigious British medical journal *Lancet Oncology* reanalyzed this study, as well as others on the subject, and concluded—again—that no link between abortion and breast cancer has been proven. Furthermore, after reviewing *all* the literature on the topic, the American College of Obstetricians and Gynecologists concluded: "There is no evidence supporting a causal link between induced abortion and subsequent development of breast cancer."

But never mind that the clear scientific consensus on the supposed link between abortion and breast cancer is that *it doesn't exist*. Opponents of choice continue to spread disinformation about the link through both legislative initiatives and taxpayer-financed Web sites. On the legislative front they have embarked on an aggressive campaign to pass laws requiring doctors to tell patients seeking abortion that the procedure increases the risk of breast cancer. Such dishonesty destroys the essential trust built in to the doctor-patient relationship, and undermines the most basic medical ethics.

Similarly inaccurate statements were posted on a National Cancer Institute Web site fact sheet, another source from which citizens have a right to expect straightforward reporting of the facts. "Some studies have reported statistically significant evidence of an increased risk of breast cancer in women who have had abortions, while others have merely suggested an increased risk," the

NCI Web site stated. This statement replaced the language which used to be there, which did give an accurate summary of the available literature on the subject: "The current body of scientific evidence suggests that women who have had either induced or spontaneous abortions have the same risk as other women for developing breast cancer." The NCI made this change after being lobbied hard by anti-choice members of Congress. Insofar as there is any basis whatsoever for the belief that abortion causes breast cancer, it derives from research showing that women who have children early in life are less likely to get the disease than women who have babies late or not at all. But by that reasoning abstinence would cause cancer. The idea that abortion causes breast cancer has zero validity.

Why, then, did the government base its "fact" sheets on misinformation supplied by anti-choice congresspeople instead of on the scientific consensus of the American Cancer Society, the *New England Journal of Medicine*, the *Lancet*, and the American College of Obstetricians and Gynecologists? Because this is an administration for whom ideology trumps science—and truth!

Fortunately, the falsehoods about breast cancer and abortion on the NCI fact sheet attracted so much attention that this time the anti-choice war machine was unable to get away with its blatant dishonesty. *The New York Times* called the fact sheet "an egregious distortion of the evidence," and the director of epidemiological research for the American Cancer Society said, "This issue has been resolved scientifically. . . . This is essentially a political debate." After some members of Congress protested the change, the NCI held a three-day conference reviewing studies on the issue, and finally, in March 2003, the NCI Web site was revised to report that the conclusion that "induced abortion is not associated with an increase in breast cancer risk" is "well-established."

Despite this action at the national level, anti-choice zealots in South Dakota and Minnesota tried to perpetuate the same bad science on their state Web sites. However, when Planned Parenthood of Minnesota/South Dakota discovered that the Minnesota Department of Health's Web site included the bogus information about a link between breast cancer and abortion, it alerted the press. Using the state's open records law, Josephine Marcotty, a reporter with the *Minneapolis Star Tribune*, obtained e-mails to and from the Minnesota Commissioner of Health revealing that political pressure from the governor and other anti-choice interests was responsible for the specious statements. The resulting public outcry caused the governor to reconsider.

Though the Minnesota Web site had still not been changed as of the time this book was going to press, the bad publicity did have an effect on South Dakota's plan to include the bogus abortion/breast cancer link on their Department of Health Website. Wanting to avoid an embarrassing Minnesota-style PR disaster, the governor and the Health Department dropped their plans, saying they did not want to "diminish the integrity and credibility" of the site.

PSEUDOSCIENTIFIC ANTI-CHOICE SYNDROME (PAS)

Another myth about abortion promoted by those who oppose it is that it causes so-called post-abortion syndrome (PAS). Anti-choice activists claim that a majority of American women who have an abortion suffer severe and long-lasting emotional trauma, similar to post-traumatic stress disorder (PTSD). This supposed psychological disorder isn't recognized by the American Psychological Association or the American Psychiatric Association. But Web sites abound with "help" for women suffering from this imaginary syndrome, and the inventors of PAS have pushed for legislation requiring that women be (mis)informed about its risks during mandatory preabortion counseling sessions.

Real science, though, shows that the emotional response to legal abortion is mainly relief. Dr. Nada Stotland, secretary of the American Psychological Association and author of *Psychiatric Aspects of Abortion*, published a commentary in the *Journal of the American Medical Association* on the topic. "There is no evidence of an abortion trauma syndrome," she says. While some women certainly have mixed feelings after an abortion, most studies have found that the emotional effects of abortion are short-lived and relatively benign. (Contrast these effects to the emotional problems that frequently appear after childbirth. Postpartum depression—PPD—unlike PAS, is a clinically recognized disorder affecting at least one out of every ten women, often with extremely debilitating results.) The more serious emotional problems that sometimes occur deserve to be dealt with compassionately, but they are rare. Women who experienced psychiatric symptoms such as depression reported having those symptoms before the procedure—the abortion itself did not contribute to their symptoms. None of this is meant to suggest that abortion is a decision to be taken lightly, but the reports of PTSD, flashbacks, depression, and suicidal tendencies are wildly exaggerated. Instead, researchers have found:

- For most women, the process of choosing abortion represents a maturing experience, a successful coping with a personal crisis.
- The crisis for most women is the unintended pregnancy, not the abortion itself.
- Ninety-eight percent of women who have abortions say they have no regrets and would make the same choice again under similar circumstances.
- More than 70 percent of women who have abortions express a desire for children (or more children) in the future.

- Fewer than 10 percent of women who have abortions experience lingering depressive symptoms, and those are often related to the experience of an unwanted pregnancy. As a comparison, this is slightly less than the percentage of women who experience postpartum depression.
- When women aren't allowed abortion, their mental health is endangered. In one study, 34 percent of women who were denied abortions reported one to three years later that the child was a burden they frequently resented.

Still, the myth of PAS has persisted for many years. In 1987, anti-choice president Ronald Reagan directed his anti-choice surgeon general C. Everett Koop to produce a report on the health effects of induced abortions. Koop followed his commander in chief's orders—but after reviewing the relevant literature could say only that there was "insufficient evidence" to determine the psychological effects of abortion. The more than 250 studies disproving the existence of PAS must have dissuaded Koop from coming to any conclusion more pleasing to the anti-choice constituency. Conversely, ideology must have prevented him from publicly coming to the conclusion to which all the facts pointed. Nonetheless, in closed-door meetings in 1988, Koop did tell members of Congress that the risk of significant emotional problems following abortion was minuscule from a public health perspective. However, he was not only unwilling to say that in public, he even chose to suppress his report—as ridiculously inconclusive as it was—because its findings didn't mesh with the president's anti-choice position. No wonder that several years later, the PAS myth still circulates. In fact, in some states it's all but required reading for pregnant women, as you'll see below.

MANDATORY COUNSELING, MANDATORY LIES

Despite the fact that PAS and other myths about the risks of abortion have been dismissed by the scientific community as political voodoo, anti-choice zealots have managed to get laws on the books in dozens of states requiring women considering abortion to undergo mandatory biased "counseling" about these "risks," along with other information designed to discourage them from getting abortions.

Most states have so-called informed consent laws on the books that are specific to abortion, requiring that women seeking abortion services listen to state-mandated lectures first. More than twenty states with these laws combine them with waiting periods, which prohibit a woman from having an abortion until she has waited a specific period of time after receiving the counseling—usually twenty-four hours. The Supreme Court's 1992 decision in *Planned Parenthood of Southeastern Pennsylvania v. Casey* made way for these laws by upholding a Pennsylvania state law requiring that health care providers give women state-prepared materials at least twenty-four hours prior to the abortion procedures.

The mandatory counseling materials vary from state to state, but often include photographs and videos of fetuses at various stages of development, lists of abortion-alternative and adoption agencies, and sensationalistic misinformation about the risks of abortion. Typically biased, inflammatory, graphic, and medically inaccurate, the materials are designed to deter women from seeking abortion. Several states, such as Texas, Minnesota, and Mississippi, have laws requiring that women be "informed" of the supposed link between abortion and breast cancer—although, paradoxically, these laws allow providers to give only medically accurate information. In 2001 alone, eighteen states introduced thirty-four measures warning women of this bogus link. Mandatory biased counseling attempts to scare vulnerable women about the potential risks of abortion. The truth is, legal first-trimester abortion has a lower complication rate than most other surgical procedures.

Real counseling—ethical and professional counseling—gives clients an opportunity to get unbiased information on all their options and to consider the options without pressure or coercion. Real counseling gives people a supportive framework in which they can make their *own* best decisions within the context of their own values and religious beliefs. That's *not* what this counseling is.

Several states require that women must return for a second appointment after the initial counseling consultation, increasing the time a woman must take away from her work and family, and the travel expenses involved when abortion providers are far away. A forced waiting period can cause some women to put off having an abortion for days or even weeks, so that they are compelled to have a later abortion, which poses increased, and unnecessary, risks. Since some clinics offer abortion services on only certain days of the week, a day of twenty-four hours can turn into a week of anxiety and missed work, further adding to the psychic and economic costs women must bear to exercise their legal and moral right to choose to end a pregnancy. All in the name of making ideology superior to medical science.

In 1992, Mississippi became the first state to enforce a mandatory delay and biased counseling, requiring a separate visit, before a woman could get an abortion. In the five months following enactment of the law there was an 18 percent increase in the proportion of abortions performed in the second trimester of pregnancy, resulting in increased health risk and greater expense to the woman.

In some states, such as Florida and Idaho, physicians are required to deliver the biased counseling personally. In others, the information can also be relayed by other professionals, such as psychologists, nurses, or physicians' assistants. Such laws go against a physician's credo: "First, do no harm." The biased materials are often labeled Informed Consent, or a Woman's Right to Know, but they are nothing more than ideologically based and misleading propaganda. In no other area of the medical profession are doctors and other medical professionals required to give their patients ideology which they identify as "information." This is a truly shocking breach of trust.

"It's a big conflict with clinical and ethical practice," says Dr. Stotland, who testified in an Alabama deposition over state law requiring biased counseling. "You don't tell patients untrue things, and make them go through unnecessary materials as an obstacle for them to make a decision about abortion."

The fact that a few states require physicians to deliver the mandatory "counseling" themselves may convince some doctors, already wary of the harassment and risk that come with being an abortion provider, to stop performing the procedure. Already, there are no abortion providers in 87 percent of counties, and these laws will ensure that there are fewer still. Requiring physicians to give out this misinformation also drives up the costs of abortion, since physicians' time is more expensive than that of other clinic workers. But that's part of the anti-choice plan to make abortion inaccessible even if they can't make it illegal.

The mandatory counseling not only treats women like moral cretins—as if a woman hadn't considered the implications of abortion and wouldn't have the ability to make a morally informed choice about her pregnancy without such biased counseling—but also turns physicians into mindless automatons, dispensing advice that is completely unscientific, and sometimes downright ludicrous. In some places, for example, physicians are required to inform a victim of rape that the "father" of the "unborn child" is liable for financial assistance if she carries the pregnancy to term.

It's no wonder the American Medical Association opposes all mandatory abortion counseling language, saying these requirements "often are not medically indicated and never are appropriate areas for codification in law." The medical profession and state laws already ensure that health care practitioners give patients accurate information regarding the risks and benefits of any treatment. Women already get informed consent about the real risks of abortion. Scare tactics like mandatory biased counseling bring the government and anti-choice ideology into the examining room, where they have no business, and where they can do a great deal of harm.

IDEOLOGICAL SCREENING FOR SCIENTIFIC COMMITTEES: THE ANTI-CHOICE LITMUS TESTS

The Bush administration has completely overhauled numerous scientific advisory committees, replacing qualified people with candidates chosen for their ideological views, not their professional credentials. Some of these appointees are in a position to do considerable damage to public health if their views prevail:

In December 2001, the Bush administration appointed a prominent advocate of abstinence-only programs, Dr. Joe McIlhaney, to the CDC director's Advisory Committee. He was appointed to this position despite the fact that in 1995, the Texas Commissioner of Health, under then-governor George W. Bush, questioned the credibility of his research, writing, "Many of the items in [Dr. McIlhaney's] presentation [on sexually transmitted diseases] are misleading and are quoted incompletely. . . . The only data which was reported in the presentation are those which supported his bias on the topics he addressed. Intellectual honesty demands that he present all the data."

In March 2002, the Bush administration appointed an anti-choice former congressman from Oklahoma, Tom Coburn, to co-chair the AIDS Advisory Council. Anti-choice groups like Focus on the Family and Family Research Council had lobbied hard for his appointment, to either the council or the position of surgeon general. Remember Coburn? It was Tom Coburn who launched the crusade to label condoms ineffective, and who has publicly stated that only sex that occurs in a monogamous, heterosexual marriage is morally acceptable. Coburn, a physician, left Congress after three terms in 2000, where he gained a reputation as a fierce opponent of reproductive health and a staunch supporter of abstinence-only education. In complete defiance of proven public health principles, he charged the Centers for Disease Control and Prevention (CDC) with a massive cover-up of the ineffectiveness of condoms, despite having no research to support his position, and successfully called for the resignation of CDC director Jeffrey Koplan.

We believe the failure of public health efforts to prevent the STD epidemic in America is related to the CDC's "safe-sex" promotion and its attempt to withhold from the American people the truth of condom ineffectiveness.

The CDC has promoted condom-use programs that have been used to educate an entire generation. Because they believed condoms would protect them during intercourse, millions of women in our country now suffer from the ravages of diseases, including pelvic infections, infertility and cervical cancer.

There is a health model that completely protects against all STDs; it is abstinence until marriage with an uninfected partner and monogamy thereafter. If we, as a medical community, are really serious about the STD epidemic, this is the message we must begin sending to our young people. We call

*upon President Bush to request the immediate resignation of Dr. Jeffrey P.
Koplan as the Director of the CDC. Only with fresh and bold leadership at
the CDC, dedicated to primary prevention as opposed to social ideology, can
we, as a country, start moving toward genuine sexual health.*

—joint statement made by Congressman (Ret.)
Tom Coburn, M.D., and Congressman
Dave Weldon, M.D., July 24, 2001

In December 2002, the administration appointed Dr. W. David
Hager, an anti-choice fundamentalist and obstetrician-gynecologist,
to sit on the Food and Drug Administration's Reproductive Health
Drugs Advisory Committee. (Actually, Hager was the president's
choice to *chair* the committee, but didn't get the top position because of public outcry.) This committee oversees the safety and
effectiveness of drugs for obstetrics and gynecology, and reviews
studies on such important topics as hormone-replacement therapy.
One of Hager's main qualifications for the post seemed to be that
he assisted the Christian Medical Association in creating a "citizens'
petition" asking the FDA to reverse its approval of mifepristone,
the "abortion pill" (formerly known as RU-486). But perhaps his
published work also spoke to his expertise on women's health matters. He coauthored a book with his wife, entitled *Stress and the Woman's
Body,* which emphasizes the restorative powers of putting Christ in
your life, and recommends specific Scripture readings to treat pre-
menstrual syndrome. In his private practice, he reportedly refuses
to prescribe contraceptives to unmarried women.

Hager was picked over two other much better qualified nominees proposed by FDA staff members—a former dean of the
University of Pittsburgh School of Public Health, and the director
of maternal fetal medicine at Massachusetts General Hospital. His
appointment led the usually restrained medical journal the *Lancet* to
comment, "Expert committees need to be filled, by definition, with

experts. . . . Any further right-wing incursions on expert panels' membership will cause a terminal decline in public trust in the advice of scientists."

In January 2003, President Bush appointed Jerry Thacker to the Presidential Advisory Council on HIV/AIDS. Whereas Hager is at least a physician, Thacker is a marketing consultant whose chief qualification for the job seemed to be his virulently homophobic views. Thacker has described homosexuality as a "deathstyle," and referred to AIDS as "the gay plague." He has promoted a type of therapy in which gays are "reformed" through religion. Just after the appointment was made public, there was a huge outcry, and Thacker withdrew his name from consideration, citing his inability to be effective amidst so much controversy.

Academics from several health-related fields have reported that when administration staff members have called them about possible committee appointments, they've had to undergo a litmus test on right-wing issues. Psychologist William R. Miller told the *Los Angeles Times* that when he was asked to join a panel that advises the National Institute on Drug Abuse, he was asked some surprising questions: Did he support abortion rights? What about the death penalty for drug kingpins? Had he voted for President Bush? He hadn't voted for Bush, and he wasn't appointed. Other academics have reported being denied positions on advisory committees because their views on embryo cell research didn't mesh with those of the administration.

When the journal *Science* published an article about stacking the scientific committees with ideologues, they were inundated with letters from readers who said that it wasn't just candidates for high-level posts who were subjected to an ideological litmus test—they were vetted for even midlevel and lower positions. "They have gone to a shocking new level when claims on loyalty are that naked," *Science* editor Donald Kennedy told me.

In fact, whole scientific advisory committees have been eliminated when their work was at odds with the administration, including one on genetic testing, and another charged with creating regulations to protect human research subjects. *The Washington Post* reported that the latter committee came under fire from the religious right because it hadn't included fetuses under a regulation pertaining to research on newborns.

The administration has made a sham of the scientific advisory system. Instead of assembling teams of experts who are qualified to offer genuine, objective, scientifically informed opinions, it has created councils of ideologues—yes men and women who rubber-stamp the views of the administration, corrupting the very concept of science and threatening the U.S. position as a global scientific leader. These appointments have potentially deadly consequences for individual Americans who place their trust in the information they receive from institutions like the CDC and the NIH.

Advisory committees are supposed to give the government and the public expert unbiased advice based on the best possible science. By stacking these important committees with right-wing ideologues instead of respected scientists, the administration is putting the health and well-being of the American public at risk.

—Senator Edward M. Kennedy (D–Massachusetts)

Scientific decision-making is being subverted by ideology, and scientific information that does not fit the Administration's political agenda is being suppressed.

—Congressman Henry Waxman (D–California), in an October 21, 2002, letter to Tommy Thompson, secretary of Health and Human Services, signed by eleven other members of Congress

DESTROYING EMBRYONIC STEM CELL RESEARCH

One of President Bush's first actions in office was to declare a ban on federal funding of most stem cell research. As a result, he has virtually halted a great deal of promising scientific research in its tracks.

Stem cells are found in early preembryos, about three to five days after fertilization, when they're called blastocysts. The blastocysts that researchers would like to use come mainly from preembryos left over from couples undergoing in-vitro fertilization treatment. IVF treatment involves stimulating the growth of several eggs in a woman, and then capturing them for fertilization outside her body, in a petri dish. In most cases, physicians fertilize many more eggs than a couple can use, and freeze the leftover eggs, which, if not used in research, would otherwise be destroyed.

There are at least one hundred thousand of these excess preembryos produced each year in the United States. The lining of these blastocysts contains about thirty stem cells, which can be removed and put into a culture dish to reproduce millions of stem cells in a stem cell "line." Embryonic stem cells have two special qualities that make them invaluable to researchers: they have the potential to develop into nearly all different types of tissues in the body, and they are self-renewing, so that large quantities can be produced for medical purposes. Researchers hope that by using the unique capabilities of stem cells, they can generate specific tissues in the body that can help repair damaged or diseased organs or tissues. Stem cell therapy could eventually be used to treat Parkinson's disease, Alzheimer's disease, sickle-cell anemia, diabetes, cancer, cardiovascular disease, spinal cord injuries, osteoporosis, and many other disorders. Potentially, stem-cell-based therapies could help at least 100 million Americans now suffering from one of these conditions.

Never before, not until 1998, has there ever been such a powerful tool, such a resource, that can give so much hope. And to have it just sitting there, right in front of us, ready to go while this debate rages on, is really, really frustrating.

—Christopher Reeve, actor, paralyzed
in an equestrian accident

Those who oppose stem cell research believe that an egg fertilized in a petri dish is a human being. All other considerations aside, these embryos are not human beings, because humans need a woman to carry and gestate the embryo for nine months to birth. Embryos can't develop by themselves. It's a woman's choice that makes an embryo a potential human being. The blastocysts that researchers would like to use are ones that women have clearly decided they will not carry to term. This choice is, of course, generally made in consultation with her spouse or partner, her doctor, and her own conscience, but ultimately it is her own. Right-wing ideologues, however, are trying to short-circuit women's power and take control of the entire reproductive process, even at the petri dish level.

On August 9, 2001, President Bush announced a "compromise" on federal funding for stem cell research, allowing scientists to use the stem cells that already existed but banning funding for any new stem cell lines. He claimed that this ban would not adversely affect research, because there were already sixty genetically diverse stem cell lines in existence that researchers could use. He was hedging his bets, appeasing his far-right allies, while at the same time trying not to alienate those in his party who believe that scientific research should continue unhindered by such extreme ideology. Nancy Reagan, whose husband has Alzheimer's, is among those who have lobbied for this research, as is Senator Orrin Hatch.

The actual effect of the ban on federal funding, despite Bush's so-called compromise, was to bring stem cell research to a virtual standstill. It soon became clear that of the sixty lines of stem cells in existence, many were not actually viable. Researchers say that fewer than ten of the sixty lines are viable, but not even all of these are available to researchers. Also, so few stem cell lines means there is very little genetic variation in the stem cells, which is crucial for researching a wide variety of diseases. As the president of the American Society for Reproductive Medicine told a Senate committee, "The president seems to have information far different from that of the bulk of the medical community."

Ronald Reagan didn't have to take care of Ronald Reagan for the last ten years.

—Michael Deaver, a Reagan advisor and confidant, after a Republican legislator told him that conservatives believe that Ronald Reagan would never have approved of embryonic stem cell research

---

Ronnie struggles in a world unknown to me or the scientists who devote their lives to Alzheimer's research. Because of this, I am determined to do what I can to save other families from this pain. . . . I believe that embryonic stem cell research may provide our scientists with many answers that are now beyond our grasp. . . . There are so many diseases that can be cured or at least helped that we can't turn our back on this. We've lost so much time already. I can't bear to lose any more.

—letter from Nancy Reagan to Senator Orrin Hatch, March 19, 2003

The decision to donate fertilized eggs for research should be left up to the couple that produced those eggs. But the policy of the present administration ensures that this vital research material will simply be destroyed. By rigidly holding onto the belief that personhood begins in a petri dish, right-wing ideologues have put obstacles in the path to finding cures and treatments for diseases affecting millions of people, and they've done it while flying in the face of public opinion. A recent poll found that 70 percent of Americans support stem cell research, including 75 percent of Catholics and 63 percent of fundamentalist Christians. For now, other countries are taking the lead in stem cell research, while our scientists are being held hostage to ideology.

It's time for all of us to wake up and realize that our medical care is being driven by someone else's religious and ideological beliefs, not by science. Politics are infecting science with censorship, misinformation, and coercion. The administration has reduced everything to the abortion issue—stem cell research, contraceptive policy, population aid, everything. As Arthur Caplan, director of the Center for Bioethics at the University of Pennsylvania, said, "Sacrificing other aspects of policy on the altar of abortion is just unfair to Americans." It is also unhealthy, and un-American.

SEVEN

WATCH YOUR MOUTHPIECE

———————◄►————————

THE RIGHT-WING SUBVERSION OF THE PRESS

*Samples of other "inflammatory rhetoric" that pro-lifers must use . . .
are: "holocaust" for America's abortion culture, "abortuary" or
"death camp" to describe the abortion clinic, "abortifacient" for
pills and IUDs, "fornication" for sex outside of marriage,
"adultery" for having an affair.*

—Joseph Scheidler, "Closed: 99 Ways to Stop Abortion,"
a primer on how to shut down abortion clinics

———————◄►————————

Women's reproductive rights are under the greatest threat we've faced in the past thirty years. I think that's news. But to the majority of the media, somehow that isn't worth reporting. In January 2003, *The New York Times* did finally take note, describing the stealthy progress of the multifaceted anti-choice strategy to take away women's reproductive rights:

> As the thirtieth anniversary of the *Roe* decision approaches, women's right to safe, legal abortions is in dire peril.

Most Americans would be shocked at the lengths American representatives are going to in their international war against women's right to control their bodies. . . .

. . . On the surface, the Bush administration's war against women's rights is a series of largely unnoted changes. It is intended to look that way. In reality, it is a steady march into the past, to a time before *Roe v. Wade,* when abortion was illegal and pregnancy was more a matter of fate than choice.

Other than that analysis—which, as is often the case when reproductive rights are covered, was in an editorial rather than on the front page—reporters and editors in major dailies and on TV have almost completely failed to connect the dots. While they may report on individual court decisions or events that affect women's freedoms, they have missed the big picture. Just about the only time the issue of reproductive rights gets ink or airtime in the major dailies or on TV is when something sudden and dramatic has happened, as when a physician or clinic worker is murdered.

Let me give you a typical, and maddening, example of how the media operates. In the two years before the post-9/11 anthrax scare, Planned Parenthood and other women's health centers were the targets of anthrax scares on over eighty occasions. Envelopes full of mysterious powders were sent to our clinics, accompanied by letters claiming the substance was anthrax, and issuing death threats. When reproductive health centers received 550 such epistles within six weeks after the anthrax attacks on the Senate, the media weren't very interested, not even during the harrowing days and weeks we spent waiting to learn whether the substances were in fact anthrax or "merely" death threats accompanied by a harmless yellowish powder. Compare that with the near-hysterical response to the anthrax hoaxes sent to Dan Rather! We were victims of a planned strategy of domestic terrorism—and we had a lot of experience to share with a nation terrorized by anthrax. In fact, we had become so adept at dealing with its psychological consequences and developing procedures for handling biological threats that a number of law enforcement entities requested copies of our protocols to incorporate into their own guidelines.

That's a story—actually two stories. But did the media cover it? Hardly. I spent half an hour talking with a reporter for *The Washington Post* about our experiences with anthrax just when the nation was reeling from the latest biological threats. "Well, call me if someone is killed," he told me. "*Then* it'll be a story."

There's something very wrong when threats to women's lives and freedoms only become news when someone is killed.

Women's reproductive rights are being covered more and more cursorily in the media, despite the fact that they've been under ever fiercer attack over the past few years. In the 1980s, when Ronald Reagan pointed his administration's big guns at Planned Parenthood and women's reproductive rights and health care, it was a national story. But after Bill Clinton was elected—partly thanks to the grassroots efforts of pro-choice women, who were energized after the *Webster* and *Casey* court decisions that eviscerated *Roe v. Wade*—the media decided the issue was passé. The press assumed that under Clinton, reproductive rights were safe, and therefore not worth covering. We became invisible in the media. Since then, even though our rights have been steadily chipped away, important reproductive rights stories have been marginalized, if they were reported at all—partly because the media has been asleep, but also because journalists have been the objects of constant manipulation by right-wing interests. Those stories that were reported were reduced to one word—abortion. And then abortion was reduced to one issue—*Roe* and when or if it would be overturned.

Those who are determined to strip away women's rights have a highly organized, multifaceted strategy to control the media, to take threats to reproductive rights off the front page. Having reaped too much negative publicity over their bombings, murders, and threats toward abortion clinics, they've shifted tactics. Now they're engaged in a slow, piecemeal dismantling of women's rights, which rarely counts as "news." Besides trying to terrify reproductive health care providers out of business, as they have in the past, they're making women's access to those providers ever more difficult by defunding them. And they're aiming their tactics not just at abortion clinics but at facilities offering family planning and reproductive health care of all kinds. They know their actions will fly right under the media's radar—until the day that we have no rights left. Then it'll be front-page news again. And then it'll be too late.

The right-wingers have also been smart in the way they've manipulated the media directly. They relentlessly monitor and harass the media, so that whenever any story appears regarding reproductive rights, reporters and editors are bombarded with hundreds of e-mails, often including threats and intimidation (some reporters have been followed home). More subtly, they've carefully skewed language to cloud and redefine women's reproductive health issues. They've pandered to the media's black-and-white concept of "objectivity" by creating controversy where none exists, and by positioning reactionaries as the other side of a "balanced" story. They've managed to talk reporters and editors into believing that the right-wing point of view never gets a voice. They've succeeded in making journalists flinch even before they write a word about choice; they've inflicted a kind of self-censorship on the media regarding reproductive rights. And they've cried "liberal bias" so many times that the media can't even present straight medical facts without feeling they have to present another "side" from anti-choice groups.

Meanwhile, if you turn on talk shows, little but the right-wing position gets heard, particularly on the radio. That's partly because the venomous contempt they spew over the airwaves to get attention is believed to be "entertaining," and it's partly because the right wing, by and large, owns the airwaves and major television corporations. Consider that Clear Channel, a consistently right-wing organization, owns twelve hundred stations around the country. The concentration of media power in a few hands has silenced progressive voices in the media. Currently ten companies own over 90 percent of all media outlets. Much of the media concentration, and the right-wing domination of the airwaves, has come about because of events that took place under Ronald Reagan. In 1986, the FCC eliminated rules on radio ownership, allowing monopoly ownership, and giving conglomerates the chance to squeeze out independent stations. Also in 1986, the D.C. Federal Court of Appeals upheld a new FCC rule refusing to require television to follow the Fairness Doctrine, which deemed the airwaves to be a "public trust" and required programs to accurately reflect opposing views. The two prevailing judges were Antonin Scalia and Robert Bork. In 1987, FCC commissioners appointed by Ronald Reagan repealed the Fairness Doctrine altogether.

CORRUPTION OF LANGUAGE

The news media not only inform us but form us. The language they use, and the topics they choose, shape and define the way people think about issues—even if that language is inflammatory and misleading, supplied by political extremists. Which particular words the media latch onto can make a huge difference: when "affirmative action" became "reverse discrimination" in the media, it was a setback for the redress of generations of racial and gender oppression. The *L* word (liberal) has become a dirty word—so much so that no politician will allow himself to be stained with it. The word "feminist" has also been demonized, associated with some apocryphal radical man-haters instead of the vast majority of women who simply believe in equal pay and equal rights. Now women have become defensive, demurring, "I'm not a feminist, but . . ." And so feminist issues themselves have become degraded and devalued. The corruption of language leads to a corrosion of thought.

The right-wingers have manipulated language to change the way the media covers issues. There's no better example of how the media recycles inherently biased language than by their use of the loaded term the anti-choice forces invented out of thin air: "partial-birth abortion."

As discussed earlier, there is no medical procedure known as partial-birth abortion. It's a sound bite, a PR gambit, and a political construct, created with the specific intention of inciting and confusing people. It's part of a strategy of misinformation designed to ban abortion procedures by changing the shape of the debate. The phrase was made up by aides to Representative Charles Canady of Florida, as you may recall from Chapter 1. Canady was subsequently appointed by Governor Jeb Bush to the Florida Second District Court of Appeals, where he now sits. He has been enormously influential in advancing the anti-choice agenda through his contribution of a phrase that has been used so often that it has entered the media lexicon. This has happened despite the fact that the American College of Obstetricians and Gynecologists denounced the phrase as a "non-medical term" that was being used indiscriminately to outlaw abortion techniques "critical to the lives and health of American women." The press has also managed to ignore the U.S. Court of Appeals for the Eighth Circuit, which in its September 1999 decision that such bans were unconstitutional, declared: "The law refers to 'partial-birth abortion,' but this term, though widely used by lawmakers and in the popular press, has no fixed medical or legal content." What it does have is a heavily loaded emotional content which is being used to sway the public despite its having been uncovered as a complete fabrication concocted by people with no expert medical knowledge.

The right wing has been clever with the media. They made up the language on "partial-birth abortion," turning it into a cartoon issue where all you saw was a fetus. It was hard for people not to be sucked in. As for the use of the term "mother," unless she has had a child, a pregnant woman is not a mother.

—Ellen Goodman, columnist, the *Boston Globe*

The best that can be said for the media is that, after extensive education efforts by pro-choice groups, some outlets now preface the use of the term "partial-birth abortion" with "so-called" or "the procedure known as," or, even more accurately, they don't refer to "partial-birth abortion" at all, but instead use the phrase "ban on abortion procedures" or the "abortion ban law." But many others still toss it around as if it were a medical fact, or inaccurately equate it with "late-term abortion." And use of the phrase is accelerating. Nearly one in ten news articles that mentioned abortion in 2003 also included the phrase "partial-birth abortion," up from 3 percent in 2001. Of those, only 10 percent use the term "so-called partial-birth abortion," meaning that in 90 percent of recent media hits, the term was accepted as having validity. Perhaps you think it's just unsophisticated small local papers that have been duped into this terminology. Wrong: four of the largest national newspapers— *The New York Times, The Washington Post, Los Angeles Times,* and *Chicago Tribune*—were even less likely than smaller papers to use the correct terminology when discussing abortion-ban legislation, with only 3.6 articles out of 100 in these papers using the phrase "so-called" with "partial-birth abortion."

When the nation's top medical and legal authorities say a term is misleading and wrong, you'd think the media would realize that it's time for a correction. But when the Center for Reproductive Rights complained to the Associated Press about the use of the term, Mike Silverman, AP's deputy managing editor, admitted that "birth" is a loaded word in the context of an abortion procedure, but said that the news service uses the term because it is instantly recognizable. When a public affairs director at a Planned Parenthood affiliate recently challenged an editor at a major daily about its use of the term, the editor heard her out, admitted the term wasn't correct, but said it was easier to use than the alternatives.

Yeah, and it was easier for Jayson Blair to make up stories from his apartment in Brooklyn than get out and do some actual, factual reporting. The press must be made to live up to a standard of accuracy, and not pass on, willy-nilly, any propaganda term that anti-choice groups have pushed into the public consciousness. They might start by refusing to grant the term "pro-life" to those who value women's lives so little.

There are many other examples of these sorts of language biases. Some of the papers covering the Unborn Victims of Violence Act have appropriated the political term "unborn child" instead of using the correct medical terms "embryo" or "fetus." In 1999, for instance, one Associated Press article reported, "Some 24 states have laws that recognize the unborn as potential victims." In reporting about the Laci Peterson murder, most stories refer to the fetus she was carrying as "the baby." Several news articles have even referred to the fetus as "Connor," the name Peterson told people she had picked out. Similarly, many news articles refer to the incident as a "double murder." The incident was a horrible tragedy, but it is a tragedy the right wing hijacked in order to advance a political agenda.

Specifically, the use of the term "unborn child" is part of the campaign to assert the primacy of the fetus over the rights of the woman carrying it. And it has been so successful that the media sometimes forgets the woman herself. In 1999, in Arkansas, Shawana Pace, a pregnant college student, miscarried after being brutally beaten by three men allegedly hired by her boyfriend. The press used her story as a lead-in for an article about Arkansas's proposed Fetal Protection Act and its federal twin, the Unborn Victims of Violence Act. While emphasizing the tragedy of the miscarriage, reports in the local *Arkansas Democrat-Gazette*, AP, and UPI neglected to describe the extent of the woman's injuries: Pace was so badly injured that she had to have her spleen removed. But the new emotionally charged phrase, "unborn baby," used to describe a fetus and elevate it to personhood, shifted the attention from the woman to the fetus—which is exactly the anti-choice agenda.

DEFINING THE DEBATE

There's an old political saying that whoever defines the issue wins the debate. Well, the anti-choice folks have become very adept at using language to reshape and redefine political issues, to the point where words end up having very little to do with reality. Take the phrase "reproductive rights," for example. Judging from the media—because of the way right-wingers have twisted the language—you'd think reproductive rights and health care have only to do with abortion. That's certainly the context of most of the media coverage Planned Parenthood receives. But abortion services are only one small piece of the many health care services Planned Parenthood provides. We're in the business of trying to prevent abortions with family planning, halting the spread of HIV/AIDS and other sexually transmitted diseases, and helping women have healthy pregnancies and babies. Our almost 900 clinics are focused on the entirety of women's reproductive health. However, the hard right's strategy is to create controversy that positions us—a group that serves more than 5 million people a year—as extremists on a political issue, instead of the trusted, credible reproductive health experts we are.

And the media has bought into the false controversy. A survey of the coverage of reproductive rights and Planned Parenthood in *The New York Times* from August 2001 to August 2002 is revealing. During that year, only four articles appeared that focused on Planned Parenthood. All were small blurbs in the National Briefing section, and all were about abortion issues. Reproductive rights in general received little feature coverage. The reason anti-choice strategists turn any topic relating to reproductive rights into a debate on abortion is simple: they know that most Americans support family planning and sex education so strongly that their only hope of eroding those rights is to confuse people about what is really at stake. They know that they aren't going to get much sympathy for cutting family planning funds, so they cry "abortion" to create controversy and sensation—and the media takes the bait. It's the oldest political trick: incite the public against one thing to distract them from another. Conflate contraception and abortion, and maybe the public won't notice that you oppose all contraceptives, including condoms, and that you want to end family planning and sex education programs, and restrict access to reproductive health care. If the issue were only about abortion, then why wouldn't its opponents work with us to reduce unintended pregnancy? Why aren't they clamoring for contraceptive research, sex education, and universal access to family planning?

Instead, they have so successfully muddied the issues on reproductive health that some reporters are practically illiterate when it comes to the topic. *The Washington Times* (like many other newspapers, I might add) is seemingly incapable of deciphering the difference between mifepristone (Mifeprex, also known as RU-486 or the "abortion pill") and emergency contraception. They confuse emergency contraception, which is intended to prevent conception and must be started within 120 hours of unprotected intercourse, with mifepristone, which can be taken up to nine weeks into a confirmed pregnancy. When one of our affiliates contacted the reporter about the mistake, he apologized and printed a correction. Shortly after, he made the same "mistake" again. When the affiliate contacted him a second time, he left a message stating in essence, "It's not my fault, it's my editor."

Another example of the media buying into the right wing's manipulations is the way the press covered Bush's reinstatement of the Reagan-era global gag rule. In announcing his support for this policy, which bans U.S. family planning aid to overseas groups that provide abortions or referrals, even if they do so with private, non-U.S. funds (see Chapter 8), Bush said: "It is my conviction that taxpayer funds should not be used to pay for abortions or advocate or actively promote abortions." That quote was reported over and over again in the media over the next couple of days—as though Bush had effected a basic change in the way our money is spent abroad.

But the media was passing along misinformation: the fact is that since 1973, when the Helms Amendment passed, preventing USAID from directly financing foreign abortion-related services, *not a single U.S. dollar* has been spent on such purposes. The media failed to report the global gag rule as an attack on family planning funding, and simply accepted, uncritically, the anti-choice characterization of the rule as preventing abortion funding. Moreover, they failed to report on the irony that family planning prevents the need for abortion in the first place. Instead, the media repeated Bush's deliberate mischaracterization of the situation, with such headlines as "Bush Halts Funding Used for Abortions" in the *Houston Chronicle*. Bush *couldn't* halt it—because it hadn't existed for nearly three decades.

When some newspapers did eventually correct the mistake, they often presented the information as a matter of opinion, not fact. For instance, the *Boston Herald* reported that "U.S. Rep. Martin T. Meehan (D–Lowell) asserted that U.S. funds are not directly used for abortions," as if this was simply his belief, his "assertion." The media's handling of the gag rule amounts to parroting, not reporting.

The Washington Post used the opportunity to run three prominent stories that examined the reactions of American abortion rights supporters and opponents, but offered no insights on the rule's overall impact abroad, which is the real heart of the matter. Once again, the press demonstrated its completely myopic view of reproductive rights issues: the discussion always has to be about abortion, even when, as is the case with reinstating the global gag rule, the issue had nothing whatsoever to do with abortion. Because the Bush administration policies compromise *all* international family planning efforts, the reproductive health of millions of women worldwide has been endangered. Now, that's a big story. But the vast majority of the articles written on the global gag rule were editorials and op-eds, not features. Feature writers, who should have been doing factual analyses of the impact of the policy on the impoverished populations who would be hardest hit, left that job to editorial writers—again, as though this was just a matter of "opinion." Why does any article that has anything to do with reproductive rights—in this case, family planning—have to be relegated to the opinion pages?

Similarly, out of six articles written on the defunding of the United Nations Population Fund, only one appeared on the front page. Again, most of the articles on this situation, which affected women all over the world, appeared in the editorial section. Why didn't the international section do a news story that looked at the dire impact of this defunding on real women?

BEYOND ABORTION:
COVERING REPRODUCTIVE HEALTH

Planned Parenthood and its affiliates are the nation's oldest and most trusted experts on the topic of reproductive health. So you would think the media would turn to us when they do stories on sexual health and family planning. Women's magazines do—and fortunately, that's where most women get their information on the subject. But thanks to the right wing's having so successfully positioned us as an abortion provider in the eyes of the press, and therefore "controversial," other media seldom call us for an informed opinion on women's health issues. The truth is that daily newspapers just don't cover women's reproductive health issues very well—or very often (unless, of course, they relate to abortion).

It's a different matter when an issue involving women's health *also* involves *men* and sex. Then the media takes note. For example, for years there were few if any major stories about the fact that in most states, women's contraceptives weren't covered under insurance plans. The Pill had been in existence for thirty-five years and was an essential part of many women's family planning, yet only one-third of insurance plans covered oral contraceptives for women—which is one reason why women spent 68 percent more than men for out-of-pocket health care expenses. To rectify this injustice, in 1996, Planned Parenthood began fighting to get state legislatures to pass contraceptive equity legislation. In 1997, the Equity in Prescription Insurance and Contraceptive Coverage Act was introduced in Congress. By the end of 2003, twenty-one states had passed contraceptive coverage bills—a stunning victory, although I doubt you read about it in your newspaper. No: it took Viagra to make the topic of insurance inequities newsworthy. As soon as Viagra came on the scene, insurance companies jumped to add it to their plans. When companies that had been unwilling to cover contraceptives agreed to cover Viagra, not even the media could resist the irony of that story, so the issue finally got reported.

Now, I applaud Bob Dole's healthy messages about sexuality. But why should it take men's sexual performance problems to get media coverage about a reproductive health issue for women? And why, even when the press did cover it, were there only 168 stories on state contraceptive coverage bills—bills affecting people in nearly three-quarters of the states in the union—compared with 1,272 on states' so-called partial-birth abortion bills?

I yearn for media coverage that digs deep, that brings clarity to real issues. For instance, just what is the real issue of choice? It isn't a euphemism for abortion. Choice is about making deliberate childbearing decisions, considering all medical and moral options. Without coercion or government interference. It's about women having an equal place at life's table. It's about truly valuing children enough to make sure they're wanted and loved.

Reporters often ask me, Why don't we sit down with the other side and find middle ground? My answer is, "I would love to. The middle ground is preventing unintended pregnancy. That's what reduces abortions. Let's talk about that."

I'd rather have smallpox than write a column on abortion, because people's minds are locked.

—Molly Ivins

"BALANCE" TILTED TOWARD THE RIGHT

One of the ways the right-wingers have been able to get attention, sometimes with dangerous outcomes, is by making use of the media's canon of "balance." In theory, it certainly is fair to get perspectives on both—or better yet, many—sides of an issue. For instance, if you're doing a story about parental consent laws, it makes good sense not just to interview politicians but to talk to some teenage girls who will be affected by the laws (something rarely done). But in practice, the media's interpretation of "balance" usually amounts to giving undue airtime and attention to a minority extremist group that opposes the position of the majority of Americans. When people who are on the fringe of an issue debate people who represent the majority, the exposure legitimizes the fringe and runs the risk of making representatives of the mainstream appear to be extremists. That's *false* balance.

Any story I write about abortion instigates a flood of e-mails from angry anti-choicers complaining about my so-called bias. Often they're complaining about being called anti-choice.

—Kristen Philipkoski, biotech reporter,
Wired magazine

Coverage of the murder of Dr. Barnett Slepian is an example of how distorted this media concept of "balance" can be. Dr. Slepian was hunted down and murdered by James Kopp, a domestic terrorist who killed him because he was a doctor who performed abortions. Kopp gunned down Slepian in his kitchen in front of his wife and children. Kopp believed that it was legitimate to murder someone with whom you disagree—not a value, obviously, that most of the rest of America shares.

After Slepian's murder, I was asked to appear on a network TV show to discuss the killing and its implications. I was told it would not be a debate. And how could it possibly be a debate? Is there "another side" to the issue of cold-blooded murder?

But by airtime, the host had found a representative from the National Right to Life Committee to oppose me. "To be fair," she explained. Predictably, my opponent immediately tried to turn the program away from the murder of a physician and into yet another abortion debate. Fairness, my eye. Would you have gay bashers on to "debate" the murder of Matthew Shepard? Give Al Qaeda operatives airtime to present their views in defense of the bombing of the World Trade Center? Sociopaths don't deserve this kind of attention. Yet this sort of thing happens to me all the time. I can't say a single word about reproductive health on television without having to be shouted down by an anti-choice extremist, even if the topic is family planning or health care. The fact is, the overwhelming majority of Americans support reproductive rights. Why should we have to engage in shouting matches with extremists who'd like to see women barefoot and pregnant in order to get our voices heard at all?

On October 23, 1998, Dr. Barnett Slepian of Buffalo, New York, was murdered by a sniper. . . . In more than 500 stories, only six labeled his killing as "terrorism" or "terrorist."

On October 19, 1998, several unoccupied buildings at the Vail ski resort were burned by arsonists. In 300 stories about this event, the word "terrorist" or "terrorism" was used 55 times.

Why are journalists 10 times more likely to give the label "terrorism" to a ski resort arson than an anti-abortion murder?

—from " 'Terrorists' Attack Ski Lodges, Not Doctors,"
Extra! December 1998

Giving extremists media attention only encourages them. The most horrifying example of this phenomenon is the case of Paul Hill, another murderer who was encouraged to violence by the media attention he received. His journey to murder might be said to have begun on March 10, 1993, when Michael Griffin, a zealous anti-abortionist, shot and killed David Gunn, a physician who worked at the Ladies Center in Pensacola, Florida. Griffin was the first terrorist to murder an abortion provider. Hill, a fundamentalist preacher, was so inspired by the incident that on March 12, he used a pay phone to call a producer of the *Donahue* show. *Donahue*, eager as the rest of the media for an outrageous debate, jumped at the chance to put the zealot on the air. On March 15, Hill appeared on the show with pro-choice activists, a physician, and David Gunn's son. Hill used the opportunity to proclaim in front of millions of viewers that the murder of David Gunn was "as good as Dr. Mengele being killed."

That, of course, is just the kind of inflammatory statement TV loves. It's no surprise that Hill became a media darling. He appeared on several TV shows over the next year. In December, he appeared on ABC's *Nightline* with Ted Koppel. Koppel, buying into the right's framing of the issue completely, opened the show by comparing the number of legal abortions with the number of violent incidents against abortion clinics. In other words, he compared a legitimate medical procedure with terrorism and violence as if they were the same: "Thirty million aborted fetuses over the past thirty years since *Roe v. Wade* was handed down by the Supreme Court. On the other side of the ledger, 7,709 incidents of violence and disruption targeting doctors and abortion clinics since 1977 . . . [including] one attempted murder and one successful murder," he intoned. While he was counting, Koppel could have mentioned the 78,000 women per year who die around the world from illegal abortions, and the untold thousands of women who died in our country before abortion was made legal.

Koppel allowed a polite conversation on an unimaginable topic—whether killing physicians who perform abortions is justifiable! As "balance," Koppel had Helen Alvare of the Catholic

Bishops' Pro-life Committee on the air—someone opposed to abortion who *didn't* think murdering an abortion provider was justifiable.

On March 8, 1994, Paul Hill was a guest on CNN's *Sonya Live,* telling viewers that Dr. Gunn's murderer was a hero who was willing to lay down his life to fulfill "the commandment of Christ." Sonya Friedman pressed him further. "But Mr. Hill, indeed, you personally are not laying down your life. One might suggest that you are offering that message to others and they may be laying down their lives." Less than five months later, that's exactly what Paul Hill did. On Friday, July 29, he arrived at the Pensacola, Florida, clinic at 6:45 A.M. with a shotgun, and hid it in the grass. At 7:27 A.M., when Dr. John Bayard Britton arrived at the clinic with his volunteer escort, James Barrett, and Barrett's wife, June, Hill shot and killed Britton and James Barrett, and wounded June Barrett. Even after his murder conviction, the media was still giving Hill a platform for his views—thanks to the help of Florida governor Jeb Bush, George W. Bush's brother, who actually allowed Hill to have a press conference prior to his execution! The media covered the press conference and quoted Hill, thus legitimizing his words and actions, and allowing him to become a martyr, and perhaps an inspiration to others who would perform similar gruesome deeds. Such stories embolden anti-choice extremists, thereby imperiling the safety, and the lives, of reproductive health care providers and their families nationwide. The Alan Guttmacher Institute reports that 82 percent of facilities that provide abortion services experience some form of harassment, including arson and death threats.

The problem of false balance occurs not just in extreme cases of murder but any time reproductive health is mentioned. How is it that Planned Parenthood, an organization with a 72 percent public favorability rating, is always described as "controversial"? Why is it that sex education, which is favored by 85 percent of parents, always needs to be discussed with "another side"? And why do birth control opponents always get a voice when 90 percent of Americans use contraception at some point in their lives to prevent pregnancies? You can't get that much agreement that today is Friday, so why should it even be presented as a "controversy" that must be "balanced"?

I often ask reporters that question. The fact is, they're intimidated by the right-wing zealots and they admit it. One TV reporter—who had to ask that her name not be used—told me, "We once did a story in which we gave Planned Parenthood two sound bites and the anti-choice people one sound bite. The anti-choice people called the reporter, the news director, the general manager, and the station owner to complain. Now we have to give exactly the same number of sound bites to both sides, no matter what the story is." And guess which story she was talking about? Again, Paul Hill and his murders of Britton and Barrett.

Even the airing of a bookstore reading on a topic related to reproductive rights has to be "balanced" by other voices. I would venture to say that this happens to very few authors. But when my first book, *Behind Every Choice Is a Story*, was published, the book contained real stories told by me and many other women about all kinds of reproductive issues, from adoption to how they learned about sex to family planning, childbearing, abortion, and public policy. In other words, it's no single-issue book. I was thrilled that C-SPAN was going to air one of my readings in Washington, D.C. Thrilled, that is, until I discovered that my presentation was part of a "package" that included one hour of me talking about the panoply of reproductive choices—and two hours of a virulently anti-abortion panel. Why, then, did that same channel give Phyllis Schlafly a three-hour interview with no "other side"? Why did they present Ann Coulter, a right-wing pundit, unopposed? Why, when challenged, did they say they have to present "both sides," when the necessity seems to apply only to presenting opposition to the pro-choice message?

The "fair balance" canon also allows the administration to kill issues it doesn't want to deal with by simply not responding. Recently, Minnesota Public Radio's *Marketplace*, which is syndicated nationally on many NPR stations, expressed interest in covering *Access Denied*, an original and important study by PPFA and others showing the impact of Bush restrictions on international family planning (see Chapter 8). A reporter from *Marketplace* did an interview with me, and since the subject was highly topical and newsworthy, I expected it to run soon thereafter. When the piece never aired, we called to ask what happened. The response from *Marketplace* was that "we made a judgment call based on the balance of the news not to go with it." We later learned the deeper reason: Bush administration officials refused to respond to *Marketplace*'s requests for an interview. When the *Marketplace* producers were left with only my interview, they feared the piece would be "unbalanced." That's all it takes to keep the American people in the dark about the results of a groundbreaking study showing the awful human toll of our current foreign policies. Don't return reporters' calls for interviews, and the story will go away.

The right-wing insistence on "balance" has even affected free speech at colleges and universities. Recently, the Women's Studies Department of an Arizona community college invited me to speak for International Women's Day. Upon hearing of the event, the college president nixed the idea, explaining that if I were to speak, they would "have to get the other side."

False balance is silencing many reasonable voices in the media, voices in the middle. Take the example of Caitlin Petre, a student at Wesleyan University, who wrote an essay for *Newsweek*'s "My Turn" column about her experiences as an escort at an abortion clinic. The sensitive, thoughtful piece was edited, Caitlin's photo taken, but three hours before the deadline, it was pulled by top editors for being "too controversial." Caitlin told me they felt it needed a balancing piece, as did *USA Today* when Caitlin subsequently submitted the piece there. Now, people write "My Turn" columns all the time, airing their opinions without a "balancing" piece. It's an opinion column, for heaven's sake. Why should the media require an "other side" only on an opinion column supporting reproductive rights?

Because they've been intimidated by a violent, threatening, and well-organized bunch of extremists. And the right has called "fouls" on the "liberal media" for so long that reporters and editors are starting to believe them.

WHAT PRO-CHOICE MEDIA?

Reporters and editors are inundated with e-mails, letters, and calls every time they write about reproductive rights issues. The right is noisier and meaner than we are, and so they get a disproportionate amount of attention. One of the right's favorite strategies is to insist that the media is too liberal and pro-choice, causing reporters and editors to bend over backward to prove that they are not.

The accusation that the media is pro-choice got front-page, four-part series treatment in a piece David Shaw wrote in 1990 for the *Los Angeles Times*. Arguing that abortion bias seeps into the news, he presented evidence that the majority of American journalists favor abortion rights and that abortion-rights supporters get more coverage than abortion-rights opponents. What he did not say is that it is not just a majority of American journalists who favor abortion rights, but a majority of the American people, period. Nor did he suggest the fact that that there are far more supporters than opponents might warrant their receiving the additional coverage. Shaw did point out, accurately, that abortion tends to be covered as a political issue, rather than as the medical issue that it is.

Abortion is indeed a medical issue, a private health issue, and it should be covered as such. Instead, it has been politicized to the extent that every mention of any reproductive health topic has to include a rebuttal by an abortion foe. The lesson reporters and editors took home from the Shaw piece was not that newspapers should begin to cover the issue with more sensitivity and depth, as a health issue, but rather that they should be darned sure to give "equal" coverage to abortion foes no matter what the topic. They've bent over backward to appease the anti-abortion side. The exception is some women's magazines, which provide service articles about health care across the spectrum of reproductive rights. They don't need a quote from the National Right to Life Committee every time they offer their readers information on the efficacy of using emergency contraception if they've accidentally had unprotected sex. Maybe that's because, well, the women's magazines are edited by *women*. By contrast, few newspapers have women publishers, and only 34 percent of newsroom supervisors are women, which could have something to do with why newspapers give such scant coverage to reproductive rights issues.

At The Washington Post *you'd be hard-pressed to find a female columnist who's writing serious political stuff. There are very few female by-lines on the op-ed page. While women abound in the Metro and National sections, molding the opinion of the country is still being done by white males. My column was under extraordinary stress from 1991, when they wanted to kill it because they thought it was strident. I went on for ten more years. Finally, my column space was filled with "Hints from Heloise."*

—Judy Mann, former *Washington Post* columnist, author of *The Difference: Growing Up Female in America*

In the mainstream news media, the prickliness about being "accused" of being pro-choice is at an all-time high. It's impossible to ever discuss abortion as a legitimate health procedure, and to provide straight facts without having to quote the "other side." Recently, a *Los Angeles Times* memo on abortion was leaked to the rest of the news media. On May 22, 2003, *Los Angeles Times* editor John Carroll sent out a memo criticizing a reporter for being biased in a front-page story he wrote about a Texas bill that would have required abortion doctors to counsel prospective patients that they might be risking breast cancer. The writer had described the bill as requiring "so-called counseling of patients." Carroll wrote, "I don't think people on the anti-abortion side would consider it 'so-called,' a phrase that is loaded with derision." He also criticized the reporter for failing to come up with a credible scientist to quote to make the case that there *is* a link between abortion and breast cancer. "I want everyone to understand how serious I am about purging all political bias from our coverage," Carroll wrote. He also added, "I'm no expert on abortion."

Well, apparently not. The reason his reporter couldn't find a credible expert to quote about the "link" between breast cancer and abortion is that there is no such link and no one with any credibility would say there is. Searching for one would be a little like looking for a credible scientific expert to say that the earth is flat (or that evolution is debatable!). Even though the mythical link between breast cancer and abortion was for a while being perpetuated on a government health Web site, before a public outcry resulted in its being removed (see Chapter 6), no evidence exists to support it. It is true that women who have children are slightly less likely to have breast cancer than women who have no children—but by that logic, we should be counseling people that sexual abstinence causes breast cancer. The reporter was absolutely correct to call it "so-called counseling," because it's a presentation of misinformation. And it's anti-abortion misinformation like this that extremists often use to intimidate women, even in clinic settings, where women look up to medical professionals as authorities. It seems perfectly reasonable to me for a newspaper to call a lie a lie. When we're dealing with science, politics shouldn't enter into the editorial process. But somehow the issues have been so distorted that speaking the truth is now considered "biased," and "political."

Eric Alterman, who stated in *What Liberal Media?* that there may indeed have been pro-choice bias in the media at one point, has observed that any such bias is now long gone. As he said on a talk show, "Ever since this was pointed out in the early 1990s . . . they [anti-abortionists] have gotten more than their fair shake. I think that journalists have bent over backwards to be fair on social issues because they know that they are social liberals. And if they don't know it, they get hit over the head by three hundred Washington organizations alone that are on their case."

But the press seems so anxious to be "fair" about abortion coverage that they're creating trends where none exist. A story in the Sunday *New York Times* on March 30, 2003, reported on an apparent wave of anti-abortion sentiment among today's kids. Illustrated with color photos of pro-choice moms and anti-choice daughters, the story seemed to describe a real social trend in which the country was turning against abortion rights. But aside from anecdotes, the piece gave only two pieces of actual data, both of which showed a drop of a few percentage points since 1992–93. Although that drop might appear significant, it's a drop from the period when pro-choice sentiment was at an all-time high. And the reason support was so high in 1992–93 was that there had been a flurry of recent court decisions that threatened to take away the right to choice, which had resulted in much greater public awareness of the issues at stake. After the modest drop-off in numbers from the 1992–93 high, polls show that support for the right to choose has remained very steady since 1995–96.

Support would probably increase to 1992–93 levels or higher if people were more aware of how perilously close we are to losing the right to choose. This was the point I made to the *Times* reporter when she called me for the story she was doing. I told her that young women, who have never known a world without choice, might well change their minds if their own rights were threatened, and also that our experience shows that support for abortion rights among college students is as robust as ever. We have over 150 campus chapters of Planned Parenthood, and the Feminist Majority has just as many—we can't keep up with the demand for new groups. I cited a study that found students who enter college anti-choice often emerge pro-choice once they have had real life experiences that give them more compassion for a woman's life. The youth of the country, like the country as a whole, remains broadly pro-choice.

The *Times* reporter chose not to quote me, my statistics, or my point of view for the story. She was evidently "quote-shopping"—finding words to fit her idea for a trend piece. Since I don't believe there is any such trend, my quote didn't fit, and could have threatened her front-page Style section story. Where's the balance and fairness there?

Or more to the point, where is that anti-abortion "trend"? Like the link with breast cancer, it just doesn't exist. And yet the media are reporting on trends and pseudoscience fabricated by extremists.

THEY'RE "PRO-LIFE," AND WE'RE "TOO CONTROVERSIAL"

Even the right to air paid-for opinion spots is unbalanced. One of the strategies right-wingers have used to chip away at women's access to safe, legal abortion is advertising. They've used paid commercials to sway public opinion about the right to choose. One of the most high-profile and costly of these campaigns was sponsored by the Florida-based Arthur S. DeMoss Foundation, which spent an estimated $100 million on television ads with the slogan, "Life. What a Beautiful Choice." The ads, which ran on ABC, CNN,

CBS, and local stations, featured smiling children running through sunny fields, while women murmured in amazement that they'd ever considered ending their pregnancies. Another ad featured a large, healthy baby lying in a crib next to a photo of an in-utero fetus, comparing them. "The difference is, the baby on the left is just born—and the baby on the right would very much like to be." One organization that ran the ads in Colorado boasted that their commercials had resulted in a statewide change of 10 percent more people favoring the anti-choice position.

In response, the Pro-Choice Public Education Project (PEP) developed its own media campaign aimed at raising young women's awareness of the importance of choice. They produced a spot called "Old Guys." In it, a group of grim, graying white men in suits trail a young urban woman throughout her day, monitoring and correcting her every move. When she drops her change into a soda machine, they grab her finger and guide it to their favorite cola. As she watches TV, they seize the remote and change the channel. When she ducks into a hip clothing store, they hand her what appears to be a maternity dress. The voice-over says, "You wouldn't want some old guys in Washington making choices for you—then why are you letting them make the most important choice of all? Fight for your right to a safe and legal abortion—while you still have it. It's pro-choice or no choice."

The local stations that ran the anti-choice ads all rejected the "Old Guys" spot, with the single exception of a station in San Francisco. All four national networks also rejected the ad on the basis that it was "too controversial." CBS said, "Because these commercials take an advocacy position on the subject of abortion, they are unacceptable for broadcast on the CBS television network." Now, why didn't they have similar complaints about the "Life" anti-choice ad? Well, ABC told the *Village Voice* that they believed that the DeMoss ad was not taking a position on a controversial issue.

So, let's see: to equate fetuses with living children isn't taking a position on a controversial issue?

Meanwhile, our affiliates report that they can't run ads on perfectly legal and necessary health services in numerous states. For instance, in parts of South Dakota, you can't run ads on emergency contraception; stories about Mifeprex, the "abortion pill," are banned from virtually all local Westchester and New York City subway stations; and our Adirondacks affiliate wasn't able to publish an ad about the availability of Mifeprex at the local affiliate. Television is full of sex, but most shows won't take ads about contraception or choice. Only magazines—with women's magazines taking the lead—are willing to publish ads about contraceptives. And only recently, in the wake of the AIDS epidemic, have newspapers been willing to accept ads that promote condoms for disease prevention. But plenty of them ran ads for escort services and other sexual services long before they accepted ads for condoms.

Where's the real balance? Where's the common sense?

"FAIR AND BALANCED": AN ETHIC, NOT A RIGHT-WING SLOGAN

The right wing has become so obsessed with claiming "fairness" and "balance" that Fox News registered "Fair & Balanced" as a trademark. The words have nothing to do with reality anymore; they've just degenerated into a right-wing slogan—and an occasion for the Fox News network to sue humorist Al Franken for his use of the phrase in the title of his book *Lies and the Lying Liars Who Tell Them: A Fair and Balanced Look at the Right.* Fox, which is widely regarded as a mouthpiece of the right, alleged that Franken "is not a well-respected voice in American politics; rather, he appears to be shrill and unstable." Franken replied that "when I read . . . shrill and unstable in

their complaint, I thought for a moment I was a Fox commentator."
Fortunately, when it became clear they were not likely to prevail, Fox
dropped the lawsuit.

The media's obsession with "balance" and "fairness" doesn't
seem to apply to Fox itself, which is owned by conservative billion-
aire Rupert Murdoch, is loaded with conservative commentators,
and has a news department headed by Roger Ailes, who used to
work for the former president Bush. Nor does the media concern
over balance and fairness extend to television talk shows in general.
The Sunday morning political talk shows are intended to reflect the
opinions at play in national debates, yet the lineup of guests is overwhelmingly white male conservatives. In the year 2000, women represented only 11 percent of guest appearances on Sunday talk shows,
dropping to 9 percent in the period following the September 11
crisis. Women—and women's issues, such as reproductive rights—
are severely underrepresented on these shows.

*There are 1,500 conservative radio talk show hosts. You have Fox News.
You have the Internet, where all the successful sites are conservative. The
ability to reach people with our point of view is like nothing we have ever
seen before!*

—Paul Weyrich, cofounder of the
Heritage Foundation

One of the right's strategies for getting such high visibility on TV
and radio talk shows is to simply shout louder than anyone else,
and to make more rude, obnoxious, inflammatory remarks. There's
a wide civility gap between us and our anti-choice opponents.
That's one of the reasons why venomous, outrageous right-wingers
receive so much airtime. Reasonable people protecting fundamental
human rights don't sound as entertaining as rabid dogs. Consi-

der that conservative commentator Ann Coulter has said that she wishes Timothy McVeigh had blown up the *New York Times* building, that all Muslims need to be converted, and that all reporters are "retarded." Not exactly sophisticated commentary, but it sells airtime. And books!

Right-wing on-air personalities get away with that kind of venom partly because their stations are owned by right-wingers. But they also play into the media's concern about its supposed "liberal bias." As Anna Quindlen said, conservatives hardly even need to bother playing the bias card anymore, "reporters have become so paranoid about accusations of bias that they work almost reflexively to refute it, frequently to the detriment of liberal institutions." The airways are full of Rush Limbaughs, Ann Coulters, Michael Savages, and other mad-dog commentators. Of course, when Michael Savage went so far as to tell a gay caller, "You should only get AIDS and die, you pig," MSNBC dropped him. Apparently there are some limits to the hatred that can be spewed. But not many.

We can't sink so low. But we need to be heard. Not only do we need to support more evenhanded talk shows but we need to start complaining about the vitriol on the air that passes for commentary. And we shouldn't apologize for airing our point of view just because someone calls it "liberal."

Democracy can't survive unless we embrace controversy. We need to air our differing perspectives, and clarify the issues. But we need real fairness. When TV networks appear to legitimize people who support murder, when right-wing extremists are given airtime but the pro-choice position is deemed "too controversial," when the media repeat inflammatory terms such as calling caring abortion providers "baby killers," and contraceptives, which prevent abortion, "baby pesticides," true debate is frozen in fear. The more bullies and screamers are allowed to corrupt the truth and to frame the issues, the more ordinary Americans feel excluded from the debate, or choose to exclude themselves. And truth is relegated to the cutting room floor.

The only way we're going to get fair media coverage, when the press is bombarded by anti-choice hard-liners, is to make ourselves heard as well. We need to be just as active in sending in calls, e-mails, and letters to newspapers as our anti-choice opponents. We need to monitor the media—including local media, radio, TV, blogs, and Web sites—and make sure corrections or responses go out right away. Complain. Compliment. Open our mouths.

Here's the hard truth: Americans must participate if they want to protect their freedom. Talk back to the media!

WEBSITE ADDRESSES FOR SOME KEY NATIONAL MEDIA OUTLETS

ABC   www.abc.com
Associated Press   www.ap.org
CBS   www.cbs.com
CNN   www.cnn.com
C-SPAN   www.c-span.org
FOX Network   www.foxnews.com
LA Times   www.latimes.com
MSNBC   www.msnbc.com
NBC   www.nbc.com
New York Times   www.nytimes.com
NPR   www.npr.org
PBS   www.pbs.org
Salon   www.salon.com
Slate   www.slate.com
USA Today   www.usatoday.com
Wall Street Journal   www.wsj.com
Washington Post   www.washingtonpost.com
Women's eNews   www.womensenews.org

EIGHT

EXPORTING EXTREMISM

———◆———

HOW ANTI-CHOICE POLICIES THREATEN
WOMEN'S LIVES AROUND THE WORLD

*HIV infection and AIDS are spreading dramatically and dispropor-
tionately among women. Today, AIDS has a woman's face.*

—UN Secretary General Kofi Annan

———◆———

Growing up near the U.S–Mexico border, I had always seen people
migrating in search of better opportunities for their families. It became clear to me early on that there was a connection between culturally appropriate family planning services and helping people
around the world better their lives. After I moved to Arizona, where
I was the CEO of Planned Parenthood of Central and Northern
Arizona, I worked with my colleagues in Mexico to develop family
planning clinics in the state of Sonora. I was touched to my core by
the community volunteers called *promotoras,* who were so committed
to helping their people that they took birth control information
door-to-door and opened their modest homes daily for consulta-
tions on contraception.

At one of the *promotoras'* homes, I met Maria, a mother of five
children under the age of seven. She was in her early twenties, but so

bent and worn that she seemed older than her years. With downcast eyes, she said, "I want to stop the babies but my husband won't let me take the Pill." The women—her peers and neighbors—told her to use an IUD. "You must do this for your own health and the well-being of your children," one told her. Maria had never considered that there was a way she could control her fertility without her husband knowing. Her face brightened, she stood up straighter, and I knew I was witnessing a quiet revolution. It was one that was being replicated in country after country where women were gaining access to birth control information and methods. Because women all over the world want the same thing—to live and provide a better life for their children.

I could see so clearly in Maria's eyes the personal meaning of the political phrase "women's rights are human rights." Reproductive rights are fundamental to both. Reproductive health care is a daily life-and-death issue for women in developing countries.

EVERY MINUTE A WOMAN DIES

Around the world, 350 million couples lack access to a range of family planning services. There are nearly 80 million unintended pregnancies per year. More than half of these result in abortion, nearly 20 million of which are performed in unsafe conditions each year worldwide, killing more than 78,000 women and filling hospital wards with women suffering debilitating illnesses from the procedures. Every minute of every day, a woman dies of pregnancy-related causes in the developing world, the majority of them preventable. In Kenya, a physician told me they measure the distance to medical care not in miles but in bleeding time—how many hours a woman will have to bleed while she travels on foot from her community to get medical care for miscarriages or unsafe abortions. In sub-Saharan Africa, reproductive health care, and the HIV/AIDS prevention integral to that care, is a matter of saving whole countries from devastation.

Until recently, the United States had taken a noble role in international family planning and health care. U.S. policies have always recognized that family planning and basic health care are essential to economic development. But now, U.S. global health care policies are being held hostage to right-wing ideology, endangering the lives of millions of women and children around the globe, and damaging our relationships with our allies in other countries. While preaching democracy, the U.S. government extorts silence in exchange for desperately needed health funds.

Beginning on his first day in office, George W. Bush has attacked international family planning programs. On that day, the twenty-eighth anniversary of *Roe v. Wade*, Bush reinstated the Reagan-era global gag rule. It was the first of many maneuvers to export anti-sex religious extremism, with devastating consequences to women's health care, population stabilization, and HIV/AIDS prevention programs in developing countries.

The international gag rule first came into being in 1984, at a conference on population held in Mexico City. President Ronald Reagan personally announced the new rules, sometimes referred to as the Mexico City policy, which denied U.S. family planning funding to any foreign nongovernmental organizations (NGOs) that provide advice, information, or referrals regarding the availability of abortion; advocate to make or keep abortion legal in their own country; conduct public information campaigns regarding the availability of abortion; provide legal abortion services; and procure or distribute equipment intended for use in inducing abortion—*even if these activities were paid for out of their own, private, non-U.S. dollars.*

Two organizations turned down U.S. grants rather than comply with the Mexico City policy: the International Planned Parenthood

Federation (IPPF), representing some 180 family planning associations around the world, and Planned Parenthood Federation of America, which has provided services in over sixty-one countries. PPFA alone lost $32.4 million per year in funding. Reagan's gag rule remained in effect from 1984 to 1992. It was such a disastrous policy that one of President Clinton's first actions in office was to rescind it. But the override lasted only as long as his term in office, after which the gag rule was reinstated by Bush.

Between 1972 and 1989, Planned Parenthood Federation of America used USAID financial assistance to provide 330 million cycles of birth control pills, 1.3 billion condoms, 14 million IUDs, and provided $92 million in financial assistance to over 439 family planning agencies around the world. The gag rule cut all USAID funding to PPFA.

Contrary to the way the media has reported on the global gag rule, it isn't just an attack on international organizations that perform abortions; it's an attack on freedom of speech and access to family planning. Funding for abortion itself had already been eliminated by the Helms Amendment, passed in 1973, which prohibited the use of any U.S. taxpayer funds for abortions overseas. The gag rule goes much further than the Helms Amendment, preventing health care providers from even *speaking* about abortion to their patients. It's censorship in the service of ideology, as well as a breach of the trust inherent in the doctor-patient relationship. The gag rule's chilling effect can't be measured—it is global bullying, coercing developing countries to follow the values and restrictions of the U.S. religious right in order to get desperately needed funding for health care programs. And this time the gag rule is being enforced much more stridently than the Reagan-Bush Sr. gag rule was.

The most important impact of the gag rule can't be measured. That is the chilling effect. It has been pushed in a very different way this time, under George W. Bush. Under the original Mexico City policy, once the policy was made by the president, the political people explicitly gave it to the career people to implement in ways that would not harm the underlying programs. "Let's continue to do the program," we were told. While damage was done, it was minimized as much as possible.

The big difference with the Bush Jr. gag rule is that it's much broader, it has a bigger agenda with zealots, if not fanatics, pushing it in a very aggressive way. In fact, even the Europeans are rolling over and being overpowered by the Bush administration. The U.S. dominates this field. No major organization involved globally does not get funding from the U.S. That's why the administration can get away with almost anything.

—Duff Gillespie, former deputy assistant
administrator, USAID

Poor women in developing countries around the world are easy targets for right-wing ideologues who would like to eliminate reproductive freedoms. They are not protected by our constitutional rights and they don't vote here. They're being subjected to international policies that parallel the U.S. anti-choice domestic agenda. For example, the administration is dismantling effective international family planning health care services and replacing them with faith-based, abstinence-only preaching programs.

Of all the anti-choice policies put into play by the religious right, the gag rule is the one that has affected more women than any other. The Reagan-Bush Sr. gag rule in the 1980s inflicted untold damage on the health and well-being of women around the world. Family planning assistance was drastically cut to such important countries as India, where U.S.-based organizations recognized that the groups that most needed support would be unable to comply with the terms of the gag rule. In many countries, women who use family planning facilities as their only health resource were left with very few medical resources, with the result that hundreds of thousands were denied proper health care. And thousands more have been put at risk of death or injury from unsafe abortions.

When a woman gets pregnant in the developing world, she may see no choice for herself [but abortion] if society or her family decides she should not be pregnant. Sexuality is a completely taboo topic—never discussed. Yet when a young girl becomes pregnant, those parents who never talked to her about sex will be the first to crucify her.

—Dr. Solomon Orero,
Kenyan obstetrician-gynecologist

lack of education?

While the ostensible purpose of the Mexico City policy was to prevent abortion, the evidence has shown that the restriction did nothing to reduce reliance on abortion. Instead, it made abortions more likely—and more dangerous. If you want to prevent abortions, you don't cut funding to groups that do contraceptive and abortion counseling, you increase access to family planning. In Russia, for instance, when contraceptives were rare, abortion was the primary method of birth control; with increased family planning, the abortion rate dropped by one-third. In Hungary, abortion dropped 60 percent with the introduction of contraceptives, and similar results can be seen in Chile, Colombia, Mexico, South Korea, Kazakhstan, and Ukraine.

In countries where abortion is legal, the gag rule results in cutting off post-abortion contraceptive counseling, the purpose of which is to prevent unwanted pregnancies from happening again. Beyond that, contraceptives are crucial for women to achieve higher socio-economic status and better health care in developing countries, and to bring their children out of poverty. If women delay childbirth, they're more likely to go to school and learn job skills that can improve their economic chances in life. Easing population growth is important to the environment, too, and to political stability. As former secretary of state Madeleine Albright put it, "International family planning . . . serves important U.S. foreign policy interests: elevating the status of women, reducing the flow of refugees, protecting the global environment, and promoting sustainable development, which leads to greater economic growth and trade opportunities for our businesses."

The Bush administration has not only reinstated the global gag rule, but has expanded its reach. Originally, the gag rule applied only to family planning funds administered by the United States Agency for International Development (USAID). But as you'll read below, Bush has extended the rule to programs receiving funding from the U.S. Department of State, too, and he has also cut funding to other important international family planning programs, including the United Nations Population Fund and the Reproductive Health for Refugees consortium. The refugees group deals with the world's most vulnerable citizens, including young women who frequently fall victim to sexual violence. We'll be telling them to "just say no."

Yes, it's true: the present administration has financed abstinence-only family planning to women who are culturally (and sometimes physically) powerless to say no; provides abstinence-only training to people who desperately need condoms to prevent unintended pregnancies and death from AIDS; and denies not just abortions but adequate contraceptive programs to people who can't afford to feed the children they already have. The gag rule and the rerouting of family planning funds to abstinence-only programs show a complete lack of sensitivity for cultural differences, not to mention a country's—and a woman's—self-determination.

Drafters [of the Global AIDS Bill] seem to want to follow the disastrous course of throwing condoms after a problem that is largely based in bad behavior. . . .

—Austin Ruse, president, Catholic Family and Human Rights Institute, April 10, 2003

It isn't easy to quantify the effects of the global gag rule, because they are insidious and difficult to track. Who knows how many poor women in Third World countries have died because they didn't have access to the condoms and information they needed to save their lives? Who knows how many have been forced to have unsafe abortions or unplanned pregnancies because the only health care clinic they could reach no longer had the funds to give out contraceptives? Who knows how many more children have been forced to live in poverty because their parents can't support them?

What we do know is that countless women and their families have suffered. Family planning clinics that refused to comply with the gag rule are struggling to meet the contraceptive and health care needs of their clients. Currently, more than 120 million women in the developing world state that they would like to space or cease their childbearing but lack the tools to do so. And while we've made great progress in global family planning over the past decades, the 6-billionth human inhabitant of the earth has already been born. One billion youth are in their prime reproductive years, with another 2 billion to follow in the next generation. The decisions these young people make about the number and timing of their children will affect our entire planetary future. With the global gag rule, we have taken a giant step backward in international family planning, population stabilization, and global relations.

We also know that the gag rule is making abortion more dangerous. Already there are 78,000 deaths from unsafe abortions each year, and the continued enforcement of the gag rule will only make that number go up. Deaths by AIDS have increased measurably, since people who don't have access to programs that provide medically accurate reproductive health information, and condoms, have neither the knowledge nor the protection they need to prevent HIV/AIDS. Under the gag rule, some countries have been unable to maintain their levels of contraceptive supplies and health care services, many clinics have closed, and family planning providers are having more difficulties working with their governments to coordinate health care.

Here are just a few examples of the impact of the gag rule since it was reinstated in 2001:

- In Ghana, 697,000 people have lost access not only to family planning services but also to voluntary HIV testing and counseling, and HIV/AIDS prevention education.
- In Cote d'Ivoire, the family planning agency has $186,000 less available for contraceptive supplies, eliminating services from nearly half its 92 distribution points.
- In Nigeria, funds for a multiorganizational health program that was to be used in seven states have been taken away.
- In Congo, the Association Congolaise pour le Bien-Etre Familial was forced to eliminate programs that served 15,739 clients.
- In Cameroon, several family planning clinics, a youth service, and a mobile health clinic have had to close.
- In St. Lucia, plans to train 218 "peer helpers" from secondary schools were scrapped; the program would have reached 12,000 school-aged children with information on preventing HIV and on sexual and reproductive health.
- In Lesotho, where one in four women is infected with HIV/AIDS, the Lesotho Planned Parenthood Association received 426,000 condoms donated by USAID between 1998 and 2000.

Now, because of their refusal to agree to the gag rule restrictions, they receive no more family planning supplies.

- The International Planned Parenthood Federation, made up of more than 150 autonomous family planning agencies working in 180 countries, lost $8 million in U.S. government funds.

Here's a closer look at how the global gag rule has affected four countries.

Zambia

Zambia is facing crushing international debt, extreme poverty (income is about $300 per capita), and a devastating rate of HIV, with nearly 2 million people—over 25 percent of its population—infected, a majority of them women. Discrimination against women contributes to the spread of HIV: girls are trained from an early age to submit to the wishes of their husbands and other family members, and there is widespread sexual abuse against girls. Zambia has a high fertility rate, at 5.9 children per woman, and one-third of girls become pregnant by age seventeen. About a third of married women use contraception, and a high proportion of births are unplanned. Zambia has a high maternal mortality rate—649 per 100,000 live births. While abortion is legal, it is hard to get because of strict requirements, and therefore botched clandestine abortion remains a major cause of maternal deaths in the country. The need for family planning in Zambia is obvious.

On the most basic level, when you take away a woman's right to be informed, you rob her of the ability to know herself, to protect herself and care for herself. You take away her dignity.

—Hilary Fyfe, president,
Family Life Movement of Zambia

Under the global gag rule, Planned Parenthood Association of Zambia, the only nongovernmental service provider in the country, had to turn down U.S. funding, which was a quarter of its budget. Programs, services, and supplies have all been scaled back, especially in the already underserved rural areas. As a result, three out of nine family planning clinics have closed, and the country lost $137,092 in contraceptive supplies. Condom distribution booths, which gave out 2.8 million condoms in 1998, have shut down. PPAZ has been unable to continue training community-based distributors and peer educators who had been working in twenty-three government clinics around the country, leaving many young people uninformed and without the necessary supplies to prevent sexually transmitted infections and unintended pregnancies.

Even faith-based organizations were affected: when PPAZ lost its funding, the Family Life Movement of Zambia, a Christian youth organization which relied on PPAZ to be sure they were providing the best information about preventing pregnancies and AIDS to their young clients, also had to cut back on its AIDS prevention work.

Kenya

Kenya has a dire need for family planning assistance: 25 percent of Kenyans survive on less than a dollar a day, and 44 percent of the 31.1 million population are fourteen years old and younger. Maternal and infant mortality rates are high; a Kenyan woman has a 1-in-36 chance of dying from pregnancy-related causes in her lifetime (compared with 1-in-14,000 in the U.S.). About 38 percent of women in Kenya have been subjected to female genital mutilation. Abortion is illegal, and yet it is practiced widely, reflecting both an unmet need for family planning and the lengths to which women will go to control their fertility. Some 3.1 million Kenyans are infected with HIV.

As a result of the global gag rule, family planning services in

Kenya, once the model for the rest of Africa, have been severely limited. Five family planning clinics, serving 56,000 poor and underserved clients, have closed. The gag rule has disrupted women's access to contraception, gynecologic and obstetric care, screening and treatment of STIs, and voluntary counseling and testing for HIV/AIDS. Poor women in slum and rural areas have been left, in some cases, with no health care at all, and no means to travel to another clinic. In rural communities, half of the agents who distributed condoms and contraceptive pills and counseled clients for maternal and child health services have been let go. One Kenyan physician said he has already noticed an increase in maternal and infant deaths, because reduced access to prenatal care means that women with pregnancy-related complications aren't being seen until it is too late.

Many people in your country see abortion as a political tool, but in my part of the world, abortion is an issue of life and death. We have to see it in the context of the woman who is living out there in a rural part of Africa who has very little information on how to prevent a pregnancy, who has even less access to contraception, but who has a twelfth or thirteenth pregnancy. She hemorrhaged after the last delivery, and barely survived. She's now pregnant, and she doesn't want to die. She comes to me, as a health provider, and tells me, "Doctor, I almost lost my life last time. I don't want this particular pregnancy." But I happen to be on projects that are funded through organizations that are funded by USAID, and I tell her that because of linkages with the American government, my dear sister or woman, I cannot help you as I believe you need to be helped. So please go and get yourself another service provider who has no linkage with American funding. But in most instances, I am the only provider in that district, so there is no other alternative for her.

—Dr. Khama Rogo, former president of the Kenya
Obstetrical and Gynecological Society, Kenya

Ethiopia

Ethiopian women face life-threateningly poor reproductive health. Ethiopia has one of the highest maternal mortality ratios in the world, with eighteen hundred maternal deaths per hundred thousand births. About 11 percent of the population ages fifteen to forty-nine have HIV/AIDS. With an average of 5.5 births per woman, only 8 percent of married women practice birth control. The abortion rate is high, even though it is illegal. More than half of all pregnant teenagers have abortions, usually performed by laypeople in dangerous, unhygienic conditions. Very early marriage, abduction of girls, and the common practice of female genital cutting expose girls to infection, death, difficult childbirths, and sexually transmitted infections. Fifty-four percent of the population is without access to any health services whatsoever.

Two of Ethiopia's family planning service providers refused to sign the gag rule. As a result, the Family Guidance Association lost more than $500,000, 14 percent of its budget, even though it does not provide abortion services, since abortion is illegal in that country. The group does, however, seek to educate local policy makers in the country about the dangers of unsafe abortions, and the role they play in Ethiopia's staggering maternal mortality rate. With the loss of funds, services to 229,947 men and 301,054 women in urban areas have disappeared. Marie Stopes International, a reproductive health provider that provided crucial post-abortion care for women who suffered illegal abortions, lost funds that were going to be used to train traditional birth attendants in women's homes, and for maternity services. Both organizations are short on contraceptives—Ethiopia has lost close to $56,000 in contraceptive supplies alone. The Ethiopian Society of Obstetricians and Gynecologists says it fears that the gag rule will reverse the few reproductive health achievements made in that country over the past few years.

Romania

Romania has an off-and-on-again history of relying on abortion for family planning, depending on the political situation of the moment. In the 1960s, Communist leader Nicolae Ceauşescu banned abortion, and sharply restricted the importation and use of contraceptives in order to increase the low birth rate. Women were rounded up at their workplaces at least every three months and given pelvic exams to check for signs of pregnancy. Nonetheless, women continued to have abortions—illegal and unsafe ones, which accounted for more than 80 percent of maternal deaths in the 1980s. We have also seen the horror of the children abandoned and uncared for as a result of these policies.

In 1989, Ceauşescu was arrested and executed. One of the very first acts of the new government was to legalize abortion and birth control, reversing the official policy of forced childbearing during the Communist era. Maternal mortality has declined dramatically ever since. But abortion rates shot up and remain high, partly because of popular myths that abortions have a beneficial "cleansing" effect, and that contraception contributes to cancer and weight gain. Romanians have a clear need for medically accurate information about family planning.

USAID funds have helped support Romania's transition to contraception instead of abortion for family planning. But the gag rule has interfered with this emerging social movement, to the detriment of women's health. With the imposition of the global gag rule, family planning has to be separated from the government abortion services. On the face of it, this might not seem to be a problem. But separating the facilities means that the family planning providers can't do post-abortion contraceptive counseling—which is precisely what women who have been relying on abortion as birth control need. If women traditionally rely on abortions, they aren't going to make a separate trip for family planning services.

But if such services are offered where the abortions are done, it's much more likely that a woman would get family planning education for the future. Another problem is that USAID-funded sex education materials in Romania have been censored so that they make no reference to abortion, which makes no sense in a place where the practice is so common. How can we convince people that there are better alternatives to abortion, if abortion can't even be mentioned?

Ever since President Bush reinstated the global gag rule, the world's poorest, most vulnerable women have paid an awful price. In the summer of 2003, the Senate voted to repeal the global gag rule by adopting the Global Democracy Promotion Act sponsored by Senator Barbara Boxer (D–California). The Senate sent a message to President Bush that the global gag rule is an extremist, ideologically driven position that is out of step with mainstream America. The House vote was very close, but under pressure from the White House, the House is unlikely to pass such an act, and Bush would surely exercise his veto if they did.

EXTENDING THE GLOBAL GAG RULE TO THE STATE DEPARTMENT: THE NOOSE TIGHTENS

Until recently, the global gag rule has only applied to non-governmental organizations. But the Bush administration has extended it to other international organizations that were previously unaffected by the rule. On August 29, 2003—taking advantage of the summer torpor that becomes most pervasive on the Friday afternoon before Labor Day weekend, when the media and the public are most likely to be distracted—President Bush issued a memorandum extending the global gag rule to all family planning funds administered by the U.S. Department of State. While it is as yet unclear which programs this will affect, most likely it will target refugee reproductive health programs.

That was just the latest of such cuts. In 2002, President Bush announced his decision to withhold $34 million that had been approved by Congress for the U.N. Population Fund. The UNFPA provides family planning services and HIV/AIDS prevention to people in 141 countries. One example of the work that the UNFPA supports is the REACH program in Uganda, which educates diverse community groups in Uganda to stop female genital cutting rituals and replace them with others that don't harm women; they've been successful in decreasing female genital mutilation by 36 percent in that country. The UNFPA has successfully worked with refugees in such countries as Afghanistan and other countries where it is difficult for U.S. program workers to enter. Historically, the U.S. has contributed as much as 50 percent of the UNFPA's budget, but the Reagan administration withheld funding based on claims that the UNFPA directly or indirectly supported coercive family planning practices in China, a claim that was never substantiated. Clinton restored U.S. funding for the UNFPA, but Bush Jr. cut it once more, again based on the fact that family planning programs operated in China, even though the administration's own investigators said that those programs were not involved in coercive family planning or abortion practices.

According to the United Nations Population Fund, the loss of $34 million from the United States will lead to 2 million unwanted pregnancies, 800,000 induced abortions, 4,700 maternal deaths, and 77,000 maternal and child deaths.

Since late fall 2002, the Bush administration has withheld assistance to the Reproductive Health for Refugees Consortium, which provides reproductive health care in refugee settings. It stopped funding an AIDS program for African and Asian refugees because the consortium includes the Marie Stopes International (MSI), the large reproductive health organization, which the administration claims supports coercive family planning and abortions in China. The consortium also includes CARE, the American Refugee Committee, International Rescue Committee, Women's Commission for Refugee Reproductive Health, Johns Hopkins Committee, John Snow International, and Columbia University's Department of Population and Family Health.

The administration told those other groups that they could continue to receive the funding—$500,000—if they dropped MSI from the group. Those groups courageously refused, and lost the grant money that would have helped prevent AIDS among refugees. The State Department then tried to do damage control by spinning it to seem as though the members of the consortium were the ones causing the trouble! "We were disappointed that for reasons of solidarity with Marie Stopes that they should refuse our money," a State Department official was quoted as saying in *The New York Times*. "We had hoped they would show more humanitarian statesmanship than that."

UNDERMINING HIV/AIDS PREVENTION

The global gag rule has already harmed HIV/AIDS prevention work through its impact on family planning services that provide information about AIDS. But the Global AIDS package proposed by President Bush in 2003, which focuses largely on abstinence-only programs, will be a huge setback to HIV/AIDS prevention efforts around the world, at a time when they are most critical.

President Bush made headlines in July 2003, when he traveled in Africa and announced $15 billion in funding to prevent

HIV/AIDS. Speaking in Botswana, Bush said that his plan to fight AIDS was "an expression of the great, good heart of the American people." He poured on his "compassionate conservative" lines: "The average citizen cares deeply about the fact that people are dying in record numbers because of HIV/AIDS," he said. "We cry for the orphan. We care for the mom who is alone. We are concerned about the plight, and therefore, will respond as generously as we can."

Bush's words sounded good. And the press bought into them, parroting his stance that he was putting the "compassion" back into conservative. *The New York Times* went so far as to write, "his stance also reflects a growing feeling in one of his core constituencies, religious conservatives, that dealing with the suffering caused by AIDS in Africa is a moral imperative. In doing so, religious groups have forged an alliance with liberal activist groups that have long called on rich nations to do more to help." This was followed by a quote by Bush stating, "I believe God has called us into action." We do have an obligation to help—but we're not meeting it. When Bush made his speech, he knew Congress was not going to give him anything near $15 billion ($10 billion in new funding). A large part of whatever new money he does get for prevention— a third—will be allocated to abstinence-only AIDS prevention programs, which are not required to comply with sound public health principles. They are even permitted to lie about the effectiveness of condoms. Teaching "just say no" to poor women in Africa—who may have little choice when it comes to choosing their sexual partners— and then lying to them about effective methods of prevention is not just unrealistic, it's cruel.

What we're seeing is an evisceration of HIV/AIDS prevention around the world, not an expansion. In most developing countries, family planning and AIDS prevention and treatment programs share facilities. Every reputable family planning organization integrates HIV/AIDS prevention efforts into everything it does—

contraception, education about reproductive health, prenatal and postnatal care for mother and child.

Restrictions aimed at excluding family planning programs housed in these clinics from receiving AIDS funding are devastating to women in developing countries the world over, and these are the women who are most vulnerable to HIV. Where women once counted for only a fraction of HIV infections, now almost 50 percent of all persons living with HIV/AIDS today are women. In sub-Saharan Africa, women account for 58 percent of all HIV-positive adults. There are many reasons for their plight. Women are more susceptible to the virus than men. With their low social status, women are unable to negotiate condom use and safer sex. Women depend on men economically for themselves and their children, and are in no position to say no. There are high rates of sexual violence and coercion by husbands and intimate partners. And even monogamous married women are vulnerable to unsafe sex and infection due to the behavior of their husbands.

Abstinence-only programs, carried out by the fundamentalist faith-based organizations favored by the administration, are not going to do such African women any good—they will only appease the far-right constituents back at home. But at what price? Programs that don't offer condoms and rely on abstinence-only messages are tantamount to death sentences for the women they serve. The Bush administration's HIV/AIDS prevention strategy, ABC—"Abstinence, Be Faithful, and Use Condoms," based on the successful Ugandan model—has shifted to A and B, with no support for C. In Uganda, rates of HIV plummeted in the 1990s, cutting infection rates by two-thirds, because of a multifaceted approach, which involved everyone from village leaders to top politicians and the media in a war against the disease, providing not only information and education but also condoms, targeting key groups such as sex workers and their clients, soldiers, bar girls, students, and others at high risk. Without condoms and family planning programs to back up the prevention messages, the programs cannot be effective. And the effect of that will be many thousands of lives lost and untold human suffering.

These cruel policies also extend far beyond Africa. In September, USAID abruptly withdrew an $8 million aid package aimed at promoting and marketing condoms and other AIDS-prevention materials in Brazil, the country hardest hit by the epidemic in the region, accounting for 52 percent of all reported cases of AIDS in Latin America and the Caribbean. The cancellation was probably motivated by social conservatives within the Bush administration who prefer an abstinence-only approach to AIDS prevention, despite the many studies that show that condoms are critical to fighting HIV infection. As in Uganda, the Brazil program specifically targeted high-risk groups such as sex workers and gay men, and called for the development of a condom used for anal intercourse. The programs had been so successful that USAID singled them out for praise just last spring. DKT International, an AIDS-prevention nonprofit that runs many programs in Brazil, predicted that the lost funds for the Brazil program, and others like them around the globe, will result in millions of new HIV-related deaths. Phil Harvey, president of DKT, said USAID offered only one explanation for halting the funding: "They said they'd changed their minds."

In August 2002, President Bush withheld more than $200 million in funding for programs to support women and address HIV/AIDS in Afghanistan. After using the issue of women in Afghanistan to support the war there, and signing legislation for the funds, Bush determined that the programs didn't need emergency funding, despite the fact that Afghan women suffer from one of the highest levels of maternal mortality in the world.

ALIENATING OUR GLOBAL PARTNERS

The global gag rule has only served to further isolate the United States in international affairs. Once a leader in family planning, and an inspiration to the world, the United States now has the reputation of being one of the most regressive, ideologically driven countries on the planet. It's hard for other nations to respect the U.S. when their essential family planning programs are cut, when commitments are not kept, and when ideology that would be unconstitutional in the U.S. is exported to developing countries. In international conferences, the U.S. has cut a lone and zealous figure, opposing progressive policies that could save many lives. For example:

Opposing sexuality education and condoms for HIV/AIDS prevention at the U.N. Children's Summit

In May 2002, the U.S. delegation to the U.N. Children's Summit tried to block the consensus among 180 nations on a global plan of action to promote children's well-being and rights, because the U.S. opposed sexuality education for teens. The U.S. delegation claimed that the phrase "reproductive health services and education" implied a right to abortion and abortion counseling, and so fought to remove the language from the agreement. In doing so, the U.S. overturned prior global agreements that established adolescents' right to information about sexual abuse, birth control, and condoms. At the summit, the U.S. delegation also opposed efforts to provide special rehabilitation for girls who are victims of war crimes, which usually means rape. The U.S. justified this position by saying that the measure would be construed as providing information about emergency contraception or abortion to girls who had been raped. Unbelievably, the U.S. delegation—led by HHS secretary Tommy Thompson, and including representatives from ultra-right-wing political constituencies such as Concerned Women for America, the Heritage Foundation, the World

Congress of Families, and former Vatican envoy John Klink—even opposed the promotion of condoms to prevent the spread of HIV/AIDS. And even the world's children's agency, UNICEF, capitulated under intense pressure from these anti-choice zealots. The U.S. position was hailed as a "huge win" by the National Right to Life organization. It was a huge loss to Americans who believe in international human rights.

Doing an about-face on support of a women's rights treaty

In February 2002, the Bush administration notified the Senate Foreign Relations Committee that the Convention on the Elimination of All Forms of Discrimination Against Women was "generally desirable and should be approved." This convention, created in 1979, requires ratifying nations to remove barriers to discrimination against women in the area of legal rights, education, employment, health care, politics, and finance. Though 170 nations had ratified it, the U.S. is the only industrialized nation that has refused. In order for the U.S. to ratify the treaty, two-thirds of the Senate must approve it. Bush's initial support of CEDAW was a positive signal that might have pushed the Senate to pass the treaty, after two decades of pressure from women's groups.

But Bush backtracked. He informed the Senate Foreign Relations Committee that a new "careful review [by the U.S. Department of Justice] is appropriate and necessary." The notification was sent by the U.S. Department of Justice, which is headed by CEDAW opponent John Ashcroft, once again dooming the ratification of a simple treaty to eliminate basic discrimination against women.

Freezing funds to the World Health Organization

In October 2002, the U.S. State Department froze about $3 million of the U.S. contribution to the World Health Organization (WHO) because of anti-choice activists' objections to the WHO research program known as the Human Reproduction Program. The action was taken following complaints by far-right constituents that the WHO conducts research on mifepristone—the "abortion pill"—with other funding sources. No U.S. monies are spent on mifepristone research, but the Bush administration withheld its contribution to WHO as a coercive tool anyway.

Reversing positions at a population conference

At the 1994 International Conference on Population and Development (ICPD) in Cairo, the United States helped forge an unprecedented global consensus. The ICPD produced a Programme of Action that is like a road map, a step-by-step plan for ensuring that all individuals in the world have education, health care—including reproductive health care—and access to family planning. And for the first time, the world's nations agreed to fully respect women and support women's empowerment as central to the world's health and development. This agreement earned the approval of 179 nations, and the acclaim of citizens' groups and religious leaders around the world. It represented a fundamental shift in the way governments approached population stabilization, environmental protection, and economic development.

The support of the U.S. Congress and the administration is crucial to the implementation of this worldwide plan of action. But since 1994, both have wavered in their commitment. In 1995, following the right-wing "Gingrich Revolution," Congress backed away from the Cairo program, sharply cutting funds for population and family planning programs overseas. In November 2002, a U.N. regional meeting was held to review the progress implementing the goals that were agreed upon at the ICPD. Representatives of the Bush administration took a firm stance that language about the public health problem of unsafe abortions be deleted from the conference document because it implied a right to *safe* abortion. The U.S. delegation insisted on abstinence-only sexuality education for teens, inserted governmental support of faith-based organizations, and opposed securing contraceptive supplies, which are in critically short supply. The delegates were some of the right wing's all-stars: John Klink, former advisor to the Vatican's U.N. mission and a leading opponent of family planning services, including condoms; Pedro Moreno, an abstinence-only proponent; and Louise Oliver, junior State Department appointee who once headed Harvard's Students for Life.

Attempting to derail an international population conference in Asia, I against 32

For most of the world, the Cairo consensus is a matter of settled policy, so the focus now is to ensure its implementation. But in December 2002, the Bush administration attempted to sabotage the Cairo Consensus—at the Fifth Asian and Pacific Conference in Bangkok. The purpose of the conference was for Asian and Pacific nations to discuss the health and well-being of their citizens and countries, and to affirm their commitment to the 1994 ICPD Programme of Action. Claiming that the agreement "promoted abortion and underage sex," the Bush administration delegates tried to strong-arm Asian nations into watering down the global consensus, and suggested substitute language that would dismantle sex education, undermine condom use in HIV/AIDS prevention, and water down policies intended to prevent and treat unsafe abortion. Moreover, they maintained that our nation's official policy is that life begins at conception—even though our nation's people, and the laws of the land, say otherwise.

The Asian and Pacific nations maintained a united front, however, challenging the administration's anti-family-planning, anti-health-education proposals. In the end, the U.S. delegation was isolated, and the Asian and Pacific nations voted 32–I against us on a progressive plan of action that affirms and strengthens previous agreements to ensure that all couples and individuals have the right to determine freely and responsibly the number and spacing of their children.

The Bush administration and its congressional allies have effectively dismantled many international family planning programs in the developing world, and alienated most of the countries in the industrialized world with their extremist anti-sex, anti-family-planning policies. These rigid, hard-right positions are not only cruel, they are politically destabilizing. We are losing allies in the international community, and it's no wonder. It's time we insist that Congress overturn the international gag rule, ratify international family planning treaties, and stop being held hostage to extremists. As with the environmental treaties that the U.S. has failed to ratify, the very future of the world is at stake. We must act now to defeat the global gag rule, and ensure that women in developing countries have a better chance at controlling their fertility, and living out their lives.

NINE

FIGHTING FORWARD

➤━◆

A NEW PRO-CHOICE CRUSADE

*No woman can call herself free who does not own and control
her own body. No woman can call herself free until she can choose
consciously whether she will or will not be a mother.*

—Margaret Sanger

With just a one-vote margin protecting Roe *in the Supreme Court,
pro-choice Americans cannot take these fundamental rights for
granted. The threats we face to our rights to choose are real and dangerous and already coming our way. This is the time for pro-choice
Americans to be heard!*

—Senator Barbara Boxer (D–California)

━━━━━━━➤◆━━━━━━━

Margaret Sanger undertook the crusade for women's freedom in
1914. Birth control and abortion were illegal then. Many women in
the U.S. died in childbirth or as a result of illegal and unsafe abortions, just as so many women in the developing world do today. By
1974, when I took my first job with Planned Parenthood, many of

us thought the battle for reproductive freedom had been won. We already had the Pill, and federally funded family planning programs for low-income women, and *Roe v. Wade* had been decided the year before. Thirty years later, we know we were wrong. Reproductive choice remains the most intensely personal and the most heatedly political issue that our country faces. And thanks to the extraordinarily vicious war on choice, our rights have been progressively rolled back ever since the day *Roe* was announced. We must not just fight back—we must fight forward.

Today many women still cannot call themselves free, particularly young and poor women, because they do not have access to the information and services they need to make choices about their reproductive futures. As we've seen throughout this book, the people who would strip women of reproductive rights are doing everything they can to take away our freedoms on many and diverse fronts: by way of the judicial, legislative, and regulatory arms of the government; through the media; through individual harassment; and even through terrorism. They have gone a long way toward succeeding, because they are both highly motivated and extremely well organized. They have taken advantage of our complacency—our false sense of security that after more than a generation, access to birth control could not possibly be taken away, and that *Roe v. Wade* will remain the law of the land. They are fueled by money and zeal, and fired by the belief that women should not be in control of their own bodies, their destinies, their dreams.

But they can only succeed if we let them.

It's time for a new pro-choice crusade to create a social and political climate so supportive of reproductive self-determination that no one will dare challenge its core value to women, men, youth, families—and to society. It is time for us to show our unequivocal passion for women's human rights. This is nothing less than a crusade for social justice.

The majority of Americans trust women to make their own morally responsible family planning decisions without the intervention of the government. Even many of those who oppose abortion for themselves still believe it is a matter of individual choice, that the government should stay out of our bedrooms and out of our doctors' offices. If everyone who claims to be pro-choice stood up and said so in unison one day, I wouldn't have needed to write this book. So don't be afraid to assert your position and don't hesitate to lay claim to the language of rights and justice. The moral high ground is ours.

IF YOU'RE PRO-CHOICE YOU'RE IN GOOD COMPANY

Americans who believe in reproductive freedoms are the majority. The people of the United States are clear, and have been unwavering for years, about the importance of family planning and sex education.

- Ninety percent of Americans support access to family planning.
- Seven in ten Americans favor increased public spending for family planning.
- Eight in ten support comprehensive sexuality education.
- Fifty-four percent of voters say it is personally important to them that abortion remains accessible.
- Seventy percent believe abortion should be legal, a decision for a woman, her doctor, and her conscience—but not the government.

A GRASSROOTS MOVEMENT: MOBILIZING FROM THE BOTTOM UP

People can change opinions by being very vocal, by writing letters and band-ing with other people, going to meetings and voicing opinions at the local level. At the school board, they should be talking against abstinence-only. The county supervisors in my county tried to pass a policy that if groups did family planning and gave any abortion information the county would de-fund them for everything else. We stopped that. It's right there in front of you at home. You can make a difference.

—Representative Loretta Sanchez (D–California)

Women's rights to reproductive freedom were won from the top down the first time, through court cases, culminating with the *Roe v. Wade* decision. This time we must fight from the bottom up—to preserve the rights we still have, to win back those we have lost, and to eliminate the barriers to women exercising those rights. The strength of our voices and our numbers can ensure that women in this country and around the world have reproductive freedom. But we will need new blood and new energy in the movement—people who are willing to roll up their sleeves and do the work. We will need to build the strength of pro-choice organizations in order to activate a massive grassroots constituency that can shape public policy. And we must commit to win.

The very core of winning our rights "from the bottom up" re-lies on each one of us assuming everyday leadership and participa-tion in our local communities, whether that means running an organization, chairing a project, or stuffing envelopes. The hard reality is that while support for pro-choice issues is high, choice will be lost unless many more supporters become activists. Mere "support" without action doesn't get us anywhere. We must build a critical mass of passionate activists whose individual actions will collectively shift the social and political climate.

We have changed the world once. We must do so again.

As a result of the advances we've already made, women have gained status and power—the power that comes from self-determination, sexual autonomy, and gender equality. This is not power to run over others but the power to achieve our goals in life, the power to achieve our potential as human beings. And that is exactly what the small but vocal minority of anti-choice activists wants to take away from us: our power and our freedom.

We're facing the toughest battle ever. At this writing, anti-choice politicians control the White House and both chambers of Congress. While pro-choice governors lead in twenty-three states, the state legislatures are overwhelmingly anti-choice. In terms of public attention, the nation has been distracted by war, fears of terrorism, and a sagging economy, and most people are unaware of how dire the threats to reproductive freedoms are at this moment in history.

We can no longer rely on the courts at either the federal or the state level to protect our right to choose. If and when George W. Bush appoints one or two new justices to the Supreme Court, and they are confirmed by the Senate, what's left of *Roe* may well vanish. If that happens and it's left to the states to decide their own laws about abortion and birth control, it's likely that conservative ones like Idaho, Louisiana, Michigan, Mississippi, Missouri, North Dakota, Ohio, Pennsylvania, Utah, West Virginia, and Wyoming will rush to deny access. Abortion rights will probably remain available in more liberal states, particularly those on the coasts, but only to those who can afford them, and those who can travel there. And, even then, availability will continue only until Congress is able to outlaw abortion throughout the nation and/or criminalize travel across state lines for abortion, as Senator Rick Santorum has already suggested doing. Abortion rights and access aside, family planning and all reproductive and sexual rights will continue to be threatened as more states adopt gag rules that reduce access to family planning services for low-income women, or eliminate their family planning programs altogether—as has already happened in the bellwether state of Missouri. The forces arrayed against a woman's fundamental human and civil right to make her own childbearing decisions aim to dismantle that right entirely.

That's why the active engagement of each and every American who values liberty and justice, not to mention the health and lives of women, is so urgent. It's time for us to raise our voices and say *enough*! Enough to elected officials who virtually disregard the beliefs of their constituents on these issues because they're in the pocket of extremists. Enough to the media, which pay far too much attention to the marginal viewpoints promoted by religious political extremist groups. Enough to the restrictive policies that are harming young and low-income women. Enough to policies that demean and humiliate women by denying our moral autonomy to make our own reproductive decisions. We've had it with policy makers who want to send women back to the second-class status we had in the 1950s and before. Enough!

Now, the question I am most often asked is "how." Well, there is no silver bullet, but there is a way. It's simple to describe, but it's not easy to do. In fact, it may well be the hardest work we have ever done, but it is the most important.

HOW TO FIGHT FORWARD: THE EXAMPLE OF CONTRACEPTIVE EQUITY

First they ignore you, then they laugh at you, then they fight you, then you win.

—Mahatma Gandhi

We've learned from experience how to fight back and fight forward even in harsh political climates. The first step is to get off the
defensive and set the agenda ourselves. When *we* set the agenda, *we*
decide what the public debate will be about. We decide the language
of the debate, too. Our campaign to require insurance companies
to provide contraceptive coverage is a model for how to do this. A
decade ago, no states required that employers or insurers cover contraceptives. It was one of the reasons why women of childbearing
age paid 68 percent more for health care than men in the same age
group. The idea to challenge this unfairness originated with one of
my former staffers, Kate Duvall, who wondered why the women she
saw every day at the health center where she worked should have to
struggle to pay for contraception. Kate, twenty-eight at the time,
knew a lot of the women went without pills because they couldn't
afford them. Out-of-pocket birth control is not cheap—especially
oral contraceptives, which cost about $30 a month—and its cost is
one reason why there are so many unintended pregnancies. Kate
asked the obvious, but crucial, question: "Why don't health care
plans cover birth control?"

Why not, indeed! For years, I had unthinkingly paid for my
birth control out of my own pocket, just glad to have it. But this
was a new generation, asking new questions, demanding new
progress. Why *wasn't* the birth control pill covered like any other
prescription drug? It's expensive for women, but a bargain for the
companies that employ them: it takes only about $360 to cover the
Pill for a year, but employers would have to pay about $20,000 to
cover a female employee's pregnancy. It made economic sense to
cover the Pill.

We looked for support in Congress, and fortunately, Senator
Olympia Snowe (R–Maine) saw our point. In 1997, after we
showed her letters from countless women, telling us how they
couldn't afford the Pill, she agreed to be a primary sponsor for what

would be the Equity in Prescription Insurance and Contraceptive Coverage Act (EPICC), requiring all insurance companies that cover other prescription drugs to cover contraceptives, too. Senator Snowe enlisted the help of Senator Harry Reid (D–Nevada) to ensure the issue had broad support. EPICC has still not become the law of the land. But, as a first step toward covering contraceptives for all women, Representative Nita Lowey (D–New York) led the 1998 campaign for contraceptive coverage to federal employees. I'll never forget when I turned on C-SPAN to watch the coverage and saw a sea of skirts—and female voices drowning out anti-choice politicians like Representative Chris Smith (R–New Jersey), who argued against the bill, saying that some kinds of contraception are abortifacients. Nancy Johnson (R–Connecticut) responded to him: "Is there no limit to your willingness to impose your [religious beliefs] on others? . . . [This] reflects a level of intrusion into conscience, into independence, into freedom, that, frankly, I have never witnessed." The vote came and the amendment passed.

The movement gained momentum, as other women joined our fight. The first of them was a pharmacist, Jennifer Erickson, then twenty-six, who discovered that the insurance plan provided by her employer—a Seattle-based drugstore chain, no less—didn't cover contraceptives. Her lawyer, Roberta Riley, of Planned Parenthood of Western Washington, filed a gender-discrimination lawsuit on her behalf in federal court, and the court ruled in her favor. Other suits followed, fast and furious: Jackie Fitzgerald, a thirty-seven-year-old working mother; Samantha Brand, a thirty-two-year-old Air Force veteran who served in the Persian Gulf; and Brandi Standridge, a twenty-three-year-old trainman, all teamed up in a lawsuit against Union Pacific Railroad to require the company to include contraception coverage for its employees. Lisa Smith Mauldin filed a complaint against her employer, Wal-Mart. Amanda Mewborn, a single mother, sued her employer, CVS. Three journalists took on Dow Jones, and reached a settlement ensuring contraceptive coverage for every employee. All these women had the courage to recognize an injustice, and stand up for what they believed was fair. Soon, as a result of women's activism, twenty-one states enacted laws that require insurers who cover prescription drugs to cover birth control.

Like those who oppose reproductive rights, we've realized we must fight for our rights on all fronts. So in the battle to win insurance equity, we're working for it in Congress, by pushing for passage of the Snowe/Reid EPICC bill; in the states, by passing state contraceptive coverage statutes or through state insurance discrimination or sex discrimination laws; and privately, by urging employers to voluntarily bring their insurance coverage of contraception up to the level of other prescription drugs to avoid being sued under civil rights laws. And we're encouraging individual women throughout the country in their successful attempts to require their employers to be fair: cover my Pills!

Thanks to all these efforts, the U.S. Equal Employment Opportunity Commission has determined that if an employer fails to include contraceptives in its prescription drug plan, that constitutes gender discrimination. More than half of all women in the U.S. now live in states with laws requiring that health insurance treat contraceptives on the same terms and conditions as other prescription drugs. And I can see us achieving 100 percent coverage by insurance plans within the next five years.

We did with contraceptive equity what we must now do for the entire reproductive rights movement: we took action. We saw the injustice, we got mad, and we decided to do something about it. We defined our goals, set the agenda on our own terms, enlisted champions, built coalitions, organized women and men around the issue, got the media's attention, and stayed with it. What we have to do to defeat the anti-choice extremists is take on other injustices, one by one, and fight forward for our agenda until we win.

THE FIGHTING FORWARD
POLICY AGENDA

- *Contraceptive equity:* Secure coverage for birth control in all prescription insurance plans.
- *Emergency contraception:* Make it universally known and available to all women so that we can reduce unintended pregnancies and abortions by half. Require hospital emergency rooms to provide it to sexual assault survivors.
- *Medically accurate sexuality education:* Change the language of all pertinent local, state, and federal laws and regulations from "abstinence-only" to "medically accurate."
- *Access to preventive family planning services for all:* Obtain full funding for domestic and international family planning, health care, birth control, STI prevention, fertility protection, prenatal care, supportive counseling, and education programs—with no gag rules. While we're at it, pass the Global Democracy Promotion Act, which would prohibit gag rules.
- *Access to abortion:* Restore Medicaid coverage for low-income women. Train the next generation of providers and make sure that laws and policies guarantee their physical safety.
- *Freedom of Choice Act:* Pass state-by-state and federal laws to guarantee that every woman has the right to choose to use contraception or not, to conceive a child or not, and to carry a pregnancy to term or not.
- *Research initiatives:* Invent better contraceptive methods, including microbicides that also prevent the spread of sexually transmitted infections. Fund fertility research to enable couples to conceive wanted pregnancies.
- *Economic justice:* Join forces with other civil rights and social justice organizations to assure that women can parlay their reproductive freedom into better lives for themselves and their families.

Our success with contraceptive equity happened slowly, over the course of six years, and it required organizing person by person, state by state. But we proved that when we recognize injustice, learn to work the system, set the agenda, and use the power of our voices, our stories, and our passion, nothing can stand in our way. Following are the simple steps we can take to fight back—and fight forward—on all the issues at stake in this war on choice.

CLEAR YOUR HEAD AND OPEN YOUR EYES

We encouraged [legislators] who do not normally support our views to support the emergency contraception bill for rape victims. How did we do it? By not snarling at them. We developed a dialogue. We said that rape victims would be left out in the cold. Elected officials don't know this stuff. They need education. Tell them you'd love to help them as their position evolves. Work it through with them to show them the options. Show them the statistics. Cultivate friendships.

—Lynn Grefe, former executive director,
Republican Pro-Choice Coalition

One of the secrets to the success of anti-choice extremists is that they've managed to make people feel ashamed of their sexuality and uncertain about their right to make their own reproductive choices. They've seared a big scarlet *A* for abortion on the consciousness of the nation, and they've managed to burn that letter on every aspect of reproductive rights and health care. We have to stop allowing right-wing extremists to be our thought police. As writer Sally Kempton has said, "It's hard to fight an enemy who has outposts in your head."

The first thing we must do to fight injustices is to see them for what they are. When women here and abroad don't have access to family planning, when rape victims can't get emergency contraception in hospital emergency rooms, when insurance companies don't cover the Pill, when young women are misinformed about their rights, when children aren't being taught medically accurate sexuality education—it's time to take notice. It's time to get mad enough to get off the defensive and take action.

Nebraska has a parental notification law for minors seeking abortion, with a judicial bypass process. The law is very specific about how petitions are to be handled, and mandates that forms and instructions are to be available to the public in all courthouses—without requesting them from a clerk. A sixteen-year-old in western Nebraska, where there is no Planned Parenthood, learned of the judicial bypass at school, and went to her county courthouse to obtain a petition. There were no forms or instructions visible in the public areas, so she went to the Clerk of the Court's office to inquire. They told her they had no such thing and gave her a marriage license form. She was, of course, very confused and upset.

Fortunately, the friend who accompanied her told her mother. Her mother told a City Council member, who in turn called Planned Parenthood in Lincoln. Lincoln PP had set up a network of attorneys to help teens with judicial bypasses, and they were able to help her petition the court in Lincoln, 250 miles away. Planned Parenthood informed the State Court Administrator's office of this occurrence, and they took steps to ensure that it did not happen again.

—Chris Funk, president & CEO of Nebraska and Council Bluffs Planned Parenthood

WAYS TO CLEAR YOUR HEAD AND OPEN YOUR EYES:

- Believe in your ability to effect change—and act on it.
- Turn off those right-wing talk shows!
- Buy pro-choice books and magazines, and pass them around to your friends; host pro-choice book club discussions.
- Log on to pro-choice organizational Web sites to get information and take action (see Resource List, Appendix B)

UNDERSTAND DEMOCRACY 101— AND WORK IT!

Cynics who complain they don't want to participate in the process because they don't like any of the politicians are hurting themselves and their country.

—Tanya Melich, author, *The Republican War Against Women*, political consultant and lifelong Republican activist, now an Independent

Fighting for our principles by participating in the democratic process is the most patriotic thing we can do. There are many ways to get involved—direct lobbying, volunteering to organize a cause-oriented grassroots group, joining e-mail alert networks, hosting house parties where pro-choice issues are discussed, or employing one of the many other tactics I suggest throughout this chapter.

However you get involved, remember that your elected representatives are supposed to work for you. But too often, they respond to those with the loudest voices, as opposed to the largest numbers. That's why we have to speak up. The right wing has long understood this principle and has used it to apply intense, effective pressure—relentlessly calling, writing, visiting, and e-mailing politicians about any issue they have targeted.

Another thing the right wing has understood is that it's often best to start small, working issues at the local level, developing strength along the way. For example, the right wing began its campaign for abstinence-only education with local school boards because school boards are very accessible to the public, and with a minimum of expense they can be easily influenced by a small but highly vocal minority. Moreover, school boards frequently become launching pads to election to city councils and state legislatures, so they are a good place to begin to educate elected officials about the issues at stake. If we employ similar tactics, we can make sure that *our* voices—representing the views of the 85 percent of parents who want their children to receive medically accurate and comprehensive sex education—are the ones that school boards hear. And of course the same kinds of tactics will work for other issues, whether local or national in scope.

Every American citizen, regardless of your stance on any particular issue, needs to take what was learned in high school civics to heart: lobby your elected officials, find out where they stand on the issues, hold them accountable, and exercise your right to vote in every primary, general, and special election at every level of government every time. The same goes for participating in the governance of the professional associations, religious denominations, and civic organizations you belong to. No effort is too large or small to make a difference. Bill Clinton started out as class president. Ronald Reagan was an official of the Screen Actors Guild. Whatever your political party or philosophical leaning, learn the process. Read up on the issues. Take part fully as a citizen of this democracy.

We have to look at the facts and tell the truth. When I point out the facts about reproductive health issues, many times women are shocked. We need to sit down with women (and men) around the kitchen table and share those facts. Then we have to get the voters to vote. Right now, in the United States of America, too few people vote, especially in primary elections.

—Roselyn O'Connell, president, National Women's
Political Caucus, and Republican activist

WAYS TO WORK DEMOCRACY 101

- There is strength in numbers: join a pro-choice organization, most of which offer easy ways to plug into the democratic process. (See Appendix B for suggestions)
- Participate in lobby days (opportunities organized by pro-choice groups to meet with or contact legislators about our agenda), letter writing, phone calls to elected officials, e-mail alerts, public meetings, legislative hearings, and other efforts to communicate with officials, whether or not they have demonstrated support for reproductive rights.
- Go to speak-outs and candidate forums—and ask specific questions about where the candidate or official stands on our agenda issues. If he or she does not give you a clear answer, press the question again!
- Visit your elected officials in person, one-on-one. Get to know them, and build relationships with them. Find out who you know whose advice they trust and enlist that person, too.

USE THE POWER OF YOUR VOICE

Women can save choice in a nanosecond if they just stand up and speak as a group. They need to do the same thing with childcare. With childcare: women drive themselves into the ground running around trying to do everything, but if we just all stood up together, we could get adequate childcare. We are so used to being women and doing what women have to do to keep their families together. We don't get mad enough. We need to fight back.

—Representative Eleanor Holmes Norton, (D–Washington, D.C.), and long-time civil rights activist

For too long, we have been silenced by people who think that "abortion" or "family planning" are dirty words. There's a kind of McCarthyism in the country right now, silencing our views on reproductive rights—just ask people who work inside the government who have been censored on the topic. For too long, sex, sexuality, and reproductive health have been taboo subjects. But the more we talk about those social issues, the closer we will be to creating a society that respects our reproductive rights.

Speak up! Your church group or your running partner is as important an audience as the one I have when I speak on television. Start in your immediate environment, and move out to the wider world.

But choose your audience. You don't need to argue with or try to persuade hardline anti-choicers. They are generally unpersuadable. It's much more important to make your pro-choice voice heard among those who are undecided. Speak to them; help them understand the validity of your views. Speak to the choir, too—we all need to be buoyed up by the support of like-minded people. And speak to those who are passively pro-choice as well. Urge them to join you in becoming an activist for choice. Educate them about how close they are to losing their rights.

However you do it—make your voice heard!

It's going to be a long war, with changing strategies, so we have to teach our children, too, to be vigilant. The language of choice has to be part of their everyday vocabulary. That way they can't be silenced without it feeling un-natural. It was the children that were the turning point in the South in the '60s and in Soweto. It has to be the children who are the turning point in this movement if we are ever to gain the momentum necessary to turn back the opposition.

—Audrey Bracey Deegan, Planned Parenthood
National Board, and Board of Planned Parenthood
of Rhode Island

WAYS TO USE THE POWER OF YOUR VOICE

- Talk to your kids' teachers, school administrators, and school board members about your support for sexuality education.
- Be active in the PTA and other school committees.
- Write a letter to the editor in your local newspaper every month—it's a commonly read page for politicians. Send a copy to every elected official you know just in case they missed it.
- Talk to your clergy about pro-choice topics; encourage them to play a leadership role on these issues in the community and suggest they give a sermon on the ethical value of choice on every Mother's Day or *Roe* anniversary. Even better, if you be-long to a pro-choice denomination, make sure that your group's views are heard in the wider community.
- Bring up reproductive rights with your friends and family, in-cluding your children. Be loud and proud in your perspective.

- Be supportive of others who are outspoken, and encourage them for their efforts in private, at meetings, and in public forums.

TELL YOUR OWN STORY

One of the most powerful ways we can create change is to tell our personal stories about reproductive rights—and the lack of them. Storytelling is an integral part of human experience, a powerful force in our lives, though history, literature, and culture. It's through storytelling that we learn to respect other points of view and gain empathy for a wider world. Stories teach and inspire us, and move us toward a better society.

The women's movement was built on stories. Women got together and talked about their real-life experiences—and learned from those dialogues about common struggles, real-life solutions, and eventually, political and social strategies for change. This form of kitchen table politics took the reality of oppression and, by unveiling the struggles of their daily lives, created a movement.

Hearing and telling stories can motivate us to become active. I have told you the story of my teenage pregnancy, and how much reproductive choice has meant to my life, and I hope it may inspire you. But far more powerful is the energy and motivation you get from uncovering your own history, and your own stories. Especially in the area of sexuality and reproductive choice, there has been so much shame that people hold their stories inside, and telling them can be a tremendously empowering act. After all, the anti-choice folks have never hesitated to tell their stories loudly and broadly, and their intent in doing so is to silence us.

Here's how New York State finally passed legislation to require hospitals to provide emergency contraception to sexual assault survivors: a constituent e-mailed her personal story to her senator, one of the state's most anti-choice. She told him she attended the same Catholic Church he does, that she is married and has three children, and that she had been raped but she'd been given emergency contraception in her hospital emergency room. She told him how relieved she had been, that in the face of this terrible assault, she did not also have to worry about becoming pregnant. She hoped her story would convince him to support the bill, which he had opposed in the past. That's exactly what happened. He voted for it, the bill passed, and is now law in New York.

Your story is your truth, and it also helps others with similar stories to feel validated. Stories can change the world. Think of the time that women including Gloria Steinem, Billie Jean King, Susan Sontag, Anaïs Nin, Susan Brownmiller, and dozens more came out as women who'd had abortions, signing a statement that was in *Ms.* magazine in the 1970s. That had a huge effect on removing the stigma of abortion. Their stories, and stories like them, changed them, changed the women around them, and helped to change the world.

Following is my daughter's best friend's story—which I learned only after I'd told my own story in my previous book, *Behind Every Choice is a Story*. It reminds me why I fight every day for reproductive rights—because they are good for children as well as for women—and it shows the importance of sharing our stories with the next generation, to inspire them to continue fighting forward.

My mother grew up in an orphanage in Waco, Texas. She always thought that if she'd just had a parent, life would've been so much different for her. But Mom never could exactly explain why her mother died. Someone told her it was a kidney infection, and all she could remember was there was a lot of blood.

Then, in 2001, in a conversation with her aunt, the truth unfolded. My grandmother had two very difficult pregnancies, once delivering a stillborn son, and another time, twins. The third baby almost killed her, and the doctor warned her not to get pregnant again, because she would not survive. Birth control was nonexistent in the 1930s, as far as she knew, and so she became pregnant again. The doctor couldn't do anything for her. My grandmother had heard there was a woman in town who could "take care of" the pregnancy. So, knowing she had three healthy children to raise, she made the only choice she could: she had an illegal abortion. Afterward, she went home to her three children, went to bed, hemorrhaged, and died.

And my mother began her life's journey as a motherless child.

—Karen Bryant

WAYS TO TELL YOUR OWN STORY

- Get together with a group of friends over coffee or wine and share your stories about reproductive rights and why you are so passionate about them.
- Ask your family members to tell you stories you don't know about your parents and grandparents regarding their life choices.
- Tell your story online—www.behindeverychoice.com, on your own Web site, or elsewhere.
- Host a house party and invite a local speaker to address pro-choice issues.
- Write a letter to your mother, daughter, or a friend about your story.
- When you write your elected officials, speak with opinion makers, or put your views in print, include your personal story. It will touch people as dry facts never can.

DON'T PLAY NICE

We fought back and defined terrorism as terrorism and we passed the FACE (Federal Access to Clinic Entrances) bill. We developed an organized clinic defense with volunteers. Bullies have to be faced down.

—Ellie Smeal, president, Feminist Majority Foundation

Our movement has a history of fierce, determined activism, starting near the turn of the century, when Margaret Sanger was arrested nine times for distributing information about birth control. In the 1960s, women ran an underground network (dubbed Jane) to provide women with safe abortion. Again and again, we've taken our case all the way to the Supreme Court to win rights for safe abortion, contraception, economic justice, freedom from violence, and more. When we were routinely harassed and sometimes violently attacked in front of our clinics, we fought back in the courts—and in the streets with clinic escorts, trained security, and media strategies.

Our movement has played tough with insider strategies (lobbying, elections, appointments, courts) and outsider strategies (clinic defense, marching, peer educators, coalition building, even civil disobedience). Nothing has deterred us from our mission, and we have left no organizing strategy unturned.

Planned Parenthood of the Capital Region (Austin, Texas) was about to break ground on its new health care facility. They had raised much of the money they needed and had secured a general contractor, Browning Construction Company, when Chris Danze, a concrete contractor who is anti-choice, got wind of the project. Danze organized a campaign to put pressure on all the subcontractors and vendors who were planning to work with Browning. Circulating the names of those whose arms he thought needed twisting, he had his Austin-Area Pro-Life Concrete Contractors and Suppliers Organization make thousands of calls and send thousands of e-mails threatening them with loss of business. One contractor logged 1,200 phone calls from Danze's group. Danze also mobilized anti-choice churches to put pressure on the subcontractors and vendors by telling them that there are more churches to build than Planned Parenthood facilities. Browning finally capitulated and pulled out.

But Planned Parenthood fought back. First they held a press conference, flanked by elected officials who stood with them, to break the story on their own terms. They declared their intent to complete the building, even if they had to serve as their own general contractor. Then Executive Director Glenda Parks took the matter to their supporters, appealing to a crowd of about five hundred at the group's annual public affairs luncheon. The event took in more than $180,000, topping all previous fundraisers. One large donor not only doubled his pledge, but, with the blessing of his Lutheran minister, vowed personally to make sure this building would be built.

Third, they asked people to use the power of their voices. So when their architect, Tom Hatch, received a call from Danze, "respectfully requesting that I not work on the 'abortion chamber,' I told him I've been working with Planned Parenthood for twenty-five years and I would respectfully ask him to stop harassing me and others on the project," he was quoted as saying in the *Austin American-Statesman*. Another newspaper, *The Austin Chronicle*, ran an editorial supporting Planned Parenthood, and calling its readers to action. The next week, over 1,500 people signed a newspaper ad to demonstrate their support for Planned Parenthood's work.

Soon an outpouring of support came in from all over the country—from donors (some offering to send a check if Planned Parenthood would tell Danze the funds were sent in his name), from contractors who said they'd be proud to build this health center, and from activists who contacted the national contractors' associations and told them that not only did they view Danze's actions as undemocratic, an attack on free speech worthy of the Taliban, and thuggery of the worst order, but that they planned to hire only those contractors who did not discriminate against reproductive health providers. This action is important because Danze says he is going national with his anti-choice boycotts. We don't intend to let him, or anyone with intentions like his, succeed.

Now is the time for us to use our collective power. With lives at stake, we can't be timid. We need to take the best lessons from our own movement's victories—and frankly from anti-choice zealots' victories—and make bold strides. That doesn't mean that we demean ourselves, or our cause, by adopting the dirty tricks and duplicitous strategies of those who will stop at nothing to oppose women's rights. Nor does it mean imitating the anti-choice extremists in their use of violence. It does mean, however, that we use every advantage, however big or small, to fight forward. We need to exercise the power and influence that we have. For example, urging senators to defeat federal court nominees who fail to affirm the Constitutional right to reproductive choices—up to and including filibustering—is absolutely the right thing to do.

A central component to effective organizing is discipline—in agendas, messages, and action. We commit ourselves to coalition building, even when it means having tough internal debates to accomplish that. And we must continue to embrace diversity in our movement. We stay focused on our mission and our message—even when our opponents use every trick to distract and divide us.

So don't play nice. The anti-choice forces certainly don't. Play smart, play strategically, and play with integrity. But play tough.

> We had a Catholic hospital that was sold to a nonreligious corporation, the Swedish Hospital system. When they took over, Swedish's CEO agreed to never do abortion services in their new hospital, and also to stop doing "elective" abortions in the ER and in the office buildings of their existing spaces. I was the chair of the pro-choice coalition in our state at the time, and demanded an appointment with the CEO. It appeared that he made those concessions to the Catholics as a kind of "good faith" gesture to solidify his relationship with the Catholics. He clearly thought that no one would care.
>
> We proved him wrong.
>
> We let him know, in no uncertain terms, that we would not allow him to squander the access that we had fought for years to secure. We let him know that serious benefactors and physicians practicing at Swedish were in an uproar over his actions, and that it was only because we were asking them to hold off that his front door was not mobbed by pro-choice protesters. We won.
>
> —Christine Charbonneau, CEO, Planned Parenthood of Western Washington

HOW NOT TO PLAY NICE

- Don't be afraid to use your power, whatever it is. If you are a student, you can creat an e-mail list to educate and motivate your peers. If you are a physician, nurse, or other health professional, become active in your professional association and organize it to support pro-choice policies and services. If you are a lawyer, volunteer to draft or analyze legislation for a pro-choice organization, or to do pro bono legal work for them. If you are a member of the clergy, give a sermon on the value of choice and pro-choice activism. If you are a parent, join—or form—a local coalition demanding comprehensive sexuality education in your schools.

- Join a march, a picket line, a protest on behalf of what you believe: numbers count!
- Spend pro-choice dollars—seek out businesses that support women's rights, avoid businesses that don't, and make sure they know why!
- Be a cyber warrior: send pro-choice messages to friends, e-mail elected officials and media outlets.
- Insist that any membership organization you belong to takes a public pro-choice stance.
- If your pharmacist doesn't fill prescriptions for emergency contraception, tell everyone you know and get another pharmacist.

LEARN FROM YOUR ADVERSARIES

I can't tell you how many members of Congress have said to me, "I agree with you but if I vote with you I'll have to raise more money for my next race." So don't just give kudos . . . punish those who vote anti-choice. People who are pro-choice must get much tougher about this. It's about prioritizing this issue every single time.

—Representative Diana DeGette (D–Colorado)

We've learned the hard way how a small group of anti-choice extremists have been able to hijack the political system. We can learn from their strategies now to protect and advance the views of the pro-choice mainstream. We need to move swiftly and surely, demanding that legislators vote for our interests and voicing outrage when the media display anti-choice bias. Then we must follow up by praising or blasting their actions.

We have to oppose anti-choice tactics at every turn. Don't let them get away with anything. If anti-choice picketers are coming to your town, then volunteer to participate in organized clinic escorting or rallies. Launch pledge-a-picketer campaigns, where pro-choice supporters commit to donating a dollar for every anti-choice extremist who shows up at their rally. Then tell the press.

Anti-choice extremists have used every local issue as an opportunity to advance their agenda—and they press their point in multiple venues. Whatever the situation, whatever the position, they let those in public office and in positions of power hear their voices. Organize your own pro-choice delegation and don't let any opportunity pass to make sure our side is represented—and heard. When local officials hear only from the opponents of choice, they respond accordingly.

Be pro-choice and proud—believe me, many who see you will cheer.

Our clinic applied for a zoning variance to expand our building to make room for our first-ever abortion service. The hearing on the parking variance was advertised and nearby neighbors notified, but no one had any inkling that any large-scale opposition was brewing. But on the day of the hearing, all the telephones were ringing with warnings that a large opposition group planned to storm the hearing and demand that no variance be granted. Our staff swung into action and managed to recruit a few dozen people to show up in support, but the opposition had succeeded in gaining the element of surprise, outnumbering us by a wide margin.

In future hearings, we were prepared. At the next hearing, about eight hundred pro-choice advocates attended, outnumbering our opponents by more than 2 to 1. In the end, the Board of Zoning Appeals approved the variance, and the chair of the board announced firmly that the hearing would be conducted on the subject of a parking variance and not on the subject of the rights of the fetus. The abortion service opened its doors a little over a year later.

—Scott Heyman, president/CEO, Planned Parenthood of Tompkins County, Ithaca, NY

WAYS TO LEARN FROM OUR ADVERSARIES

- Don't wait to be asked to speak up. If you see an anti-choice injustice, take action. And get your friends to do the same.
- Volunteer a couple of hours per week or month to stuff envelopes, pass out flyers, or otherwise help out a pro-choice organization.
- Make a donation to a worthy cause—and sign up for a monthly sustaining donation that's taken directly out of your checking account. Spending the equivalent of a latte each day will make you a large donor for most organizations.
- Ask obstetrician/gynecologists whether they provide abortions and patronize only those who do provide the full range of care to their patients.
- Get the agenda in advance for your local school board meetings. Attend frequently and get to know the people. Organize a group to lobby the board or to speak if sex education or stu-

dent health programs are on the agenda. Initiate agenda items when they need to be addressed.

BE PERSISTENT

The big problem is that people think they can't be activists and that one person can't make a difference. They think they need money, skills, and influence, but they don't. One ticked-off person can cause a lot of trouble, particularly on the Internet.

With e-mail campaigns, your e-mails had better be good, so people won't delete them. Start with friends who know and like you and write something short and to the point that gets them angry. Don't write a page. There's a lot of competition, so just give people a graf and make it personal. Always start with your base, an audience that knows, likes, and trusts you.

—John Aravosis, founder/president,
Wired Strategies

Again, we can take a page from the right, and be persistent. Whenever they have a piece of legislation that fails or a nominee who doesn't get an appointment, they bounce right back with the same initiative, and the same nominees. We must realize that even if we lose small battles, or have setbacks, we can keep on fighting—and win in the future. The Violence Against Women Act was introduced two times before its final passage, and the Nineteenth Amendment that gave women the right to vote took a hundred years before it was ratified. We can wear them down with our efforts, our numbers, and our courage. A tried and true battle strategy is to draw a different map to change the field of engagement if the current one isn't conducive to victory.

Lois Abraham and Jane Roberts—two women who just got mad—started the "viral marketing" campaign to get 34 million people to donate $1 each to the United Nations Population Fund after President Bush defunded it by that amount. Calling the campaign "34 Million Friends of UNFPA," they spread it by e-mail, phone, fax, and media stories across the country and internationally. They've raised almost $2 million from over 100,000 donors (many of whom will become activists) in just over a year and a half. In addition to the money and friends they have generated, the value of the public awareness they've created is incalculable. There have been news stories and editorials in most major papers and numerous electronic outlets. Organizations like the Audubon Society and People For the American Way sent e-mails to their constituents, and contributions flowed in from around the world. Lois and Jane are persistent. They intend to keep going until they reach their goals.

WAYS TO BE PERSISTENT

- Call your school board members, local politicians, and representatives often enough that they know your name and where you stand.
- Get pro-choice resolutions passed by city councils, county boards, and other local entities.
- Don't let the anti-choice people get away with lies, distortions, and harassment. Speak up right away. Let them know you are watching, and taking names.
- Monitor school boards and courses; complain if they do not include medically accurate and comprehensive sex education.
- Don't leave home without your politics: take flyers, brochures, and other pro-choice materials to share in your church, day

care, supermarket bulletin board, coffee group, and other places you go.
- If you lose a campaign, make plans to start another one.
- Monitor government Web sites, such as the CDC [www.cdc.gov] and the NIH [www.nih.gov] and give them hell when they misrepresent reproductive health issues.
- Let no attack go unanswered.
- Let no false accusation go unchallenged.

WEAR THE SHIRT

I was working in Orange County in the labor movement, supporting candidates. I was looking at proposed maps after redistricting and saw that California was getting a new Congressional district and it was where I lived. I found out the front-runner was lukewarm on many issues I cared about, like choice. I kept complaining to my husband about this. Finally he said, "Instead of complaining about it, why don't you do something?" So I decided to run for Congress. Some people think it's egotistical or self-aggrandizing to think that you could do a better job than someone else running for office. But there is no shame in taking it to the next level.

—Representative Linda Sanchez (D–California)

I once had a long conversation with the staff of a Planned Parenthood clinic in a small town in rural Arizona. We provided our staff with Planned Parenthood shirts to wear as uniforms in order to recognize their professional status. They told me that every day they had to decide whether to wear their shirts on the way home, because when they stopped at the store or to pick up their kids, people always wanted to talk with them about Planned Parenthood or choice issues.

I told them that that is exactly the most important time for them to wear their shirts! It demonstrates publicly who they are and what values they hold dear. This story became a metaphor for me, and I now look for all the ways I can "wear the shirt," to publicly demonstrate my support for Planned Parenthood and for choice. Show that you're pro-choice, and you're proud.

> Midland, Texas, has a huge Christian music fest every year. I go, wearing my shirts such as "I am the face of pro-choice America," "I spy sexism," and the like. During one of this year's performances, the male singer of the group was telling a story in between songs about a teenage girl who got pregnant, insinuating how improper it was. I called out, "What about the guy?" Being present at rallies such as this is important: we must show our faces, show that we are here—yes, even in Dubya's hometown—and we stand for choice.
>
> —LuAnn Awtrey, fund-raising coordinator,
> Planned Parenthood of West Texas, Inc.

WAYS TO "WEAR THE SHIRT"

- Put a pro-choice link on your Web site.
- Add a pro-choice message to your business card.
- Wear pro-choice T-shirts to the gym, put pro-choice bumper stickers on your car, and put up yard signs.
- Give the gift of reproductive freedom: buy organizational memberships for friends and family.
- Send pro-choice greeting cards for holidays, birthdays, Mother's Day.

TAKING BACK THE MEDIA BY TALKING BACK

We have to take back the media. The airwaves belong to the people of the United States. Both sides of an issue should be aired, not just the hate and venom of the right wing. They have fomented animosity toward government and poisoned the system.

—Representative Louise Slaughter (D–New York)

We must, in the end, create our own media ventures producing and disseminating programming on a wide range of reproductive and sexual-health-related policy issues, so that the airwaves are not ruled by the voice of the right wing. Instead of waiting for entrenched media conglomerates to support a reasoned voice in a world of Rush Limbaugh, Bill O'Reilly, Ann Coulter, and Pat Buchanan, we'll create our own "pro" media operations—pro-woman, pro-choice, pro-freedom, pro-child. Until the day comes when we have succeeded in that ambitious goal, however, we can make sure that the existing media, hostile or uninspired as they may be, hears from us, often and eloquently.

The general public is so busy taking care of life and its many challenges that they live by "sound bites," and the anti-choicers have done a masterful job of defining their side through sound bites, especially on radio.

When I worked at the Decatur affiliate we were often asked to be on a radio call-in show. The shows seemed to become increasingly hostile, with the radio personality seeming to buy into and even encourage the anti calls. It wasn't that we minded the calls as much as it was that the encouragement seemed to be coming from the station. Rather than refuse to do the shows, we asked to meet with the station manager and

the talk host. They kindly listened, expressed that they had no
intention of leaving the impression we had, and in fact were
unaware that they were doing it. After that the tenor of the
talk show changed and became less hostile.

—Karla Peterson, interim CEO, Planned Parenthood of
East Central Illinois

WAYS TO TALK BACK TO THE MEDIA

- Complain about anti-choice commentators or bias. You can
  call, write, or e-mail, but do it right away, as the media moves
  fast.
- Call in to talk shows. Challenge any speaker who opposes reproductive choice and voice support for those who advocate for
  choice.
- Call your local reporters to give them news tips, complain
  about biased reporting, or thank them for fair reporting on an
  issue you care about.
- Patronize alternative print, electronic, and Web-based media.
  Share information about these outlets with friends.
- Publish! There is always a venue for good ideas: school newspapers, weekly national news magazines, organization newslet-
  ters, teen magazines, parent magazines, Web sites, newspaper
  opinion pages, letters to the editor, columns of all kinds.
- Monitor national media Web sites, such as those maintained by
  major TV networks and newspapers, and talk back to them
  regularly. Point out anti-choice bias and insist they correct it.
  Respond when they have survey questions on issues you care
  about. Praise programming that has positive messages about
  sexual responsibility, birth control, and choice. See page 198 for
  how to reach the major media Web sites.

TAKE AN ACTION EVERY DAY

I constantly talk about these issues. Friends joke that I am unable to talk to someone at a party without bringing up the issue of choice!

—Emily Goodstein, founder, George Washington University Vox (Voices for Planned Parenthood) Chapter

Small everyday acts add up to a big difference. Pledge to take at least one action every day to advance reproductive rights and access to care. Only with persistent, vocal, visible action will we get our message across to policy makers, media, and other Americans. Pick any one of the actions suggested above, or make up your own, but do something every day. Live your convictions and turn them into action.

You should never assume that what you know or can do isn't valuable. I hold "teach-ins" on campus. I invited a teacher who had an illegal abortion in 1960, and my mother, who had a legal one in 1990 but because she didn't have money to pay for it had to struggle to get access. We called the program "Two Women, Two Eras." So much of what the two women had to go through was the same. Poor women in America today are basically choiceless.

I've also organized discussions at the residence houses on campus. Every Friday, the tradition is to have tea at 4 P.M., so you know people will be there. It's easier to go to a group than have them come to you. If I can't get actual women to speak, I use a documentary produced by the National Network of Abortion Providers. It's called "Legal but Out of Reach." I've designed some questions like "What does choice mean to me?" that raise awareness about the need for pro-choice activism.

> Women's bodies are war zones in this country and I'm not one to shy away from a fight when the lives of so many women are on the line.
>
> —Jenna McKean, age 23, Smith College senior

FREEDOM'S VANGUARDS

The rooster crows but the hen delivers.

—Former Texas governor Ann Richards

We have the passion, the skills, the energy, and the commitment. Now it's time to set the agenda and accomplish our goals. A movement has to move to be powerful! A new pro-choice crusade will create a new people's movement. We will see hands across the country for choice. People will raise the issues at every debate, every town hall, every public appearance of every candidate or elected official. We won't let a judge get confirmed who doesn't support a woman's right to make her own reproductive decisions. We will advance policies and services that guarantee all women reproductive rights and every woman access to reproductive health care.

We need concentrated outreach efforts by a broad cross-section of people and organizations. Young men and women must join organizations, work in campaigns, and take part in the democratic process. If they don't, they are leaving the field to people who have a very different vision of what America should look like.

—Senator Hillary Clinton (D–New York)

Not everyone can do everything I've suggested. But everyone can do something. And every single act, large or small, makes a difference. All our actions, taken together, will secure reproductive freedom as a fundamental human and civil right today and for the next generation. You will be freedom's vanguards in this fight to win the war on choice.

APPENDIX A

WOMEN'S REPRODUCTIVE
HEALTH TIMELINE: 1910s–APRIL 2004

———————▶ ◀———————

For a full analysis and up-to-date Women's Reproductive Health Timeline, visit http://member.plannedparenthood.org/site/PageServer?pagename=timeline.

1910s
- Birth control and abortion are illegal in the U.S.
- Margaret Sanger opens the first birth control clinic in the U.S., the founding of what would become the Planned Parenthood Federation of America. She is arrested and indicted under New York State's 1873 Comstock Law, which forbids the dissemination of birth control information.

1920s
- The Nineteenth Amendment to the U.S. Constitution is ratified— women win the right to vote. But they haven't won the right to use birth control.

1930s
- The Comstock Laws are liberalized, allowing the importing of contraceptives.
- The American Medical Association officially recognizes birth control as an integral part of medical practice and education.

1940s
- Representatives from more than twenty nations form the International Planned Parenthood Committee.

1950s

- The International Planned Parenthood Federation is launched at a conference in Bombay.
- The American Law Institute's Model Penal Code recommends that states allow licensed physicians to perform abortions if two physicians certify in writing that pregnancy threatens the woman's physical or mental health, results from rape or incest, or the fetus is gravely deformed. Opposition to such reform of the anti-abortion laws begins to take shape.

1960s

- The U.S. Food and Drug Administration approves the sale of oral steroid pills for contraception.
- President John F. Kennedy defines population growth as a "staggering" problem. He formally endorses reproductive research to make new knowledge and methods available worldwide.
- The U.S. Supreme Court, in *Griswold v. Connecticut*, strikes down state laws prohibiting the use of contraceptives by married couples.
- As a central element of his administration's War on Poverty, President Lyndon Baines Johnson singles out family planning as one of four critical health problems in the nation.
- Sherri Finkbine is refused an abortion even though she had been prescribed thalidomide, which has caused serious birth defects. Mrs. Finkbine flees to Sweden to obtain an abortion.

1970s

- Congress passes and President Richard Nixon signs into law Title X of the Public Health Services Act, providing support and funding for family planning services and educational programs and for biomedical and behavioral research in reproduction and contraceptive development.
- Congress repeals most of the provisions of the federal Comstock Laws.
- On January 22, 1973, the U.S. Supreme Court decides, in *Roe v. Wade*, that the constitutional right to privacy extends to a woman's decision, in consultation with her physician, to have an abortion.

- A series of other Supreme Court decisions—*Eisenstadt v. Baird, Doe v. Bolton, Planned Parenthood of Central Missouri v. Danforth, Bellotti v. Baird, Bellotti v. Baird II, and Carey v. Population Services International*—expand access to contraception and abortion services for adults and minors.
- The National Right to Life Committee is organized by the U.S. Catholic Conference's Family Life Division, which is administered by the National Conference of Catholic Bishops.
- Congress passes the first Hyde Amendment, which prohibits the use of federal Medicaid funds for abortions for poor women while continuing to allow these funds to be used for pregnancy, delivery, and child care costs.
- The Republican party adopts its first anti-choice platform. The Democratic party adopts its first pro-choice platform.
- In their continuing failure to decisively overturn *Roe v. Wade* through the courts or by constitutional amendment, anti-abortion factions increasingly target family planning providers around the country with harassment and terrorism, including barricades, bombings, arson, stalking, death threats, kidnapping, and finally, over the years, anthrax hoaxes and assassination.

1980s

- Ronald Reagan, the first U.S. president with political commitments to the anti-choice movement, is elected. A major goal of Reagan's administration is to stack the federal judiciary, especially the U.S. Supreme Court, with appointees who demonstrate clear antipathy to reproductive rights.
- Congress passes the Adolescent Family Life Act (AFLA), also known as the chastity law.
- At the 1984 United Nations Population Conference in Mexico City, the Reagan administration announces its so-called Mexico City policy, which denies U.S. family planning funds to most overseas nongovernmental organizations that use their non-U.S. funds for abortion services, counseling, or referral.
- Violent attacks on family planning and abortion clinics escalate.

While four incidents had occurred in 1983, thirty major attacks are reported in 1984, including bombings, arson, and attempted bombings and arson.

- President Reagan proposes the "gag rule" for Title X–funded clinics, similar to the Mexico City policy, which forbids clinics from counseling a client about abortion—even if the client specifically asks for such information, and even if withholding the information would endanger her health.
- The George H. W. Bush administration makes clear its intention to continue support for the Mexico City policy, the domestic gag rule, and other anti-family-planning, anti-abortion policies of the Reagan years. On his first working day in office, he declares his solidarity with anti-choice extremists and calls for passage of the so-called Human Life Amendment.
- In 1989, hundreds of thousands of pro-choice advocates converge on Washington, D.C., and hold pro-choice events across the country.
- In July 1989, the U.S. Supreme Court's *Webster v. Reproductive Health Services* decision sets the scene for a possible reversal of *Roe v. Wade* and a return to the days of illegal abortion.

1990s

- The U.S. Supreme Court rules in *Ohio v. Akron Center for Reproductive Health* and in *Hodgson v. State of Minnesota* that states may require notification of one or both parents before a teenager may have an abortion, as long as she has the option of a judicial bypass.
- The U.S. Supreme Court upholds the Title X gag rule in *Rust v. Sullivan,* thus permitting government censorship of doctors and women.
- In April 1992, more than 750,000 women and men join the March for Women's Lives in Washington, D.C. to demonstrate their support for choice.
- While reaffirming the right to abortion, *Planned Parenthood of Southeastern Pennsylvania v. Casey* outlines a weaker standard of review, allowing restrictions unless they constitute an undefined "undue burden" to the woman. Four of the nine justices argue that *Roe* should be overturned outright.

- On the twentieth anniversary of *Roe v. Wade*, newly inaugurated President Bill Clinton—the first pro-choice president in twelve years—reverses the Title X family planning gag rule, rescinds the Mexico City policy, lifts the ban on the importation of mifepristone, permits privately funded abortions in overseas military hospitals, and lifts the ban on the use of fetal tissue for medical research.

- Anti-abortion extremists shoot and kill David Gunn, M.D., an abortion provider in Pensacola, FL; George Wayne Patterson, M.D., an abortion provider in Mobile, AL; John Bayard Britton, M.D., an abortion provider, and James Barrett, his volunteer escort, in Pensacola, FL; Shannon Lowney, a receptionist at Planned Parenthood League of Massachusetts, and Leanne Nichols, a receptionist at a Preterm clinic, in Brookline, MA; and Barnett A. Slepian, M.D., an abortion provider in Amherst, NY. In a bombing of a women's reproductive health center in Birmingham, AL, police officer Robert Sanderson is killed and nurse Emily Lyons is maimed and permanently disabled.

- In 1994, Congress enacts the Freedom of Access to Clinic Entrances (FACE) Act. FACE makes it a federal crime to use or attempt force, the threat of force, or physical obstruction to injure, intimidate, or interfere with providers of reproductive health care services or their patients.

- In *National Organization for Women v. Scheidler*, the U.S. Supreme Court rules that the Racketeer Influenced and Corrupt Organizations (RICO) Act can be used against violent anti-abortion protesters who attempt to eliminate access to abortion by using extortion and intimidation to drive the clinics out of business.

- The United Nations International Conference on Population and Development (ICPD) is convened in Cairo, Egypt. More than 160 official government delegations negotiate a Programme of Action for addressing population and advancing women's health and economic empowerment over the next two decades.

- In April 1996, President Bill Clinton vetoes an abortion ban passed by Congress.

- Congress establishes a multimillion-dollar federal fund to support programs exclusively teaching abstinence until marriage.

- In 1997, the Equity in Prescription Insurance and Contraceptive Coverage

Act—to require health insurers to cover contraceptive services in the same way they cover other prescriptions and medical services—is introduced in Congress. Six years later, twenty-one states will have enacted laws that require insurers that cover prescription drugs to cover birth control. But the federal law is yet to be enacted.

- In 1997, PPFA takes the lead to ensure that emergency contraception becomes recognized as a basic part of reproductive health care.

2000s

- In its 2000 decision in *Stenberg v. Carhart,* the U.S. Supreme Court holds unconstitutional a Nebraska law that could have been used to ban many abortion procedures.
- The U.S. Food and Drug Administration approves mifepristone for use as an abortifacient, providing women with a medical alternative to surgical abortion.
- On January 22, 2001, the twenty-eighth anniversary of *Roe v. Wade* and President George W. Bush's first full day in office, the president reimposes the global gag rule, restricting funding for international family planning.
- In June 2003, citing the right to privacy established in 1965 in *Griswold,* the U.S. Supreme Court strikes down Texas's Homosexual Conduct law, which had criminalized oral and anal sex by consenting same-sex partners.
- In October 2003, Congress passes, and in November 2003 President Bush signs, an abortion ban that ignores women's constitutional right to make decisions about their own bodies and health and is the first federal law to criminalize abortion.
- In April 2004, hundreds of thousands of women and men from all walks of life participate in the March for Women's Lives: Washington, D.C.

The future is in our hands.

THE WAR ON CHOICE:
DECEMBER 2000–NOVEMBER 2003

———————➤◀———————

(For a full analysis and up-to-date chronology of the ongoing war on choice, visit www.plannedparenthood.org/library/facts/030114_waronwomen.html)

December 22, 2000   Extremist anti-choice zealot John Ashcroft is nominated for U.S. attorney general.

December 29, 2000   Anti-choice Wisconsin governor Tommy Thompson is nominated to be secretary of Health and Human Services.

January 22, 2001   On his first day in office, the twenty-eighth anniversary of *Roe v. Wade,* President Bush revives President Ronald Reagan's Mexico City policy and restores a global gag rule on international family planning assistance, preventing nongovernmental organizations in countries that receive U.S. international family planning assistance from using their own money—not that supplied by the U.S.—to provide abortion services, counseling, or referrals, or to lobby to change abortion laws.

April 9, 2001   In his first budget, President Bush strips contraceptive coverage from the insurance plans offered to federal employees. Congress reinstates it.

May–September 2001   President Bush nominates the following anti-choice nominees to U.S. Courts of Appeals:

- Texas Supreme Court justice Priscilla Owen, described by *The New York Times* as being "so eager to issue conservative rulings in cases before her on the Texas Supreme Court that she has ignored statutory language and substituted her own views."

- Michael McConnell, who has expressed his opposition to *Roe v. Wade* on numerous occasions and his belief that the U.S. Constitution does not protect a woman's right to choose. On November 15, 2002, the U.S. Senate confirmed the nomination.
- District court judge Dennis Shedd, who refuses to state that he believes that the Constitution guarantees a woman's right to choose or to declare that he will protect our fundamental rights when interpreting the law. The Senate confirmed the nomination on November 19, 2002.
- Lavenski Smith, former executive director of the anti-choice Rutherford Institute of Arkansas, which has consistently opposed abortion and has called on the U.S. Supreme Court to reverse *Roe v. Wade*. The Senate confirmed the nomination on July 16, 2002.
- Federal district court judge Charles Pickering, who, in 1976, chaired the Human Rights and Responsibilities Subcommittee of the National Republican party Platform Committee, which approved a plank protesting the Supreme Court's decision in *Roe v. Wade* and called for an amendment to the U.S. Constitution banning abortion.
- Judge Carolyn Kuhl, who has a long record of anti-choice advocacy.
- Federal district court judge D. Brooks Smith, who has not demonstrated that he understands or is committed to protecting women's rights, the right to privacy, reproductive freedoms, and other basic civil rights. The Senate confirmed the nomination on July 31, 2002.

October 11, 2001   In his FY2003 budget, President Bush increases annual funding for unproven and dangerous "abstinence-only" education programs to $135 million.

November 30, 2001   President Bush names abstinence-only education proponent Patricia Funderburk Ware to head the Presidential Advisory Council on HIV/AIDS.

March 1, 2002   Bush appoints an outspoken opponent of condom use and staunch supporter of abstinence-only education, former representative Tom Coburn (R–Oklahoma), to the President's Advisory Council on HIV/AIDS.

President Bush also names the cofounder of the anti-condom Medical Institute, Joe McIlhaney, to the council.

March 5, 2002 The Bush administration announces new rules making fetuses but not pregnant women eligible for prenatal care in the State Children's Health Insurance Program, thus elevating fetuses and reducing women to mere "host" status.

May 2002 U.S. representatives at the U.N. Children's Summit oppose sexuality education and the use of condoms for HIV/AIDS prevention by claiming that the phrase "reproductive health services and education" implies a right to abortion and abortion counseling.

July 22, 2002 President Bush withholds $34 million in funding for birth control, maternal and child health care, and HIV/AIDS prevention from the United Nations Population Fund.

July 25, 2002 Equating embryos with children, the Bush administration announces that approximately $900,000 is available in the FY2002 Labor-HHS appropriations bill to support public awareness campaigns for embryo "adoption."

August 2, 2002 President Bush withholds more than $200 million that was approved by Congress for programs to support women and address HIV/AIDS in Afghanistan.

September 6, 2002 President Bush names Dr. Freda McKissic, the director of Virginity Rules and anti-condom and abstinence-only proponent, to the CDC Advisory Committee on HIV and STD Prevention.

October 2002 President Bush freezes $3 million in funding to the World Health Organization (WHO) in response to anti-choice objections to the WHO's Human Reproduction Program.

HHS Web sites remove scientific findings of the National Cancer Institute, which prove that, contrary to anti-choice propaganda, abortions do not increase the risk of breast cancer.

The Bush administration gives "human status" to embryos in the Health and Human Services Secretary's Advisory Committee on Human Research Protection Charter.

October 7, 2002 HHS Secretary Tommy Thompson names Dr. Alma Golden, a Texas-based pediatrician and longtime abstinence-only proponent, to the position of deputy assistant secretary of population affairs, which oversees the implementation of Title X, the nation's family planning health service program.

November 2, 2002   The Bush administration reverses the U.S. position supporting the Cairo Programme of Action developed at the 1994 International Conference of Population and Development, which affirmed the right of all couples and individuals to determine freely and responsibly the number and spacing of their children and to have the information and means to do so.

November 25, 2002   The National Cancer Institute Web site posts a "revised" fact sheet that suggests an unproven link between abortion and breast cancer, even though the best available evidence, from large population-based cohort studies, shows that induced abortion has no net effect in putting women at increased risk for developing breast cancer.

December 2, 2002   The Centers for Disease Control and Prevention Web site posts a "revised" fact sheet that downplays the long-established effectiveness of condoms.

December 24, 2002   The Bush administration appoints religious extremist David Hager, M.D., who is noted for prescribing biblical Scripture to cure PMS and for his opposition to prescribing contraceptives to unmarried women, to the Reproductive Health Drugs Advisory Committee of the Food and Drug Administration.

Also appointed to that committee are Joseph B. Stanford, M.D., who refuses to prescribe contraceptives of any sort; Susan A. Crockett, M.D., a board member of the American Association of Pro-Life Obstetricians and Gynecologists; and Vivian Lewis, M.D., who has called for more stringent controls on mifepristone.

January 2003   U.S. Agency for International Development (USAID) joins the administration's efforts to censor government and government-funded Web sites in a cable directing USAID-funded programs and publications in missions around the world to reflect the policies of the Bush administration.

January 7, 2003   Bush renominates right-wing extremists to circuit courts of appeals: federal district court judge Charles Pickering, Texas Supreme Court justice Priscilla Owen, and Los Angeles Superior Court judge Carolyn Kuhl, all of whom had been rejected by the

Senate because of their abysmal records on a host of issues, including trying to roll back women's fundamental civil and human rights.

February 3, 2003   Despite increasing demand for family planning services as more and more U.S. families are squeezed by the struggling economy, President Bush's proposed FY2004 budget provides no increase for the Title X family planning program, but does include a proposed 83 percent increase over 2002 levels for unproven abstinence-only education programs. The same budget prohibits federal funds for abortions for women in prison, except in cases of rape and when the woman's life is endangered, and for women who depend on the federal government for their health care benefits, including poor women and federal employees. This budget also includes the president's global gag rule, which would prohibit the provision of abortion services or counseling and lobbying for abortion rights by agencies that accept U.S. foreign aid.

August 29, 2003   President Bush extends the global gag rule to all international family planning programs, even though earlier in the summer, the Senate voted overwhelmingly (53–43) to repeal it by adopting the Global Democracy Promotion Act (Senate Amendment 1141 to S. 925), authored by Sen. Barbara Boxer (D-California).

October 22, 2003   Congress passes a reckless and dangerous ban on abortion, which provides no safeguards for women's health and is opposed by the American College of Obstetricians and Gynecologists, the American Nurses Association, and the American Medical Women's Association.

November 5, 2003   Surrounded by smiling men with not a woman in sight, President Bush signs into law a reckless, dangerous, and blatantly unconstitutional abortion ban that will harm women by ignoring their constitutional right to make decisions about their own bodies. Attempting to broaden the "civil rights" protection of fetuses while creating a potential conflict of interest in his responsibility to protect access to abortion clinics, U.S. Attorney General John Ashcroft assigns responsibility for the ban's enforcement to the justice department's civil rights division and begins aggressively defending the ban.

APPENDIX B

RESOURCE LIST

———◄—

Activist/Membership Organizations
Advocates for Youth—www.advocatesforyouth.org
Programs that help young people make informed and responsible decisions about reproductive and sexual health.

AIDS Action—www.aidsaction.org
Dedicated to the development of sound policies in response to the HIV epidemic.

Alliance for Justice—www.afj.org
Works to advance the cause of justice for all Americans.

American Association of University Women—www.aauw.org
Promotes education and equity for women and girls.

American Civil Liberties Union (ACLU)—www.aclu.org
Defends the individual rights guaranteed by the Constitution and U.S. laws.

Americans United for Separation of Church and State—www.au.org
Defends separation of church and state in the federal and state courts.

Black Women's Health Imperative (formerly National Black Women's Health Project)—www.blackwomenshealth.org
Promotes the improved health status of African-American women.

Catholics for a Free Choice—www.cath4choice.org/indexengflash.htm
Engages in advocacy on issues of gender equality and reproductive
    health.

Center for Reproductive Rights (formerly Center for Reproductive Law
    and Policy)—www.crlp.org
Dedicated to ensuring that all women have access to reproductive health
    services.

Coalition of Labor Union Women—www.cluw.org
National organization for women within the labor movement.

Cover My Pills—www.covermypills.org
Planned Parenthood-sponsored advocacy for equality in prescription in-
    surance contraceptive coverage.

Feminist Majority Foundation—www.feminist.org
Seeks to empower women through research, the sharing of information,
    and effective action.

International Planned Parenthood Federation (IPPF)—www.ippf.org
Promotes sexual and reproductive health and rights internationally.

International Women's Health Coalition (IWHC)—www.iwhc.org
Works to protect the health of girls and women worldwide.

Leadership Conference on Civil Rights and Leadership Conference on
    Civil Rights Education Fund—www.civilrights.org
Promotes national policies that support civil rights and social and eco-
    nomic justice.

Mexican American Legal Defense and Educational Fund—www.maldef.org
Latino litigation, advocacy, and educational outreach.

NAACP (National Association for the Advancement of Colored People)—
    www.naacp.org
Dedicated to ensuring the political, educational, social, and economic
    equality of minority groups.

NARAL Pro-Choice America—www.naral.org
Facts and news on all aspects of abortion rights.

National Abortion Federation—www.prochoice.org
Provides information on options for pregnant women and how to take
    action on abortion issues.

National Asian Pacific Women's Forum—www.napawf.org
Advocates equality and empowerment of Asian and Pacific-American
    women.

National Asian Women's Health Organization (NAWHO)—www.nawho.org
Works to protect the reproductive health and rights of Asian-American
    women and families.

National Council of Jewish Women—www.ncjw.org
Dedicated to improving the quality of life for women, children, and families.

National Council of Negro Women—www.ncnw.org
Advances the quality of life for African-American women, their families,
    and communities.

National Gay and Lesbian Task Force—www.ngltf.org
Works for the civil rights of gay, lesbian, bisexual, and transgender people.

National Latina Institute for Reproductive Health—www.latinainstitute.org
Advocates reproductive health and rights for Latinas, their families, and
    their communities.

National Organization for Women (NOW)—www.now.org
Advances women's rights and promotes the goal of equality.

National Partnership for Women and Families—www.nationalpartner
    ship.org
Uses public education and advocacy to promote fairness in the workplace
    and quality health care.

National Women's Law Center—www.nwlc.org
Uses litigation and advocacy to support women.

People for the American Way—www.pfaw.org
Works to defend constitutional liberties.

PFLAG (Parents, Families and Friends of Lesbians and Gays)—www.
pflag.org
Supports gay, lesbian, bisexual, and transgendered persons, their families,
and friends.

Planned Parenthood Federation of America (PPFA)—www.planned
parenthood.org
The world's largest and most trusted voluntary reproductive health care
organization and advocate.

Planned Parenthood Federation of America-International—www.planned
parenthood.org/global
PPFA international services program and international advocacy program (PPGP).

Population Action International—www.populationaction.org
Working to strengthen public awareness and political and financial support worldwide for population programs grounded in individual rights.

Religious Coalition for Reproductive Choice—www.rcrc.org
Works to ensure reproductive choice as a part of religious liberty.

saveROE—www.saveroe.com
PPFA advocacy information and activist resources to advance reproductive health.

Sierra Club—www.sierraclub.org
Promotes the responsible use of the earth's ecosystems and resources.

Vox®:Voices for Planned Parenthood—plannedparenthood.org/vox
Mobilizing young people in support of reproductive health and rights.

YWCA—www.ywca.org
Empowers women and girls through a wide range of services and programs.

Research and Education Organizations

The Alan Guttmacher Institute (AGI)—www.agi-usa.org
Research on all topics related to women's reproductive health.

American College of Obstetricians and Gynecologists (ACOG)—
www.acog.org
The nation's leading group of professionals providing health care for
women.

American Medical Women's Association (AMWA)—www.amwa-doc.org
Organization of 10,000 women physicians and medical students dedicated
to serving as the unique voice for women's health and the advancement
of women in medicine.

Association of Reproductive Health Professionals (ARHP)—
www.arhp.org
Fosters research and advocacy to improve reproductive health.

Emergency Contraception—ec.princeton.edu
In English and Spanish; EC providers in each state, FAQs contains a di-
rectory.

Fairness and Accuracy in Reporting (FAIR)—www.fair.org
Media watch group; offers well-documented criticism of media bias and
censorship.

International Women's Media Foundation—www.iwmf.org
Explores obstacles women journalists face and the impact of women on
media decision making.

Kaiser Family Foundation—kff.org
Philanthropy focused on health policy; source of facts and analysis.

Mediachannel.org—www.mediachannel.org
Concerned with the political, cultural, and social impact of the media.

National Campaign to Prevent Teen Pregnancy—www.teenpregnancy.org
Features reading lists, publications, and a section specifically for teens.

National Coalition Against Domestic Violence—www.ncadv.org
National information and referral center for battered women and their
   children.

Native American Women's Health Education Resource Center—www.
   nativeshop.com/nawherc.html
The first resource center on a reservation; programs in health and civil
   rights.

OutProud—www.outproud.org
The National Coalition for Gay, Lesbian, Bisexual and Transgender Youth;
   information and support.

PLANetWIRE.org—www.planetwire.org
Background on reproductive rights, health, education, women, the environment.

Planned Parenthood Federation of America (PPFA)—www.planned
   parenthood.org
Reproductive and sexual health information.

Sexuality Information and Education Council of the United States
   (SIECUS)—www.siecus.org
Disseminates information about sexuality, promotes comprehensive sex
   education.

teenwire.com[SM]—www.teenwire.com/index.asp
Produced by PPFA for teens needing information about sexual health.

United Nations Population Fund (UNFPA)—www.unfpa.org
World's largest international source of funding for population and reproductive health programs.

Government Web Sites for Monitoring and Information

Centers for Disease Control and Prevention—www.cdc.gov

Daily Federal Register—www.archives.gov/federal_register/publications/
         about_the_federal_register.html

The Library of Congress—www.loc.gov

National Cancer Institute—www.cancer.gov

National Institutes of Health—www.nih.gov

President's Advisory Council on Bioethics—www.bioethics.gov

Thomas, Legislative Information on the Internet—www.thomas.loc.gov

Title X: All related information—opa.osophs.dhhs.gov

The United States House of Representatives—www.house.gov

The United States Senate—www.senate.gov

The White House—www.whitehouse.gov

ENDNOTES

Chapter 1—Good Ol' Boys and the Bad Old Days

page 1   "I say watch me" On the Emmitt McCauliff program, "The
         Talk Show that Hell Hates," AM KSTL 630, August 1998.

page 1   "damn careless in the first place" May 12, 1994 In an
         Education and Labor subcommittee meeting on Labor
         Management Relations.

page 1   "power to restrict abortion" Stahl, Lori. October 22, 1994.
         "Surprisingly, Abortion Hasn't Made Election Issue List."
         Dallas Morning News, p. A32.

page 2   "to be illegal" November 1, 1995. *USA Today*.

page 3   "that surrounds it" "Randall Terry, Founder of Operation
         Rescue says, 'Partial-Birth Abortion is a Political Scam, but a
         Public Relations Goldmine.'" September 15, 2003. U.S.
         Newswire [Online]. (Accessed November 11, 2003). http:
         //releases.usnewswire.com/GetRelease.asp?id=141-09152003.

page 4   "partial-truth abortion" Kennedy, Miranda. 2000. "Partial
         Truth Abortion Coverage: Media Adopt Rhetoric of 'Fetal
         Rights.'" [Online]. (Accessed August 4, 2003). http://www
         .fair.org/extra/0003/partial-abortion.html.

page 7   87 percent... money and time Henshaw, Stanley, and
         Lawrence B. Finer January/February 2003. "The Accessibility

of Abortion Services in the United States, 2001." Perspectives on Sexual and Reproductive Health, 35(1).

page 9   have to perform them *Maher v. Roe,* 432 U.S. 464 (1977).

page 12   "of American women" American College of Obstetricians and Gynecologists. February 3, 2002. Statement on so-called Partial-Birth Abortion laws by the American College of Obstetricians and Gynecologists. ACOG news release.

page 18   highest teen pregnancy rate Meckler, Laura. April 30, 1998. "Teen Birth Rate Drops in 1990s." The Associated Press.

page 19   Planned Parenthood in Connecticut Thomas, Helen. December 22, 1999. "Backstairs at the White House." United Press International.

page 19   nicknamed him "Rubbers" Hines, Cragg. August 10, 1992. "Thorny Issue of Abortion Plagues GOP Politics; Bush Stance Took Sharp Turn in 1980." *Houston Chronicle,* p. A1.

page 20   "cannot be legislated" Bush, Barbara. 1994. *Barbara Bush: A Memoir.* (New York: St. Martin's Paperbacks), p. 163.

page 20   "should be overturned" National Broadcasting Company (NBC). January 19, 2001. *Today.* Transcript.

page 20   "middle [on abortion]" Simon, Mark. July 1, 1999. "Ex-Provost Lends a Hand to Bush, GOP Condoleezza Rice Appears at Peninsula Fund-raiser." *San Francisco Chronicle,* p. A17.

Chapter 2—Barefoot and Pregnant

page 29   "keep her barefoot" "Van Dalsem Offers Formula for Handling 'Nosey' Women." August 28, 1963. *Arkansas Gazette.*

page 35   IUDs as abortifacients Copy of draft Frist Amendment to S. 2328 in files of Planned Parenthood Federation of America, Government Relations Department, Washington, D.C.

page 36   Vitter ... family planning funds Alpert, Bruce. October 12, 2001. "Vitter Gives Up Plans to Offer Controversial Anti-abortion Bill; Measure Falls Short in House Panel Vote." *Times-Picayune* (New Orleans).

page 36   mandatory reporting law Texas Department of Health. TDH

Rider II. "TDH Child Abuse Screening, Documenting, and Reporting Policy for Contractors/Providers," chapter 261, Family Code (2003).

page 37 "and emergency contraception" American Life League. "STOPP International's Plan for Defeating Planned Parenthood." STOPP International. [Online]. (Accessed October 3, 2003). http://www.all.org/stopp/plan.htm.

page 37 Bush supported family planning Bush, George. February 24, 1969. Congressional Record, vol. 115(4) p. 4207.

page 37 restored the coverage Administration Budget Request. 2001. Government-Wide General Provisions. Title VI—General Provisions, Sec. (630)(a), 11.

page 39 "prejudice and persecutions" Haney, Robert. 1960. *Comstockery in America: Patterns of Censorship and Control* (Boston: Beacon Press).

page 39 in colonial America Tone, Andrea. 1997. *Controlling Reproduction: An American History* (Wilmington, Delaware: Scholarly Resources Inc.).

page 39 Pilgrim women were pregnant Kempner, Martha. 2001. "Toward a Sexually Healthy America: Abstinence-Only-Until-Marriage Programs that Try to Keep Our Youth 'Scared Chaste.'" New York: Sexuality Information and Education Council of the United States.

page 39 performed by midwives Boston Women's Health Book Collective. 1998. *Our Bodies, Ourselves for the New Century* (New York: Touchstone).

page 39 "became a battleground" Faludi, Susan. 1991. *Backlash, The Undeclared War Against American Women* (New York: Anchor Books Doubleday), p. 413.

page 40 *Griswold v. Connecticut Griswold v. Connecticut,* 381 U.S. 479 (1965).

page 41 *Eisenstadt v. Baird Eisenstadt v. Baird,* 405 U.S. 438 (1972).

page 42 pregnancies went down Piccinino, Linda J. 1994. "Unintended Pregnancy and Childbearing." From Data to Action: CDC's Public Health Surveillance for Women, Infants, and Children." Hyattsville, MD: CDC, pp. 73–82.

page 42   and child mortality National Center for Health Statistics. 1967. Vital Statistics of the United States,1965: vol. II—Mortality, part A. Washington, D.C.: U.S. Government Printing Office.

page 42   "cannot afford them" Nixon, Richard. July 18, 1969. Special Message to the Congress on Problems of Population Growth.

page 42   "public health matter" Bush, George. February 24, 1969. Congressional Record, vol. 115(4) p. 4207.

page 42   5 million women AGI. 2002. Family Planning Annual Report: 2001 Summary, Submitted to the Office of Population Affairs, Department of Health and Human Services.

page 43   services for newborns Forrest, Jacqueline, and Renée Samara. 1996. "Impact of Publicly Funded Contraceptive Services on Unintended Pregnancies and Implications for Medicaid Expenditures." Family Planning Perspectives, 28(4), pp. 188–195.

page 43   57 percent less . . . in 1980 AGI. February 20, 2002. Unpublished memorandum to Planned Parenthood Federation of America.

page 46   "of family planning" P.L. 572, Ninety-first Congress (1970). Title X: Population Research and Voluntary Family Planning Programs.

page 47   "Title X funds" Concerned Women for America. "Efforts Renew to Deny Family Planning Funds to Agencies That Offer Abortions." The Guttmacher Report. [Online]. (Accessed August 25, 2003). http://www.agi-usa.org/pubs/journals/gr010501.pdf.

page 48   "of the patient" American Medical Association. H5-989 Freedom of Communication Between Physicians and Patients.

page 48   "an unwanted pregnancy" American Psychological Association. (Accessed October 3, 2003). Council Policy Manual: N. Public Interest—part I. [Online]. http://www.apa.org/about/division/cpmpubint.html?CFID=2450539&CFTOKEN=93056960.

page 48   "of free speech" National Association of Social Workers.
           2002. Position on The Right to Privacy/Social Services and
           Civil Rights.

page 49   *Rust v. Sullivan Rust v. Sullivan.* 500 U.S. 173 (1991).

page 50   and Northern Arizona *Babbitt v. Planned Parenthood of Central and
           Northern Arizona.* 789 F. 2nd 1348 (1986).

page 52   or reproductive health Minnesota SF 431 (2003).

page 52   referring for abortions New Jersey AB 1078; SB 1073
           (2002).

page 52   Legislation was introduced Rhode Island 98—H 7525
           (1998).

page 52   115,000 Texas women The Associated Press. June 27, 2003.
           Texas News Briefs.

page 52   2.3 percent . . . Newswire. June 26, 2003. "Planned
           Parenthood Affiliates Sue State over Unconstitutional
           Restrictions to Family Planning Funding for Low-Income
           Women; Political Move Increases Likelihood of Unwanted
           Pregnancies."

page 53   "about preventing abortion" The Associated Press. June 27,
           2003. Texas News Briefs.

page 53   "constitutionally protected right" WL 21800213. 2003.
           W.D.TEX.

page 53   "not be deterred" Brooks, Karen. August 5, 2003. "Judge
           Delays Cuts in Abortion Clinic Budgets; Ruling Forces
           Factions Back to Court." *Star-Telegram* (Fort Worth/Dallas),
           p. 3.

page 54   "expected standard of behavior" August 1, 2000. "The Re-
           publicans; Excerpts from Platform Approved by Republican
           National Convention." *The New York Times,* p. A16.

page 54   education and counseling HHS. June 19, 2003. Federal
           Register, 68(118).

page 54   outside of marriage Republican National Committee. "A
           Responsibility Era." 2000 platform. [Online]. (Accessed
           October 3, 2003). http://rnc.org/GOPInfo/Platform/
           2000platform3.htm.

page 55   sexually transmitted infections Kirby, Douglas. 2001. "Emerging Answers—Research Findings on Programs to Reduce Teen Pregnancy." Washington, D.C.: National Campaign to Prevent Teen Pregnancy.

page 55   Golden . . . family planning program HHS. June 19, 2003. Federal Register, 65(118).

page 56   "for their weekend party" Golden, Dr. Alma. Remarks at the SPRANS Community-Based Abstinence Education Grantee Meeting, Washington, D.C. [Online]. (Accessed November 2002). http://128.248.232.90/archives/mchb/abstinence 2002/text/session5.

page 56   measures for abstinence-only programs Waxman, Henry A. July 8, 2003. Letter from Representative Henry A. Waxman, ranking minority member, Committee on Government Reform, to secretary of Health and Human Services Tommy G. Thompson.

page 57   Opportunity Reconciliation Act NOW. "The Illegitimacy Ratio." Welfare and Poverty. [Online]. (Accessed September 11, 2003). http://nowldef.org/html/issues/wel/ill ratio.shtml.

page 57   out-of-wedlock pregnancies NOW. "What Congress Didn't Tell You: A State-by-State Guide to the Welfare Law's Hidden Reproductive Rights Agenda." Welfare and Poverty. [Online]. (Accessed September 11, 2003). http://nowldef.org/ html/issues/wel/congress.shtml.

page 57   American family—two HHS. 2002 TANF Annual Report to Congress, pp. 188–90.

page 58   rates of abortion NOW. "Reproductive Rights and Welfare." Welfare and Poverty. [Online]. (Accessed September 11, 2003). http://nowldef.org/html/issues/wel/advrepro.shtml.

page 59 $300 million . . . promoting marriage Toner, Robin. March 13, 2002. "Bush's Proposal on Welfare Draws Fire from Democrats." *The New York Times*, p. 20.

Chapter 3—Abstinence of Common Sense

page 61   "easily than latex condoms" Ornstein, Charles. June 6, 2001.
             "Report to Spur Discussion of Sex: Surgeon General Focuses
             on Behavior, Lifelong Education." *The Record* (Bergen County,
             NJ), p. A8.

page 62   fifty-eight percent . . . are rapidly increasing Kaiser Daily
             Reproductive Health Report. December 15, 1999. "Sex
             Education: Two New Studies Look at Abstinence-Only
             Trend." [Online]. (Accessed October 4, 2003). http://re-
             port.kff.org/archive/repro/1999/12/kr991215.1.htm.

page 63   lower rates of teen pregnancy and . . . infections AGI. 2001.
             "Teenage Sexual and Reproductive Behavior in Developed
             Countries—Can More Progress Be Made?" New York: Alan
             Guttmacher Institute [Online]. (Accessed October 7, 2003).
             http://www.agi-usa.org/pubs/euroteen_or.html.

page 63 $700 million . . . on abstinence-only education NCAC—
             National Coalition Against Censorship 2001. "Abstinence-
             Only Education: Why First Amendment Supporters Should
             Oppose It." [Online]. (Accessed August 5, 2003). http://
             www.ncac.org/issues/abonlypresskit.html.

page 63   more than half the schools Alan Guttmacher Institute, "Sex
             and Pregnancy Among Teenagers." Facts in Brief—Sexuality
             Education. [Online]. (Accessed August 25, 2003). http://www.
             agi-usa.org/pubs/fb_sex_ed02.html.

page 65   "reduce teen pregnancy" Kirby, Douglas. 2002. "Do
             Abstinence-Only Programs Delay the Initiation of Sex Among
             Young People and Reduce Teen Pregnancy?" Washington,
             D.C.: National Campaign to Prevent Teen Pregnancy, p. 6.

page 65   surveyed 527 undergraduates Mundell, E.J. June 23, 2003.
             "No Sex Until Marriage? Don't Bet On It, Study Finds."
             Reuters. [Online]. (Accessed August 25, 2003). UCSF—
             University of California at San Francisco Children's Hospital,
             http://www.ucsfhealth.org/childrens/cgi-bin/print.cgi.

page 67   psychological issues . . . sex AGI. "Sex and Pregnancy Among

Teenagers." Facts in Brief—Sexuality Education. [Online]. (Accessed August 25, 2003). http://www.agi-usa.org/pubs/fb_sex_ed02.html, p. 3.

page 67   1 to 5 percent . . . sexual information NCAC. 2001. "Abstinence-Only Education: Why First Amendment Supporters Should Oppose It." [Online]. (Accessed August 5, 2003). http://www.ncac.org/issues/abonlypresskit.html, p. 6.

page 67   "and coping skills" The Henry J. Kaiser Family Foundation. 2000. "Sex Education in America—A View from Inside the Nation's Classrooms." Menlo Park, California, p. 4.

page 68   85 percent of parents Zabarenko, Deborah. September 26, 2000. "Parents, Teachers Want More Covered in Sex Ed." The Associated Press.

page 68   eight in ten . . . in junior high SIECUS. "Public Support for Comprehensive Sexuality Education." [Online]. (Accessed September 2, 2003). http://www.nonewmoney.org/public.htm, p. 1.

page 69   nearly half . . . sexually transmitted infections The Henry J. Kaiser Family Foundation. 2000. "Sex Education in America—A View from Inside the Nation's Classrooms." Menlo Park, California, p. 4.

page 71   two times lower Berne, Linda, and Barbara Huberman, eds. 1999. "European Approaches to Adolescent Sexual Behavior and Responsibility." Washington, D.C.: Advocates for Youth.

page 71   with 55 per thousand nationally The Associated Press. August 11, 2003. "Majority of North Carolina School Districts Only Teach Sexual Abstinence for Pregnancy, STD Prevention." Raleigh News and Observer.

page 75   a third of ninth graders MMWR. 2002. "Youth Risk Behavior Surveillance—United States," 2001, 51(SS-4), Atlanta, GA: Centers for Disease Control and Prevention, p. 13.

page 78   Dr. Julie Gerberding Anderson, Larry. August 3, 2003. "Opposing Opinion Pieces Debate Merits of Abstinence-

Only Sex Education." [Online]. *Atlanta Journal-Constitution.* (Accessed August 7, 2003). http://www.kaisernetwork.org/daily_reports/rep_repro.cfm.

page 79   CDC erased . . . Web site Waxman, Henry A., et al. "Examples—Abstinence-Only Education." "Politics and Science—Investigating the Bush Administration's Promotion of Ideology over Science." [Online]. (Accessed October 4, 2003). http://www.house.gov/reform/min/politicsandscience/example_abstinence.htm, p. 2.

page 80   "not appointed by this administration" Meckler, Laura. June 29, 2001. "White House Frustrated with Satcher." The Associated Press.

page 80   "wrong places in the wrong ways" Connolly, Cecil. June 29, 2001. "Surgeon General Urges Thorough Sex Education." *The Washington Post,* p. A1.

page 80   "at the lowest grade possible" U.S. Newswire. May 14, 2003. "Advocates for Youth Commends New Surgeon Generals' Support for Comprehensive Sex Education."

page 81   "continuing through high school" U.S. Newswire. May 14, 2003. "Advocates for Youth Commends New Surgeon Generals' Support for Comprehensive Sex Education."

page 81   "about all of the issues" U.S. Newswire. May 14, 2003. "Advocates for Youth Commends New Surgeon Generals' Support for Comprehensive Sex Education."

page 82   until after they're in office Shogren, Elizabeth, and Douglas Frantz. December 10, 1993. "School Boards Become the Religious Right's New Pulpit; Education: Alliances of Conservative Christian Parents, Political Groups Take Control of Panels, Spark Battles." *Los Angeles Times,* p. A1.

page 84   contained inaccurate medical information Connolly, Cecil. July 26, 2002. "Judge Orders Changes in Abstinence Program; La. Groups Found to Be Promoting Religion." *The Washington Post,* p. A3.

page 84 $130 million per year Dailard, Cynthia. February 2002. "Abstinence Promotion and Teen Family Planning: The

Misguided Drive for Equal Funding." Alan Guttmacher
Institute Report on Public Policy, New York: Alan Guttmacher Institute, 5(I).

Chapter 4—State of the Uterus

page 88   to that of the pregnant woman Unborn Victims of Violence
            Act of 2001, 503 U.S. 107 (2001).

page 89   about embryo "adoptions" HHS. July 25, 2002.
            "Announcement of the Availability of Financial Assistance
            and Request for Applications to Support Development and
            Delivery of Public Awareness Campaigns on Embryo
            Adoption." Federal Register, p. 48654–60.

page 90   "by the wayside" CSPT. January 26, 2003. "Back to the
            Drawing Board." Transcript.

page 91   "the unholy one" "Is It True that 'No One Knows When Life
            Begins'?" ChristianAnswers.Net. 1998. [Online]. http://www.
            christiananswers.net/q-sum/q-life026.html.

page 91   trimester, or viability *Roe v. Wade,* 410 U.S. 113 (1973).

page 91   an "undue burden" on the woman *Planned Parenthood of
            Southeastern Pennsylvania v. Casey,* 505 U.S. 833 (1992).

page 92   time of implantation American College of Obstetricians
            and Gynecologists. July 1998. Statement on Contraceptive
            Methods.

page 93   "in the womb" Unborn Victims of Violence Act of 2001,
            503 U.S. 107 (2001).

page 93   and Connor's Law Holland, Jesse J. July 8, 2003. "Re-
            publicans, Democrats Argue of Possible Effects of Possible
            Fetus Homicide Law." The Associated Press.

page 94   "but that's irrelevant" Eilperin, Juliet. July 19, 2003. "Bills to
            Change Fetus's Status Gain Support: Measures Expanding
            Crime Victim Designation Called Backdoor Curbs on
            Abortion Rights." *The Washington Post,* p. A2.

page 94   separate legal "person" Eilperin, Juliet. July 19, 2003. "Bills
            to Change Fetus's Status Gain Support: Measures Expanding

Crime Victim Designation Called Backdoor Curbs on Abortion Rights." *The Washington Post*, p. A2.

page 95 during her pregnancy Center for Reproductive Rights. July 2003. "Fetal Personhood/Unborn Victims Legislation." [Online]. http://wwwcrlp.org/tools/print_page.jsp.

page 95 and minority women Schroedel, Jean Reith. 2000. *Is the Fetus a Person? A Comparison of Policies Across the Fifty States* (Ithaca, NY: Cornell University Press), p. 53.

page 95 from unreasonable searches Center for Reproductive Rights: In the Courts. October 3, 2003. *Ferguson v. City of Charleston.* [Online].http://www.reproductiverights.org/crt_preg_ferguson.html.

page 96 "forms of violence against women" Federal News Service. July 8, 2003. "Prepared Testimony of Juley Fulcher, Public Policy Director, National Coalition Against Domestic Violence." Given before the House Committee on the Judiciary Subcommittee on the Constitution.

page 97 Health Insurance Program HHS—Department of Health and Human Services. March 5, 2002. "State Children's Health Insurance Program; Eligibility for Prenatal Care for Unborn Children." Federal Register, p. 9936–39.

page 97 principle of fetal personhood Mothers and Newborns Health Insurance Act, S. 1016 (2001).

page 97 of U.S. senators Senators Corzine, et al. August 2, 2001. Letter to President Bush voicing opposition to a draft policy developed by the Department of Health and Human Services that would allow states to define "an unborn child" eligible for health coverage under the State Children's Health Insurance Program.

page 98 eligible for anesthesia "Hospital Seeks Help from State with Medicaid Bills." May 4, 1999. The Associated Press.

page 99 not covered by other programs Goldreich, Samuel. October 10, 2002. "Democrats Block FDA Nominee to Seek Action on Health Bill." *Congressional Quarterly Daily Monitor.*

page 100   "of God's creations" Snowflakes Embryo Adoption Program. [Online]. http://www.snowflakes.org/.

page 101   daughter was diabetic Pope, Charles. March 1, 2003. "Nethercutt Faced with Tough Decision in Cloning Vote." *Seattle Post-Intelligencer,* p. A2.

page 101   "within the womb" Nightlight Christian Adoptions. [Online]. http://www.nightlight.org/cafs.htm.

page 102   "and yours alone" AIA—The American Infertility Association. "The Frozen Embryo Dilemma—A Matter of Privacy, Responsibility, and Choice." Fact Sheet. [Online]. (Accessed September 19, 2003). http://www.americaninfertility.org/faqs/aia_frozenembryo.html.

page 103   "in this tragedy" Kjos, Les. June 23, 2003. "Analysis: Florida Seeks Guardian for Fetus." United Press International.

page 105   "the 'big two' " Coppersmith, Sam. August 10, 2003. "If Gay Marriage Upsets You, Then Don't Have One." http://liberaldesert.blogspot.com/2003_08_17_liberaldesert_archive.html.

page 106   "on biblical tradition, un-Christian" Jordan-Simpson, Emma. May 2003. "Psalm 139—If I Make My Bed in Hell, Thou Art There." Clergy Voices—Planned Parenthood Federation of America, Inc.

page 106   what they wanted Carmen, Arlene, and Howard Moody. 1973. *Abortion Counseling and Social Change: From Illegal Act to Medical Practice* (Valley Forge, PA: Judson Press), p. 27.

page 106   one thousand . . . abortions Davis, Flora. 1991. *Moving the Mountain: The Women's Movement in America Since 1960* (New York: Simon & Schuster), p. 165.

page 109   the fifth month Maguire, Daniel C. 2001. *Sacred Choices: The Right to Contraception and Abortion in Ten World Religions,* (Minneapolis: Fortress Press), p. 36.

page 109   a good Catholic Goodstein, Laurie. October 4, 1995. "Pope Is Popular, His Teachings Are Not; Majority of American Catholics Polled Say Church Is 'Out of Touch' with Their Views." *The Washington Post,* p. A14.

page 110   than Protestant women Henshaw, Stanley K., and Kathryn

Kost. July/August 1996. "Abortion Patients in 1994–1995: Characteristics and Contraceptive Use." Family Planning Perspectives, 28(4).

Chapter 5—A Chill Wind Blows

page 113   "illusion of reality" *Planned Parenthood of Southeastern Pennsylvania v. Casey,* 505 U.S. 833 (1992).

page 114   "realize their dreams" Bruni, Frank. 2002. *Ambling into History: The Unlikely Odyssey of George W. Bush* (New York: Harper-Collins).

page 115   "snowfall in Miami" Holmes, James Leon. December 24, 1980. "Abortion Issue, Letter Forum." *Moline Daily Dispatch.*

page 115   *25,000* pregnancies Stewart, Felicia, and James Trussell. 2000. "Prevention of Pregnancy Resulting from Rape." *American Journal of Preventive Medicine,* 19(4), pp. 228–9.

page 117   *Stenberg v. Carhart* in 2000 *Stenberg v. Carhart,* 530 U.S. 914 (2000).

page 117   to overturn *Roe* FDCH Political Transcripts. January 16, 2001. "U.S. Senator Patrick Leahy (D–VT) Holds Confirmation Hearing for Attorney-General Designate John Ashcroft."

page 117   "for such legislation" United States of America, Department of Justice. Brief of Amicus Curiae supporting reversal. *Women's Medical Professional Corp. et al. v. Taft,* 162 F. Supp. 2d 929 (S.D. Ohio 2001) 2002 (No. 01–4124).

page 119   "They'll say, 'What's that?'" Sontag, Deborah. March 9, 2003. "The Power of the Fourth." *The New York Times Magazine,* p. 40.

page 121   "emancipation of women" U.S. Newswire. April 6, 1994. Remarks by President at Resignation Ceremony of Justice Blackmun.

page 121   17 percent . . . unsafe, illegal abortions Gold, Rachel Benson. 2003. "Lessons from Before *Roe:* Will Past Be Prologue?" The Guttmacher Report on Public Policy, 6(1), pp. 8–11.

page 122   eleven times safer than childbirth Gold, Rebecca Benson.

1990. "Abortion and Women's Health: A Turning Point for America?" New York: The Alan Guttmacher Institute.

page 122   relatively recent "right" *Griswold v. Connecticut,* 381 U.S. 479 (1965).

page 123   "beget a child" *Eisenstadt v. Baird,* 405 U.S. 438 (1972).

page 123   privacy in the bedroom *Lawrence v. Texas,* 123 S. Ct. 2472 (2003).

page 123   laws criminalizing women Fox News. April 22, 2003. "Raw Data: Excerpts of Santorum's AP Interview." [Online]. (Accessed June 13, 2003). http://www.foxnews.com/story/0,2933,84862,00html; MSNBC. *Hardball.* Transcript.

page 124   "the contraceptive case—and abortion" The Associated Press. April 22, 2003. Senator Rick Santorum's comments on homosexuality in an Associated Press interview.

page 125   covered by Medicaid *Maher v. Roe,* 432 U.S. 464 (1977); *Poelker v. Doe,* 432 U.S. 519 1977; *Harris v. McRae,* 448 U.S. 297 (1980).

page 125   were also upheld *Planned Parenthood of Kansas City, Missouri, v. Ashcroft,* 462 U.S. 476 (1983).

page 125   act was invalid *Thornburgh v. American College of Obstetricians and Gynecologists,* 476 U.S. 747 (1986).

page 126   since the Vietnam war Baum, Geraldine, and Peter Marker. April 10, 1989. "Abortion Rally Draws 300,000." *New York Newsday,* p. 5.

page 126   coverage of reproductive-rights issues Lacayo, Richard. May 1, 1989. "Whose Life Is It? The Long, Emotional Battle over Abortion Approaches a Climax as the Supreme Court Prepares for a Historic Challenge in *Roe v. Wade.*" *Time,* p. 20.

page 127   "chill wind blows" *Webster v. Reproductive Health Services,* 492 U.S. 490 1989.

page 127   blocked most of those "Abortion: Rage over *Roe.*" April 25, 1992. *The Economist,* p. 22.

page 128   "ban abortions outright" Lacayo, Richard. February 3, 1992. "Taking Aim at *Roe v. Wade.*" *Time,* p. 16.

page 130   not available in 87 percent Alan Guttmacher Institute. 2002.
             (Accessed September 12, 2003). "Facts in Brief: Induced
             Abortion." [Online]. http://www.agi-usa.org/pubs/fb_
             induced_abortion.html.

page 131   "can take place" Robertson, Pat. "Dear Fellow Americans."
             [Online]. (Accessed October 1, 2003). http://www.pat
             robertson.com/PressReleases/supremecourt.asp.

page 133   National Right-to-Life Committee "Pro-Lifers Hope 'Partial-
             Birth' Ban Will Challenge Court Ruling." Townhall.com: Con-
             servative News and Information [Online]. http://www.town
             hall.com/news/politics/200309/CUL20030922a.shtml.

page 134   refused to hear it Kirkland, Michael. April 28, 2003. "Court
             Rejects S.C. Abortion Rules Dispute." United Press
             International.

page 135   Third Circuit U.S. Court of Appeals *Pittsburgh Post-Gazette*
             June 30, 2002. p. C7.

page 135   "with the queers" Aron, Nan. May 19, 2003. "You Too Can
             Be a Judge." *Los Angeles Times,* part II, p. 11.

page 136   amendment to overrule *Roe v. Wade* WomensNews. February 9,
             2002. "Bush Judicial Nominee Opposed Family Planning,
             ERA."

page 136   amendment to ban abortion PR Newswire. February 7,
             2002. "Justice for All Project Opposes Nomination of
             Charles Pickering to the Fifth Circuit Court of Appeals."

page 136   legislation to outlaw abortion Culbreth, Michael. November
             13, 1984. "Baptists End Annual Session with Resolution
             Approvals." *Clarion-Ledger.*

page 136   mixed-race couple Volz, Matt. May 30, 2003. "Pickering:
             Nomination Battle a Matter of Principle." The Associated
             Press.

page 136   Texas Supreme Court campaign Aron, Nan. May 19, 2003.
             "You Too Can Be a Judge." *Los Angeles Times,* part II, p. 11.

page 137   necrophilia and bestiality Alliance for Justice. "Alliance for
             Justice Report in Opposition to the Nomination of William

H. Pryor to the United States Court of Appeals for the Eleventh Circuit." [Online]. (Accessed August 21, 2003). http://www.independentjudiciary.com/resources/docs/Pryor%20Final%20AFJ%20Report%206_10_03.pdf.

page 137 "slavery was made unconstitutional" Holmes, James Leon. December 24, 1980. "Abortion Issue, Letter Forum." *Moline Daily Dispatch.*

page 137 "authority of the man" Clift, Eleanor. May 9, 2003. "Capitol Letter: Off Message Again." *Newsweek.*

page 137 "on reconsideration abandon it" United States of America, Department of Justice. Brief of Amicus Curiae in Support of Appellants. *Thornburgh v. American College of Obstetricians and Gynecologists,* 476 U.S. 474 (1986) (Nos. 84–495, 84–1379).

page 137 abortion with patients American Academy of Medical Ethics. Brief of Amicus Curiae in Support of Respondent. *Rust v. Sullivan,* 550 U.S. 173 (1991) (Nos. 89–1391, 89–1392).

page 138 Court of Appeals for the Tenth Circuit "Bush Wants to Place Anti-Separationist Law Professor on Federal Court; George W. Bush; Brief Article." June 1, 2001. Americans United for Separation of Church and State, p. 15.

page 138 "take constitutional law seriously" McConnell, Michael. January 22, 1998. "*Roe v. Wade* at 25: Still Illegitimate." *Wall Street Journal,* p. A18.

page 138 "misinterpretation of the Constitution" "The America We Seek: A Statement of Pro-Life Principle and Concern." 1996. First Things, 63, pp. 40–44.

page 138 issue enough thought "An Unacceptable Nominee." January 29, 2003. *The New York Times,* p. A24.

Chapter 6—Anti-Choice, Anti-Science
page 146 "prescription for safe sex" family.org. (Accessed September 30, 2003). "Complete Marriage and Family Home Reference Guide." [Online]. http://www.family.org/docstudy/solid/a0006253.html.

page 146 distributed to sailors Brandt, Allan M. 1985. *No Magic Bullet:*

A Social History of Venereal Disease in the United States Since 1880 (New York: Oxford University Press).

page 146   "put it in" Tone, Andrea. 2001. *Devices and Desires—A History of Contraceptives in America* (New York: Hill and Wang).

page 147   1991 study de Vincenzi, Isabelle. 1994. "A Longitudinal Study of Human Immunodeficiency Virus Transmission by Heterosexual Partners." *New England Journal of Medicine*, 331(6), 341–46.

page 147   12 partners became infected Saracco, A., et al. 1993. "Man-to-Woman Sexual Transmission of HIV: Longitudinal Study of 343 Steady Partners of Infected Men." *Journal of Acquired Immune Deficiency Syndrome*, 6(5), pp. 497–502.

page 147   40,000 new cases Leff, Lisa. "CDC's HIV Prevention Plan Faces Criticism." July 28, 2003. The Associated Press.

page 147   threat of losing funds Clymer, Adam. December 27, 2002. "U.S. Revises Sex Information, and a Fight Goes On." *The New York Times*, p. 17.

page 147   does not promote sexual activity Centers for Disease Control and Prevention. September 1999. "Condoms and Their Use in Preventing HIV Infection and Other STDs." Fact Sheet.

page 147   emphasizes condom failure rates CDC. December 2, 2002. "Male Latex Condoms and Sexually Transmitted Diseases." Fact Sheet.

page 148   "a 'born-again virgin'" Block, Jennifer. September 1, 2003. "Science Gets Sacked." *The Nation*, 277(6), p. 5.

page 148   USAID . . . from its Web site United States House of Representatives, Committee on Government Reform—Minority Staff, Special Investigations Division. August 2003. Politics and Science in the Bush Administration. [Online]. http://www.house.gov/reform/min/politicsandscience/pdfs/pdf_politics_and_science_rep.pdf.

page 149   in his abstract Goode, Erica. April 18, 2003. "Certain Words Can Trip Up AIDS Grants, Scientists Say." *The New York Times*, p. A10.

page 149   investigated at least eight AIDS groups Margasak, Larry.

November 16, 2001. "Federal AIDS Prevention Money Is Paying for Sexually Explicit Workshops, Investigators Say." The Associated Press.

page 149 guilty on both counts Ornstein, Charles. June 14, 2003. "AIDS Group Told to End Classes." *Los Angeles Times,* part II, p. 1.

page 149 three times in one year Sherman, Mark. August 16, 2003. "Gov't. Again Reviews HIV Prevention Group." The Associated Press.

page 149 Guttmacher . . . also audited "Our Opinions: Anti-Condom Claims Dangerous." August 22, 2003. *Atlanta Journal-Constitution,* p. A18.

page 150 as a "conspiracy" "House Approves Labeling Condoms with Warnings about HPV Infection." May 26, 2000. *AIDS Policy and Law,* 15(1).

page 150 not prevent HPV Wetzstein, Cheryl. August 25, 2003. "Officials question HPV program." *The Washington Times,* p. A6.

page 150 HHS Appropriations Bill "Condom-Labeling Plan Is Deleted from Cervical Cancer Bill." October 27, 2000. *AIDS Policy and Law,* 15(20).

page 151 the CDC Web site CDC. January 23, 1998. "1998 Guidelines for the Treatment of Sexually Transmitted Diseases." *Morbidity and Mortality Weekly Report,* 47(RR-1), pp. 1–116.

page 152 "deadlier breast cancer" Slobodzian, Joseph A. April 1, 1999. "Philadelphia Transit Authority, Religious Group Settle over Pulled Ads." *Philadelphia Inquirer.*

page 152 "fifty percent or more" Virtue Media. (Accessed August 5, 2003). "Positive Solutions." [Online]. http://www.virtue media.org/solutions.htm.

page 152 "abortions . . . breast cancer" Melbye, Mads, et al. 1997. "Induced Abortion and the Risk of Breast Cancer." *New England Journal of Medicine,* 336(2), pp. 81–5.

page 152   "development of breast cancer" The American College of
            Obstetricians and Gynecologists. July 31, 2003. "ACOG
            Finds No Link Between Abortion and Breast Cancer Risk."
            ACOG News Release.

page 152   "suggested an increased risk" National Cancer Institute.
            November 25, 2002. "Early Reproductive Events and Breast
            Cancer." NCI Fact Sheet (revised).

page 153   "developing breast cancer" National Cancer Institute. March
            6, 2002. "Abortion and Breast Cancer." NCI Fact Sheet
            (original).

page 153   "distortion of the evidence" "Abortion and Breast Cancer."
            January 6, 2003. *The New York Times*, p. A20.

page 153   "a political debate" Simon, Stephanie. March 24, 2002.
            "The Nation." *Los Angeles Times*, p. A26.

page 153   is "well-established" National Cancer Institute. March 25,
            2003. "Early Reproductive Events and Breast Cancer
            Workshop." NCI Summary Report.

page 155   "no evidence of an abortion trauma" Stotland, Nada L.,
            M.D. October 21, 1992. "The Myth of the Abortion
            Trauma Syndrome." *Journal of the American Medical Association*,
            268(15), pp. 2078–9.

page 155   every ten women Ziporyn, Terra. 1984. " 'Rip van Winkle
            Period' Ends for Puerperal Psychiatric Problems." *Journal of the
            American Medical Association*, 251(16), 2061–63, 2067.

page 155   a personal crisis Lazarus, Arthur. 1985. "Psychiatric
            Sequelae of Legalized First Trimester Abortion." *Journal of
            Psychosomatic Obstetrics & Gynaecology*, 4(3), pp. 140–50.

page 155   the abortion itself Adler, Nancy E., et al. 1990. "Psy-
            chological Responses after Abortion." *Science*, 248(4951),
            pp. 41–4.

page 155   ninety-eight percent of women Dagg, Paul K. B. 1991.
            "The Psychological Sequelae of Therapeutic Abortion—
            Denied and Completed." *American Journal of Psychiatry*, 148(5),
            pp. 578–85.

page 155   70 percent of women Torres, Aida, and Jacqueline Darroch Forrest. 1988. "Why Do Women Have Abortions?" *Family Planning Perspectives,* 20(4), pp. 169–76.

page 156   10 percent of women Adler, Nancy E. 1989. University of California at San Francisco, Statement on Behalf of the American Psychological Association Before the Human Resources and Intergovernmental Relations Subcommittee of the Committee on Governmental Operations, U.S. House of Representatives, pp. 130–40.

page 157   more than twenty states Allen Guttmacher Institute [Online]. "State Policies in Brief: Mandatory Waiting Periods for Abortion." (Accessed October 1, 2003). http://www.agi-usa/pubs/spib-MWPA.pdf.

page 157   1992 decision *Planned Parenthood of Southeastern Pennsylvania v. Casey,* 505 U.S. 833 (1992).

page 158   18 percent increase Center for Reproductive Rights. 2002. "Access to Abortion: Mandatory Delay and Biased Information Requirements." [Online]. (Accessed October 1, 2003). http://www.crlp.org/tools/print_page.jsp.

page 160   liable for financial assistance e.g., Ky. Rev. Stat. Ann. § 311.725; Neb. Rev. Stat. § 28-237.

page 160   "for codification in law" American Medical Association. "AMA opposition to 'Procedure Specific' Informed Consent." House of Delegates Resolution 226 (A-98).

page 161   "present all the data" United States House of Representatives Committee on Government Reform—Minority Staff Special Investigations Division. August 2003. *Politics and Science in the Bush Administration,* p. 6.

page 162   "genuine sexual health" Coburn, Representative (Ret.) Tom, M.D. and Representative Dave Weldon, M.D. "The Truth about Condoms: Joint Statement." [Online]. (Accessed September 9, 2003). http://www.family.org/cforum/hot issues/A0016989.html.

page 163   "advice of scientists" United States House of Representatives Committee on Government Reform—Minority Staff

Special Investigations Division. August 2003. *Politics and Science in the Bush Administration,* p. 27–8.

page 163   "the gay plague" Squatriglia, Chuck. January 23, 2003. "Gays Shocked at Bush Choice for AIDS Panel." *San Francisco Chronicle.*

page 163   he wasn't appointed Zitner, Aaron. December 23, 2002. "The Nation; Advisors Put Under a Microscope." *Los Angeles Times,* p. 1.

page 163   of the administration Weiss, Rick. September 17, 2002. "HHS Seeks Science Advice to Match Bush Views." *The Washington Post,* p. A1.

page 164   "public at risk" Zitner, Aaron. December 23, 2002. "Advisors Put Under a Microscope." *Los Angeles Times,* p. 1.

page 164   "is being suppressed" Waxman, Representative Henry A., et al. October 21, 2002. Letter from Congressman Henry Waxman and eleven other members of Congress to secretary of HHS Tommy Thompson.

page 165   in vitro fertilization treatment National Institutes of Health. 2002. "Stem Cell Information." [Online]. (Accessed September 30, 2003). http://stemcells.nih.gov/infoCenter/stemCellBasics.asp.

page 165   one hundred thousand of these Foubister, Vida. November 13, 2000. "Extra Embryos: What Is Their Future?" *AMNews.*

page 166   "really, really frustrating" Blitzer, Wolf, et al. August 9, 2001. CNN Wolf Blitzer Reports. Transcript #080900CN.V67.

page 166   sixty genetically diverse Toner, Robin. August 10, 2001. "The President's Decision: The Reaction; Each Side Finds Something to Like, and Not." *The New York Times,* p. A17.

page 167   "bulk of the medical community" United States House of Representatives Committee on Government Reform— Minority Staff Special Investigations Division. August 2003. Politics and Science in the Bush Administration. "Examples— Stem Cells." (Accessed October 9, 2003). http://www.house.gov/reform/min/politicsandscience/example_stemcells.htm.

page 167   "last ten years" Keating, Raymond J. October 1, 2002.

"Suozzi Budget Shows Style, But Where's the Substance?" *Newsday*, p. A34.

page 168   63 percent of fundamentalist Christians Moore, Mary Tyler and Christopher Reeve. July 17, 2001. "U.S. Must Seize Stem-Cell Promise." *Newsday*, p. A29.

Chapter 7—*Watch Your Mouthpiece*

page 169   "having an affair" Scheidler, Joseph. 1985. *Closed: 99 Ways to Stop Abortion* (Regnery Books: Chicago).

page 170   "fate than choice" "The War Against Women." January 12, 2003. *The New York Times*, sec. 4, p. 14.

page 170   over eighty occasions National Abortion Federation. June 30, 2003 (Accessed October 5, 2003). "Incidents of Violence and Disruption Against Abortion Providers." [Online]. http://www.prochoice.org.

page 170   550 such epistles Lewin, Tamar. November 30, 2001. "Suspect Named in Fake Anthrax Mailings to Abortion Clinics." *The New York Times*, p. B6.

page 174   "medical or legal content" *Carhart v. Stenberg*, 192 F. 3rd 1142, 1999 8th Cir.

page 179   "actively promote abortions" Bush, George W. January 22, 2001. Memorandum for the Administrator of the United States Agency for International Development Subject: Restoration of the Mexico City Policy.

page 179   the *Houston Chronicle* Roth, Bennett. January 23, 2001. "Bush Halts Funding Used for Abortions." *Houston Chronicle*, p. A1.

page 180   belief, his "assertion" Miga, Andrew, and Laurel Sweet. January 23, 2001. "Bush Move Sparks Abortion Firestorm." *Boston Herald*, p. 1.

page 180   rule's . . . impact abroad Allen, Mike. January 23, 2001. "Bush Reverses Abortion Aid; U.S. Funds Are Denied to Groups that Promote Procedure Abroad." *The Washington Post*, p. A1.

page 180   any article . . . family planning Walsh-Childers, Kim. May/June 1997. "Sexual Health Coverage: Women's, Men's, Teen and Other Specialty Magazines; A Current-Year and

Ten-Year Retrospective Content Analysis." *Columbia Journalism Review,* sup., p. I.

page 181   68 percent more Alan Guttmacher Institute. 1994. "Uneven and Unequal." New York: AGI.

page 181   twenty-one states Center for Reproductive Rights. (Accessed September 8, 2003). "2003 Mid-Year Legislative Report." [Online]. http://www.reproductiverights.org/st_leg_summary 0703.html.

page 184   "an anti-abortion murder?" " 'Terrorists' Attack Ski Lodges, Not Doctors." December 1998. Extra! [Online]. http://www.fair.org/extra/9812/buffalo-wail.html.

page 185   "Mengele being killed" Risen, James, and Judy Thomas. 1998. *Wrath of Angels: The American Abortion War* (New York: Basic Books).

page 185   "one successful murder" American Broadcasting Companies, Inc. December 8, 1993. *Nightline.* Transcript #3273.

page 186   "laying down their lives" Cable News Network, Inc. March 8, 1994. *Sonya Live.* Transcript #500.

page 186   82 percent of facilities Henshaw, Stanley, and Lawrence Finer. 2003. "The Accessibility of Abortion Services in the United States, 2001." Perspectives on Sexual and Reproductive Health, 35(I), pp. 16–24.

page 187   90 percent . . . to prevent pregnancies United States Department of Health and Human Services. 2000. "Healthy People 2010 Objectives for Improving Health." [Online]. (Accessed October 6, 2003). http://www.healthypeople.gov/document/html/objectives/09-03.htm.

page 189   David Shaw wrote Shaw, David. July I, 1990. "Abortion Bias Seeps into News." *Los Angeles Times,* p. AI.

page 190   women are only 34 percent American Society of Newspaper Editors. 2003. "Tables from the 2003 Newsroom Employment Survey." [Online]. (Accessed October 6, 2003). http://www.asne.org/index.cfm?id=4456.

page 191   "no expert on abortion" Carroll, John, ed. May 22, 2003. "Memo on Abortion and Liberal Bias." *Los Angeles Times.*

page 192   "on their case." MSNBC. June 2, 2003. *Hardball.* Transcript.

page 192   story in the Sunday *New York Times* Hayt, Elizabeth. March 30, 2003. "Surprise, Mom: I'm Against Abortion." *The New York Times,* sec. 9, p. 1.

page 196   "a Fox commentator" Italie, Hillel. August 13, 2003. "Franken Makes Light of Fox Slogan Lawsuit." The Associated Press.

page 196   11 percent . . . dropping to 9 percent The White House Project. 2001. "Who's Talking? An Analysis of Sunday Morning Talk Shows." New York: The White House Project.

page 196   "we have ever seen before" Bai, Matt. October 12, 2003. "Think Tank." *The New York Times Magazine,* p. 84.

page 197   reporters are "retarded" Quindlen, Anna. July 28, 2003. "Why Even Try the Imitation?" *Newsweek,* p. 64.

Chapter 8—*Exporting Extremism*

page 199   "AIDS has a woman's face" Annan, Kofi. December 29, 2002. "In Africa, AIDS Has a Woman's Face." *The New York Times,* sec. 4, p. 9.

page 200   350 million couples United Nations Population Fund. 1997. "The State of World Population, 1997—The Right to Choose: Reproductive Rights and Reproductive Health." [Online]. (Accessed November 5, 1999). http://www.un pfa.org/swp/1997/swpmain.htm.

page 200   80 million . . . 20 million . . . 78,000 The Alan Guttmacher Institute. 1999. "Sharing Responsibility: Women, Society and Abortion Worldwide."

page 200   of them preventable U.S. Agency for International Development. 1999. "International Population and Family Planning Assistance: Answers to 10 Commonly Asked Questions." [Online]. http://www.info.usaid.gov/pop_health.

page 201   Mexico City policy Global Gag Rule Impact Project. 2003. "What You Need to Know about Global Gag Rule Restrictions." [Online]. http://www.populationaction.org/

resources/publications/globalgagrule/GagRule_restrictions 3.htm.

page 202   around the world UNFPA. "A Matter of Choice." [Online]. http://www.unfpa.org/about/brochure/main2.htm

page 202   for abortions overseas Foreign Assistance Act of 1961 22 U.S.C. 2151 (1961).

page 206   "in bad behavior" Ruse, Austin. April 11, 2003. "Friday Fax." Catholic Family and Human Rights Institute. [Online]. www.priestsforlife.org.

page 206   120 million women Ross, John A., and William L. Winfrey. "Unmet Need for Contraception in the Developing World and the Former Soviet Union: An Updated Estimate." 2002. *International Family Planning Perspectives,* 28(3): pp. 138–43.

page 207   family planning supplies GGRIP. 2003. "Access Denied: U.S. Restrictions on International Family Planning, Executive Summary," p. 4.

page 208 $300 per capita GGRIP. 2003. "Access Denied: U.S. Restrictions on International Family Planning, Impact of the Global Gag Rule in Zambia," p. 1.

page 208   "away her dignity" Bluey, Robert B. September 25, 2003. "Abortion Advocates Claim Pro-Life Policy Is Costing Lives." CNSNEWS.com [Online]. http://www.cnsnews.com.

page 209   infections and unintended pregnancies Satcher, David. 2001. "The Surgeon General's Call to Action to Promote Sexual Health and Responsible Behavior—2001." Office of the Surgeon General: Rockville, MD, pp. 13–15.

page 209   fourteen . . . and younger GGRIP. 2003. "Access Denied: U.S. Restrictions on International Family Planning, Impact of the Global Gag Rule in Kenya," p. 1.

page 209   1-in-14,000 Centers for Disease Control and Prevention. 2001. "Healthy People 2010: Maternal, Infant and Child Health." Atlanta, GA: CDC.

page 209   38 percent of women U.S. Department of State. June 1, 2001. "Kenya: Report on Female Genital Mutilation (FGM) or Female Genital Cutting (FGC)." [Online]. http://www.state.gov/g/wi/rls/rep/crfgm/10103pf.htm.

page 211   per one hundred thousand births WHO. 2003. "Maternal Mortality in 1995: Estimates developed by WHO, UNICEF, UNFPA." [Online]. http://www.who.int/disasters/stats/detail.cfm?indicatortypeID=137&countryID=64.

page 211   11 percent have HIV/AIDS USAID Ethiopia. 2003. "Fact Sheet on HIV/AIDS in Ethiopia." [Online]. http://www.usaidethiopia.org/HPN/HIV_AIDS.htm.

page 211   8 percent . . . practice birth control Central Statistical Authority. 2000. "Ethiopia: 2000 Demographic and Health Survey Key Findings." Addis Ababa: privately printed.

page 211   it is illegal GGRIP. 2003. "Access Denied: U.S. Restrictions on International Family Planning, Executive Summary. The Impact of the Global Gag Rule in Ethiopia," p. 2.

page 211   fifty-four percent . . . whatsoever Social Watch. 2003. "Commitment 7: To Provide Access to Health Care Services for All by 2000." [Online]. http://www.socwatch.org.uy/en/documentos/pdfsInforme2003/commitments/commitment72003_eng.pdf.

page 212   80 percent . . . in the 1980s United Nations Population Division, Department of Economic and Social Affairs. 2002. "Romania." [Online]. http://www.un.org/esa/population/publications/abortion/doc/romania.doc.

page 214   U.S. Department of State Bush, George W. 2003. "Memorandum for the Secretary of State." [Online]. http://www.whitehouse.gov/news/releases/2003/08/200308209-3.html.

page 214   people in 141 countries UNFPA. 2002. Annual Report 2001. [Online]. http://www.unfpa.org/about/report/2001/index.htm.

page 214   36 percent in that country UNFPA. FAQs on FGC. [Online]. (Accessed May 23, 2003). http://www.unfpa.org/gender/faq_fgc.htm.

page 215   "statesmanship than that" Swarns, Rachel. August 27, 2003.

"U.S. Cuts off Financing for AIDS Program, Provoking Furor." *The New York Times,* p. A8.

page 216 "as generously as we can" Donnelly, John. July 11, 2003. "Bush Promises U.S. Help in Africa's AIDS Battle." *Boston Globe,* p. A8.

page 216 "us into action" Stevenson, Richard. July 12, 2003. "Bush Has Praise for Uganda in Its Fight Against AIDS." *The New York Times,* p. A4.

page 217 58 percent of all HIV-positive adults Joint United Nations Programme on HIV/AIDS (UNAIDS). 2002. Report on the Global HIV/AIDS Epidemic: July 2002. Geneva: UNAIDS.

page 217 by two-thirds Hogle, Janice, ed. 2002. "What Happened in Uganda? Declining HIV Prevalence, Behavior Change, and the National Response." USAID: Washington D.C.

page 218 52 percent . . . and the Caribbean U.S. Newswire. September 15, 2003. "U.S. Cancels HIV/AIDS Program for Brazil; Move Fits U.S. Pattern of Politicizing Aid Targeted for Life-Saving HIV Programs Worldwide."

page 218 highest levels of maternal mortality UNICEF. November 6, 2002. "Afghanistan Is Among Worst Places on Globe for Women's Health, Say UNICEF and CDC." [Online]. http://www.unicef.org/newsline/02pr59afghanmm.htm.

page 220 "huge win" Andrusko, Dave. 2002. "Huge Pro-Life Win at Children's Summit," National Right to Life News. [Online]. http://www.nrlc.org/news/2002/NRL06/un.html.

page 220 "should be approved" Thomas, Helen. July 26, 2002. "President Has Deserted Women's Rights." *Houston Chronicle,* p. A42.

page 220 "is appropriate and necessary" Thrupkaew, Noy. September 23, 2002. "Money Where His Mouth Is." *The American Prospect,* (13)17.

page 220 froze about $3 million Maloney, Carolyn, et al. October 31, 2002. Letter to Secretary Colin Powell, U.S. Department of State. Congress of the United States.

page 221   around the world UNFPA. "A Matter of Choice." [Online].
             (Accessed December 17, 2002). http://www.unfpa.org/about/
             brochure/main2.htm.

page 222   "abortion and underage sex" Dao, James. December 15,
             2002. "At U.N. Family-Planning Talks, U.S. Raises Abortion
             Issue." *The New York Times,* sec. 1, p. 4.

page 222   begins at conception Joshi, Vijay. "An Anti-Life Crusade."
             December 20, 2002. *The New York Times,* p. A38.

page 222   voted 32–1 Joshi, Vijay. December 17, 2002. "U.S. Stance
             on Abortion and Condom Use Rejected at Population
             Conference." The Associated Press.

Chapter 9—Fighting Forward
page 224   "be a mother" Sanger, Margaret. 1920. *Woman and the New
             Race.* (New Jersey: Brentano's), p. 94.

page 226   not the government Lake Snell Perry & Associates and
             American Viewpoint. March 2002. "A Presentation of
             Findings Based on a National Survey of 1,375 Registered
             Voters and Four Focus Groups." National Survey: Planned
             Parenthood Federation of America, Washington, D.C: PPFA.

page 228   overwhelmingly anti-choice NARAL Pro-Choice America
             Foundation. 2003. "Positions of Governors and State
             Legisatures on Choice." Who Decides? A State-by-State
             Review of Abortion and Reproductive Rights.

page 230   68 percent more for health care Women's Research and
             Education Institute. 1994. "Women's Health Care Costs and
             Experiences." Washington, D.C.: WREI.

page 230 $20,000 . . . female employee's pregnancy The Alan
             Guttmacher Institute. "The Cost of Contraceptive Insurance
             Coverage." Issues in Brief. [Online]. (Accessed October 8,
             2003). http://www.agi-usa.org/pubs/ib_4-03.html.

page 231   abortifacients *The NewsHour with Jim Lehrer.* July 23, 1998.
             "Making Nice; Courting Diversity; Abortion Politics; Dia-
             logue."

page 232   cover birth control Center for Reproductive Rights. "Contra-

INDEX